# F. Scott Fitzgerald's Fiction

# F. Scott Fitzgerald's Fiction

## "An Almost Theatrical Innocence"

JOHN T. IRWIN

Johns Hopkins University Press

*Baltimore*

Johns Hopkins University Press
2715 North Charles Street
Baltimore, Maryland 21218-4363
www.press.jhu.edu

Library of Congress Cataloging-in-Publication Data
Irwin, John T.
F. Scott Fitzgerald's fiction : "an almost theatrical innocence" / John T. Irwin.
pages cm
Includes bibliographical references and index.
ISBN 978-1-4214-1230-6 (hardcover : acid-free paper) — ISBN 978-1-4214-1231-3
(electronic) — ISBN 1-4214-1230-6 (hardcover : acid-free paper) —
ISBN 1-4214-1231-4 (electronic) 1. Fitzgerald, F. Scott (Francis Scott), 1896–1940—
Criticism and interpretation. I. Title.
PS3511.I9Z668 2014
813'.52—dc23        2013018547

A catalog record for this book is available from the British Library.

*Special discounts are available for bulk purchases of this book. For more information,
please contact Special Sales at 410-516-6936 or specialsales@press.jhu.edu.*

Johns Hopkins University Press uses environmentally friendly book materials,
including recycled text paper that is composed of at least 30 percent
post-consumer waste, whenever possible.

*As always, for Meme, my beloved,*
*and for the twins Matthew and Sophia Saccone*
*in hopes that one day they may receive*
*as much enjoyment from reading Fitzgerald's fiction*
*as their Nonno has*

# CONTENTS

The present book completes a trilogy examining the work of four writers, each of whom, I contend, had been influenced in a special way by Platonic idealism. The first two volumes—*The Mystery to a Solution: Poe, Borges, and the Analytic Detective Story* and *Hart Crane's Poetry: "Appollinaire lived in Paris, I live in Cleveland, Ohio"*—appeared in 1994 and 2011, respectively. This third volume, while addressing the overall topic of the trilogy, is also the result of a professional lifetime spent studying and teaching the works of my favorite twentieth-century American fiction writer, F. Scott Fitzgerald. For a variety of reasons, as I've tried to make clear in the following chapters, Fitzgerald's work has always deeply moved me. And this is as true now as it was fifty years ago when I first picked up *The Great Gatsby*. I can still remember the occasions when I first read each of his novels, remember the time, place, and mood of those early readings, as well as the way each work seemed to speak to something going on in my life at that moment. Because the things that interested Fitzgerald were the things that interested me and because there seemed to be so many similarities in our backgrounds, his work always possessed for me a special, personal authority; it became a form of wisdom, a way of knowing the world, its types, its classes, its individuals.

One of the most powerful emotional effects of *The Great Gatsby* that has grown with each passing year is that sudden swelling of the spirit its most poetic passages (the end of chapter 6 and the end of the last chapter) produce, an effect resembling that created when the Andante theme in Gershwin's *Rhapsody in Blue* (written during the same year Fitzgerald was finishing *Gatsby*) suddenly emerges, its serene beauty set off by the more frenetic earlier part of the work, a feeling of discovery and rediscovery: "So this is what it sounds like to be an American"—this soaring ambition, this spaciousness, this hope of an infinite second chance. Nick Carraway describes Gatsby's imagination as "gorgeous," but I have always felt that that was Fitzgerald describing his own prose. When Yeats edited *The Oxford Book of Modern Verse* in the late 1930s, he included as the first modern poem Walter Pater's description of the Mona Lisa from *The Renaissance*, which he re-lineated as if it were verse; and what Yeats found in Pater's prose, I find in Fitzgerald's.

At one time, when I was writing my first critical book, I thought that Faulkner's *Absalom, Absalom!* was the greatest American novel of the twentieth century, but now (and for a couple of decades past), I've thought this honor belonged to *Tender Is the Night*. I was delighted to rediscover recently that Weldon Kees, to my mind the most interesting poet of his generation, seemed to share this opinion. In a May 1951 letter to a friend, the novelist Anton Myrer, Kees, disparaging "Fitzgerald's more thick-headed detractors," wrote, "I have always been enormously moved by the last pages of *Tender* in their compression and as a triumph of dealing with years that are too sad to insist upon. The boys who see this book as a 'parable of the artist being destroyed' by the haute bourgeoisie leave me limp. It is queer how people without the remotest understanding of the tragic sense of life react to a book that is soaked in it" (153). And given that one of the criteria I use to judge greatness in literary art is a work's power to break one's heart, then by that standard I know of no work I would place above *Tender*. All of which ultimately goes to say, as you no doubt suspect, that what follows is a labor of love.

I want to thank my friend and colleague Professor Howard Egeth of the Psychology Department at the Johns Hopkins University for originally suggesting to me during lunch one day at the Hopkins Club that, given my interest in the social theatricality of interpersonal relationships in Fitzgerald's fiction, my discussion of these might well benefit from taking a look at Erving Goffman's *The Presentation of Self in Everyday Life*. I also want to express my appreciation to Professors Jackson R. Bryer, Ruth Prigozy, Scott Donaldson, and James L. West, whose work on Fitzgerald over the years has set the standard of scholarship and criticism at a high level and kept it there.

I also wish to thank the editor of the *Southwest Review*, where chapter 1 of the present book originally appeared as an essay entitled "Compensating Visions: *The Great Gatsby*," and the editor of *Raritan*, where chapter 2 originally appeared as an essay entitled "Is Fitzgerald a Southern Writer?," for permission to use them here.

# F. Scott Fitzgerald's Fiction

# CHAPTER ONE

# Compensating Visions
# in *The Great Gatsby*

L
IKE MANY READERS of my generation, I first became a fan of Fitzgerald's fiction when I read *The Great Gatsby* in college. At the time I thought it was the best book I had ever read, and indeed at the time it probably was. Some fifty years later, it is still one of my favorite American novels and Fitzgerald my favorite American fiction writer. Before reading *Gatsby* the first time, I had only been as deeply moved by a work of fiction once before in my life. In my senior year of high school, when I should have been studying for midterm exams, I stayed up three nights in a row reading Dickens's *A Tale of Two Cities*. What has remained with me from my first experience of these two books is the uncanny equivalence of their heroes—the high romantic Sydney Carton and the late romantic Jay Gatsby. In each case the attempt to preserve a self-sustaining image of desire, the category of Desire per se, turns out to be a matter of greater importance in the characters' respective stories than their attempt to possess the object of their desire. Sydney Carton renounces the possible possession of Lucie that might result from Darnay's death in order to keep his desire intact as desire, even if that means dying to save Darnay's life. Perhaps he suspected, being a good romantic, that the object of desire, even if wholly possessed, could never be as personally, as privately, his own as his self-created *image* of that object.

Death protects Carton not only from the disillusion of possession but also from the wandering or waning of desire through prolonged nonpossession, a simultaneous foreclosure of the object of desire and of Desire itself. But that foreclosure involves a characteristic foreshadowing. Dickens says that at the moment of his death Carton "looked sublime and prophetic" (357), and the subsequent description of his prophetic vision centers on Carton's survival in the memories of Lucie, Darnay, and their descendants, a mnemic survival embodied in Lucie and Darnay's child, a son named Sydney:

I see that child who lay upon her bosom and who bore my name, a man winning his way up in that path of life which once was mine. I see him winning it
so well, that my name is made illustrious there by the light of his. I see the blots
I threw upon it, faded away. I see him, foremost of just judges and honoured
men, bringing a boy of my name, with a forehead that I know and golden hair,
to this place—then fair to look upon, with not a trace of this day's disfigure-
ment—and I hear him tell the child my story, with a tender and faltering voice.
(358)

Not only a son but a grandson as well to bear his name and be the custodian
of his story, the living vessel of memory. And this ghostly fathering requires
not the loss of his seed but simply the loss of his head. In imagining what Carton's vision at the moment of death might have been, the omniscient author
gives Carton (and us as the guardians of his interest) the prefigured compensation for his sacrifice, which is to say, gives us a compensatory prefiguration.

As I said, looking back on my first reading of A Tale of Two Cities and The
Great Gatsby, what I remember most is the equivalence of their emotional
impact. And yet at first glance what seems most striking now is the difference
in the deaths of the two heroes. True, each loves an idealized woman who is
married to another man, and each loses his life for that woman's sake; but
where Carton willingly sacrifices himself to save Darnay and preserve Lucie's
marriage, Gatsby unwittingly gives up his life for Daisy and Tom. This is not
to say that Gatsby wouldn't have done everything he could to shield Daisy
from the consequences of the hit-and-run accident, even to the point of sacrificing his life to protect her from George Wilson's revenge, but rather that
Gatsby would never have intended his death to cement the marriage of Tom
and Daisy. Yet it seems to do just that by turning that relationship into one
of mutual, though differing, complicity in manslaughter and murder. For not
only is Daisy responsible for the accidental death of Tom's mistress (a fact she
conceals from Tom); she is also responsible in a real sense for Gatsby's death
by allowing Tom to believe that Gatsby ran down Myrtle. The result of this
deception is that Tom betrays Gatsby's identity to George Wilson, knowing
full well Wilson intends to kill the person he thinks is both his wife's lover
and murderer.

In one sense Gatsby is Sydney Carton survived into another era, an era in
which the compensatory prefigurations of romantic idealism have become
ironic. The difference in the visions each narrator imagines for his hero at the
moment of death is a measure of the distance between the two. As opposed

to Carton's "sublime and prophetic" vision with echoes of Revelation ("I see a beautiful city and a brilliant people rising from this abyss" [357]), Nick Carraway's version uses the biblical trope of a new heaven and new earth to an entirely different purpose:

> He must have felt that he had lost the old warm world, paid a high price for living too long with a single dream. He must have looked up at an unfamiliar sky through frightening leaves and shivered as he found what a grotesque thing a rose is and how raw the sunlight was upon the scarcely created grass. A new world, material without being real, where poor ghosts, breathing dreams like air, drifted fortuitously about . . . like that ashen, fantastic figure gliding toward him through the amorphous trees. (126)

Yet it is also a measure of the shared tradition of the two books that the need for prefigured compensation is honored in *Gatsby*: Nick's final "vision" of the "old island . . . that flowered once for Dutch sailors' eyes—a fresh, green breast of the new world" is equated with "Gatsby's wonder when he first picked out the green light at the end of Daisy's dock," the light that symbolizes, according to Nick, Gatsby's belief in "the orgastic future that year by year recedes before us" (140–41). It is not clear that Nick's final vision is, in terms of its content, any more successful (any less disillusioned) than Gatsby's final vision of a "new world, material without being real." What success Nick's vision achieves is more a matter of its form, a form that seems to master or contain this disillusion—the figuration's ability to step back and circumscribe itself as figuration, to look at itself looking.

The vision begins with Nick's looking imaginatively through the eyes first of the Dutch sailors and then of Gatsby at the objects of their desire, an object that is figured in the former case as the fresh, green breast of the virgin continent and in the latter as an idealized woman symbolized by a green light. Nick then takes a step back from this to see that the object of desire the vision presents to the sailors and to Gatsby is an unattainable, illusory one, an object that exists not in the future but in the past. Nick says Gatsby didn't know that what he sought "was already behind him, somewhere back in that vast obscurity beyond the city, where the dark fields of the republic rolled on under the night" (141). What this step back from the vision reveals is the inevitable disillusionment that inhabits the figuration of the original object of desire (represented here by the maternal breast as partial object), which is to say, the figuration of the origin of Desire itself in the infant's first expressing, first crying out, what it hungers for—a self-projected image that, as we pursue it, continually "recedes before us" (141) like our own shadow. Yet Nick's vision doesn't rest with this disillusionment; he takes another step back to look at himself in the act of observing Gatsby as Gatsby gazes at the symbol of desire. Nick realizes that Gatsby's belief in the green light, the orgastic future, is not simply a personal obsession but a national characteristic, a trait that Nick himself shares: "It eluded us then, but that's no matter—tomorrow we will run faster, stretch out our arms farther. . . . And one fine morning—" (141). In thus affirming the power of that illusion of attaining the ultimate (i.e., original) object of desire after having just admitted that that object is in the past and therefore beyond the reach of the will, Nick acknowledges that at their origin figuration and desire are linked by an illusory equation: *the illusion that the object (goal) of desire is an object (a finite thing with an image, a discrete, particular entity that can be represented or figured forth).*

But Nick, precisely in refusing to specify the thing we seek in the orgastic future, to say what the "it" is that has eluded us in the past but that will be ours tomorrow when we run faster and stretch out our arms farther, emphasizes that the original object (goal) of Desire is not an object and that consequently the quest for it is nonclosable, a fact evoked in Nick's vision by the open-ended syntax of the dream: "And one fine morning—." (In "The Diamond as Big as the Ritz" [1922] Fitzgerald is even more explicit about the objective indeterminacy of that "radiantly imagined future": "flowers and gold, girls and stars, they are only prefigurations and prophecies of that incomparable, unattainable young dream" [*Short Stories* 195].) In his description of the Dutch sailors' first glimpse of the virgin continent, Nick makes it clear that what the voyagers see is not so much the physical object of their desire as the possibility that any physical object—something with a visual image, something available to "aesthetic contemplation" like those "vanished trees" that "had once pandered in whispers to the last and greatest of all human dreams"— could actually be "commensurate" to man's "capacity for wonder" (140): they fall prey to *the illusion that there exists a partial object that could equal the indeterminate totality of Desire, that the "incomparable" could somehow be "commensurate."*

The final moment of Nick's vision accepts as inevitable both the disillusion of that quest for the unattainable object and the persistence of the illusion that the original object of Desire is something physical (the illusion that grounds the relationship between figuration and Desire itself by allowing us to image our desire as the continuing incentive to its attainment). Or as Fitzgerald says of his hero's attachment to the idealized woman in "Winter

Dreams" (1922), the story he completed just before beginning work on *Gatsby* and that was a trial run for the novel's theme, "No disillusion as to the world in which she had grown up could cure his illusion as to her desirability" (*Short Stories* 228). The only cure for that illusion is death, the destruction of figuration. Nick's last words sum up the paradox of our condition: "So we beat on, boats against the current, borne back ceaselessly into the past" (141). Setting our wills against the flow of time to seek that shadow-object of desire that we project before us, we are carried by the passage of time imperceptibly backward, against our wills, toward that object (goal) of Desire lying behind us, toward that "vast obscurity" traditionally associated with the romantic sublime, that Whitman variously called night, sleep, death, the mother, the sea, though he knew that its essence was to transcend all names.

From our retrospective viewpoint we can characterize the prophetic vision that ends *A Tale of Two Cities* as a compensatory prefiguration, but for the narrator of the book that vision was still very much a prefigured compensation, an imaginative glimpse of objects and events that lay waiting in the future, real things that could be reached by the action of time and the will. What distinguishes Nick's vision is precisely its final sense of *not* being prefigured compensation. Nick undercuts the physical objects of desire that are imaged in the visions of the Dutch sailors and of Gatsby, indicating the inadequacy of these partial objects to the absolute nature of Desire, and in his own vision of the endlessly renewed quest for the orgastic future, he pointedly refuses to specify any physical object to be attained in that future—all of which points to Nick's sense that the only compensation connected with his vision lies in the act of figuration itself. Sydney Carton sacrifices his life for goals that, according to the narrator's vision, are clearly worth the sacrifice; but Gatsby loses his life, according to Nick's vision, in the attempt to maintain the illusory but indispensable belief that there exist attainable goals worth sacrificing one's life for, that there exists some form of individual self-interest beyond death.

For Nick, Gatsby's "sacrifice" validates in some sense the mode of unending hope. Nick's final judgment of Gatsby locates his greatness not in any achievement but in a capacity: a "heightened sensitivity to the promises of life," Nick calls it, "an extraordinary gift for hope, a romantic readiness such as I have never found in any other person and which it is not likely I shall ever find again" (6). This "extraordinary gift for hope," for imaginative projection, as idealized by Nick, is simply the mode of compensatory prefiguration freed from the necessity of having to be prefigured compensation as well. It is freed from questions of the attainability or reality of the imagined object of desire, and forever immune from disillusion because this capacity knows how to keep itself always in "readiness" to act without ever committing itself to action. In *This Side of Paradise* (1920) Fitzgerald says that his hero's "favorite waking dreams" were those in which "it was always the becoming he dreamed of, never the being" (24).

A form of this self-sustaining because self-withholding readiness, this endless holding in reserve, is Nick's own normal temperament. At the start of the novel Nick says that his natural inclination is "to reserve all judgements" because "reserving judgements is a matter of infinite hope" (5), hope that is endless because circular, having become an end in itself. Yet if, as Nick suggests, Gatsby betrays this romantic readiness, this infinitely hopeful holding in reserve, by embodying the ideal in Daisy, by wedding "his unutterable visions to her perishable breath" so that "the incarnation was complete" (86–87), then Nick himself betrays that reserving of judgments that he says is "a matter of infinite hope" by writing Gatsby's story, by incarnating the ideal of infinite hopefulness in Gatsby. As Daisy is Gatsby's object of desire, the focus of his imaginative gaze, so Gatsby is Nick's object of desire, the object whose literal and figurative "keeping in view" is the basis of Nick's narrative. Because of this analogy on the scopic level between the Gatsby–Daisy and Nick–Gatsby relationships, the story of Gatsby and Daisy as Nick tells it thematizes the problematic, reciprocal nature of imaginative vision and personal visibility: the problem of an individual imagination (a limited, first-person narrator) who, though his insights are linked to a physical sight that necessarily entails his (social/theatrical) visibility, seeks a "keeping in view" of the physical object of desire so absolute that it demands omniscience, with its concomitant invisibility (either because of the narrative viewpoint's ubiquity or because of the invisibility of what is to be observed—the contents of a human heart), an omniscience that makes him, in effect, a direct intellectual descendant of Emerson's trope of the "transparent eyeball."

All of which tends to remind us how much the story of *The Great Gatsby* is Nick's own story, and not just in the obvious sense of its being the narrative of Nick's involvement with Gatsby and his friends during the summer of 1922 (indeed, a privileged involvement since it is precisely this relationship that allows Gatsby's story to exist as a narrative at all), nor just in the sense that Nick, in fleshing out the sketchy account that Gatsby gives of his life, draws on his own personal history, motives, and emotions to understand what he has seen and been told, inevitably making Gatsby's story in crucial ways resemble his own. Certainly, the parallels between narrator and hero are real and numerous—their Midwestern backgrounds, their service in the war, a mutual admiration for Daisy and dislike of Tom, the seeking of their fortunes in the East, their unsuccessful pursuits of Daisy and Jordan—and given these parallels, Nick would have been encouraged to interpret Gatsby's inner life in light of his own. Indeed, Nick not only feels that he knows more of Gatsby's story than anyone else in the novel but that he understands that story even better than does Gatsby himself, understands it because in the very attempt to narrate Gatsby's story Nick reenacts what he takes to be its central action—the individual imagination's effort to equal the absolute nature of Desire (by producing an absolute image), in effect, the imagination's attempt to become God. It is precisely in these terms that Nick imagines the process by which James Gatz transformed himself into Jay Gatsby: The boy's "imagination had never really accepted . . . his parents" as his own, and "so he invented just the sort of Jay Gatsby that a seventeen year old boy would be likely to invent, and to this conception he was faithful to the end" (76–77). Like "a son of God," Gatsby "sprang from his Platonic conception of himself" (77) in an act of imaginative autogenesis. And later, when Gatsby incarnates the ideal of Daisy, wedding "his unutterable visions to her perishable breath," Nick says that Gatsby knew "his mind would never romp again like the mind of God" (86).

Yet in his pursuit of that limited, perishable incarnation, Gatsby intends nothing less than a godlike act: through his powers of imagination and will in the service of boundless desire, he aims to repeat the past and change it. Yet what is narration if not this same attempt to repeat the past and change it if in no other way than by rendering the ephemeral flow of time lasting and endlessly repeatable in words? Though, of course, Nick intends much more than that. His narrative will not only repeat the past but transform its significance, showing us that what people had taken to be the sordid death of a parvenu bootlegger was in fact the magnificent failure of an aristocrat of the imagination in his most ambitious undertaking—a failure in act that is partially redeemed by Nick's explanation of the ideal that animated Gatsby's quest. For all of Nick's expressed disapproval of Gatsby—he says at the start that Gatsby "represented everything" for which he had "an unaffected scorn" (6)—and for all of his efforts as a first-person narrator, as a private individual, to maintain an objective distance between himself and his protagonist, Nick must finally adopt Gatsby's own quest for a godlike imaginative power. He must accept a degree of imaginative participation in Gatsby's life—one of those "privileged glimpses into the human heart" (5)—that is tantamount to divine omniscience, accept it not for his own sake but for Gatsby's. Seeing Gatsby's dream in ruins, his imaginative life destroyed by Daisy's shallow incomprehension and Tom's malice, Nick performs his own godlike act. Looking into Gatsby's heart by looking into his own, Nick does what God is supposed to do in judging man: he sees not only action but intention. Where others had "guessed" at Gatsby's "corruption" (120), that "foul dust" that "floated in the wake of his dreams" (6), Nick sees the "incorruptible dream" (120) that Gatsby conceals. In their final meeting, Nick's omniscient insight into Gatsby's life, his imaginative summing up of that life, expresses itself in a godlike last judgment: a conditional unconditional absolution (recall that the material on Gatsby's childhood that Fitzgerald cut out of the novel became the story he titled "Absolution"):

> "They're a rotten crowd," I shouted, across the lawn. "You're worth the whole damn bunch put together."
> I've always been glad I said that. It was the only compliment I ever gave him, because I disapproved of him from beginning to end. (120)

And later, when the murdered Gatsby is suspected of Myrtle Wilson's death and there is no one to defend his name or mourn his passing, Nick says, "It grew upon me that I was responsible, because no one else was interested—interested, I mean, with that intense personal interest to which everyone has some vague right at the end" (127–28)—the kind of intense personal interest that in our tradition has its idealized personification in the notion of a personal god who considers every individual to be uniquely valuable, whose eye, as the hymn says, is on the sparrow, so you know he watches me.

In a 1939 letter in which he sketched the plot of *The Last Tycoon*, Fitzgerald commented on a later version of this technique whereby a limited, first-person narrator becomes during the course of the novel an omniscient narrator. Remarking that the love affair between Stahr and Kathleen (who was called Thalia at that stage of the writing) is "the meat of the book," Fitzgerald says that he will treat the affair "as it comes through to Cecelia," the daughter of Stahr's partner, who is herself in love with Stahr: "That is to say by making Cecelia at the moment of her telling the story, an intelligent and observant woman, I shall grant myself the privilege, as Conrad did, of letting her imagine the actions of the characters. Thus, I hope to get the verisimilitude of a first person narrative, combined with a Godlike knowledge of all events that happen to my characters" (*Correspondence* 547). But "the privilege" that

Fitzgerald grants Nick is not simply this "Godlike knowledge of all events" but that further "privileged" glimpse "into the human heart," that special insight into Gatsby's imagination that Nick gains by having, as it were, to look through Gatsby's eyes—to duplicate Gatsby's apotheosis of the individual imagination—in order to tell Gatsby's story. (Nick makes it clear that this privileged insight applies only to Gatsby, to the imaginative quester, and not to the object of Gatsby's desire: "I had no sight into Daisy's heart" [9], Nick says.) But where Gatsby willingly gives himself to this godlike imaginative mode, Nick is drawn into it against his will in order to redeem Gatsby. (As children in school we learned the saying that if you want to have a friend, you have to be a friend, but the peculiarly American inflection of this wisdom as regards the friendship of Nick and Gatsby seems to be that if you want to have a god, you have to be a god.) Having seen this mode lead in Gatsby's case to disillusion and death, Nick begins the novel by recoiling from it: "When I came back from the East last autumn I felt that I wanted the world to be in uniform and at a sort of moral attention forever; I wanted no more riotous excursions with privileged glimpses into the human heart." But he adds, "Only Gatsby, the man who gives his name to this book, was exempt from my reaction" (5).

It is precisely this symmetry (not to say fusion) of the process of narration and the content of the narrative, this ultimate coincidence between the problems of figuration, or imaginative sight, involved in the narrator's vision of the hero on the one hand and in the hero's vision of his object of desire on the other that gives *The Great Gatsby* its special force, just as it does to the best of Fitzgerald's fiction—works in which the interplay of physical sight and imaginative insight for narrator and hero is balanced against the interplay of visibility and invisibility (and their differing vulnerabilities) associated with these two types of vision.

# CHAPTER TWO

# Fitzgerald as a Southern Writer

A T ONE POINT in my working life I moved from a city in the northeast to a town in the deep South and from teaching American literature to editing a magazine. I hadn't been in my office at the *Georgia Review* for more than a week when I received a phone call from the university's retired dean of students, a venerable Southern personage who served as a self-designated official greeter and vetter of the Southernness of new faculty members. At one point, our conversation went like this: "Mr. Irwin, where are you from, sir?" "Why, from the South, sir." (As you can see, we were employing that exaggerated courtesy Southerners often fall into when they sense they may have to do some serious insulting before the conversation is through.) "Where in the South, sir?" asked the dean. "From Texas, sir." "Well, Mr. Irwin, here in Georgia we don't consider Texas, Florida, or Virginia as part of the South."

I sometimes wonder if that conversation had been the reason why a few months later, when I was writing the preface to my first book, a book on that most Southern of writers, William Faulkner, I felt it necessary to document my Southern roots at some length. You see, I knew a secret that I hadn't told the dean: that though I was born and raised in Texas and my mother's family had been there since the days of the Republic, I was the product of a mixed marriage. My father was from Brooklyn, New York. Worse yet, his father, as a teenager fresh off the boat from Ireland, had served in the Union Navy during the Civil War. Suffice it to say that as a child growing up, there were always at least two opinions at our dinner table about the correctness of the Civil War's outcome. Perhaps this is one of the reasons I was particularly attracted to Fitzgerald's fiction, for while I was born and raised in the South with a Southern mother and Northern father, he was born and raised in the North with a Northern mother and a Southern father, and I've always felt this symmetry in our parentage and regional upbringings was one of the things that made his fiction speak to me in a more personal way and that gave me, so I felt, a special insight into his work.

Recall for a moment Fitzgerald's family background. His maternal grandfather, Philip McQuillan, had been born in Ireland and had moved in 1857 from Galena, Illinois (where U. S. Grant had been an unsuccessful storekeeper before the Civil War), to St. Paul, Minnesota, ultimately making his fortune there in the wholesale grocery business and becoming a respected figure in the community. McQuillan's wholesale grocery business gets translated in his grandson's fiction into the wholesale hardware business of Nick Carraway's family, a business founded by Nick's great-uncle, who had come to their unnamed Midwestern city in 1851 and who had, like J. P. Morgan, sent a substitute to the Civil War. Philip McQuillan's daughter Mollie married Edward Fitzgerald in 1890, and their son was born six years later. Edward Fitzgerald was from Rockville, Maryland, and was related on his mother's side to some of Maryland's oldest families—the Scotts, Ridgelys, Dorseys, and Keys. Francis Scott Key was the brother of F. Scott Fitzgerald's great-great-grandfather. To say that Edward Fitzgerald and his family were Southern sympathizers during the Civil War would be an understatement. As a boy, Edward, who was born in 1853, guided Confederate "spies across the Potomac," helped "a sniper with Mosby's guerrillas to escape," and watched "General Jubal Early's troops march past" the family farm in Montgomery County "on their final attempt to seize the Federal capital," as André Le Vot notes (5). Add to that the fact that Edward's first cousin was Mary Suratt, and I think you'll admit you don't get more Southern than that unless you're related to Traveler.

Edward Fitzgerald filled young Scott's head with tales of his boyhood adventures in the war, and one of Scott's first stories, "The Room with the Green Blinds," written when he was fourteen and published in his school magazine, imagines, as Fitzgerald's biographer Matthew Bruccoli describes it, "another version of the fate of John Wilkes Booth" (*Grandeur* 29). While two of the first four of Fitzgerald's juvenile stories had Civil War settings (the other was titled "A Debt of Honor" and concerned, in Bruccoli's words, "a Confederate soldier who is pardoned by General Lee for falling asleep on sentry duty and redeems himself by an act of heroism" [*Grandeur* 28]), only two short stories from his career as a professional writer are set during the Civil War—the humorous "The Night before Chancellorsville" published in *Esquire* in 1934 and the very late tale "The End of Hate" published in *Collier's* in June 1940. The latter is based on one of his father's boyhood memories of a Confederate trooper captured by Union soldiers and hung up by his thumbs. The story concludes on the night of Lincoln's assassination, when the trooper, who had had his thumbs amputated by a Union surgeon whose sister had rescued the Confederate, comes to take revenge on the doctor for what he feels was an unwarranted mutilation, only to have the surgeon's sister, with whom the trooper has fallen in love, intervene and affect a reconciliation when she announces her intention to marry him. At the end of the story the protagonist realizes that the boardinghouse where he has been staying in Washington for the last few days, which was full of Southern sympathizers, must have been the place where Lincoln's assassination was being planned. That is, it must have been the boardinghouse of Edward Fitzgerald's first cousin, Mary Suratt.

From these stories of Fitzgerald's, one gets the impression of a writer who was a Civil War buff and whose sympathies, imaginative and otherwise, lay with the South, an impression confirmed by a passage in his first novel, *This Side of Paradise*, in which Fitzgerald's alter ego, Amory Blaine, discusses his preference for heroic losers with his intellectual mentor, Monsignor Darcy:

> "I was for Bonnie Prince Charlie," announced Amory.
>
> "Of course you were—and for Hannibal—"
>
> "Yes, and for the Southern Confederacy." He was rather skeptical about being an Irish patriot—he suspected that being Irish was being somewhat common—but Monsignor assured him that Ireland was a romantic lost cause and Irish people quite charming, and that it should, by all means, be one of his principal biasses. (31)

Yet there is certainly no sense in which Fitzgerald could be said to be a Southern writer on the grounds either of an ongoing preoccupation in his fiction with the War between the States as material or of a consistent setting of his fiction in the South. The Southernness of Fitzgerald's writing lies elsewhere, and he gives us a clue to what this regional quality meant for his fiction, as well as to its familial and social origins, when he describes his family background in a July 1933 letter to John O'Hara:

> I am half black Irish and half old American stock with the usual exaggerated ancestral pretensions. The black Irish half of the family had the money and looked down upon the Maryland side of the family who had, and really had, that certain series of reticences and obligations that go under the poor old shattered word "breeding" (modern form "inhibitions"). So being born in that atmosphere . . . I developed a two-cylinder inferiority complex. (*Letters* 503)

Clearly, for Fitzgerald the opposition between North and South in his family background was aligned with the opposition between money and class. His Northern mother had the money, his Southern father had the breeding. His mother was a first-generation American, his father's great-grandfather's brother had written "The Star Spangled Banner." His mother's inherited money was from trade, his father had been born and raised on the family farm. (Indeed, the very word "breeding" suggests a class of people who gained their livelihood from land and livestock and whose hobbies involved the selective mating of dogs for hunting and horses for racing.) So whatever national issues Fitzgerald would have considered as the causes of the Civil War, whether slavery or states' rights, he would certainly also have thought that one of its causes was that inevitable struggle for political supremacy that occurred in many Western countries entering the modern period between those people whose power and position were based on the ownership of land and those whose wealth derived from manufacturing and trade, the inevitable struggle for the upper hand between agriculture and industry.

No matter which civil war, English or American, it was a struggle in which the forces of manufacturing and trade inevitably defeated those of agriculture, a war in which money beat breeding. And Fitzgerald would have seen a personification of these two sides (and the inevitable outcome of their struggle) in his own parents. Though Mollie McQuillan, as the daughter of a wealthy wholesale grocery merchant, had been educated in a convent school and then sent east to complete the finishing process at Manhattanville College in New York, the process apparently hadn't taken. All the biographical accounts agree that Fitzgerald's mother was a woman whose behavior was often odd and sometimes willful, whose dress was eccentric, whose carriage was awkward, whose appearance was homely, and whose social conduct frequently involved the making of casual remarks of such frankness as to suggest either a lack of imagination of the feelings of others or a lack of care. To Fitzgerald, his mother always seemed a peasant who had inherited money, and we know that he grew to manhood feeling a sense of embarrassment about her. This doesn't mean that he didn't love her or that he ever doubted the depth and constancy of her love for him. Indeed, at the time of her death in 1936, he wrote a friend that his mother was "a defiant old woman, defiant in her love for me in spite of my neglect of her, and it would have been quite within her character to have died that I might live" (*Letters* 541). But in his adult years he felt that many of his own character flaws were the direct result of her permissiveness in raising him.

Fitzgerald's father, on the other hand, was every inch a gentleman—gracious Southern manners, impeccably groomed, a natural storyteller with a taste for romantic poetry, and possessed of a highly developed sense of honor that he tried to instill in his son. When Dick Diver reminisces about *his* father in *Tender Is the Night*, it is essentially Fitzgerald recalling his own parent: "His father had been sure of what he was," having been raised "to believe that nothing could be superior to 'good instincts,' honor, courtesy, and courage" (232). Edward Fitzgerald was also, as all accounts agree, a miserable failure in business. From the collapse of his wicker furniture business in St. Paul in 1898 to his losing his job as a soap salesman for Procter & Gamble in Buffalo ten years later, it was one long downward trajectory. Fitzgerald's biographers generally agree on the word "ineffectual" as the kindest characterization of Edward, while Fitzgerald himself described Dick Diver's father, who came "of tired stock" (232), as "one of those about whom it was said with smug finality in the Gilded Age: 'very much the gentleman, but not much get-up-and-go about him'" (232). For the rest of his life, Fitzgerald remembered the day when his father was fired by Procter & Gamble: "That morning he had gone out a comparatively young man, a man full of strength, full of confidence. He came home that evening, an old man, a completely broken man. He had lost his essential drive, his immaculateness of purpose. He was a failure the rest of his days" (Bruccoli, *Grandeur* 22). In a 1926 letter to his agent, Harold Ober, Fitzgerald, describing his father's life as "a 'failure,'" claims that his father has "lived always in mother's shadow and he takes an immense vicarious pleasure in any success of mine" (*Letters* 393).

Needless to say, in the marriage of Mollie and Edward, it was Mollie who was the strong one, and this strength was augmented by Edward's business reverses and the family's increased dependence on her money. Growing up, Fitzgerald would have seen his sense of the outcome of the Civil War replayed in the relationship between his parents. And inasmuch as Fitzgerald was both his mother's and his father's son, one could say that this sense of the Civil War had become incorporated into his psyche, that Fitzgerald sober, who could be charming, witty, thoughtful, and ingratiating, was very much Edward the Southern gentleman's son, and that Fitzgerald drunk, when alcohol had dissolved "that certain series of reticences and obligations that go under the poor old shattered word 'breeding' (modern form 'inhibitions')," was Mollie's son, and in a dual sense, for Fitzgerald's willful, often outrageous behavior when intoxicated, which grew out of a deep sense of insecurity and inferiority, was not only a more exaggerated version of character traits inherited from his mother (for example, the sense that one could get away with anything so long as one had money to pay the damages) but was also directed by Fitzgerald toward family and friends as a test of whether they loved him with the same unquestioning love that his mother had, loved him no matter how he behaved.

## 2

It is inevitable that when a child's parents come from regions as different as the American North and South, this difference should become, subtly or not, an aspect of the child's upbringing. And certainly the earlier in the twentieth century the child was born, the truer this would have been. Indeed, in my own family this sense of a regional difference at work in the raising of children was unmistakable. My father was seventeen when he came to Texas from Brooklyn in 1910. He lived there the rest of his life and loved the state, and I never met a Texan who had known him that didn't love him, but in their minds (and in his own mind as well) he remained to the end of his days a Yankee. Now I never heard my father say that he thought Southerners were losers, though remember he was the son of a man who got his introduction to this country by participating in a war where boys from the North and South had fought it out to the bitter end and the Southerners had lost. What my father *did* say that gave me the impression that that was what he thought were things like this: he would reminisce about the first time he had visited my mother's hometown in south central Texas, a small town named Cuero, and when he was asked what it was like, he recalled that on Saturday mornings all the men and boys in the town came down to the main street to see, in my father's words, "which one could spit the farthest."

My father's main concern about my brother and me was that being born and raised in the South and having a Southern heritage we would lack energy, lack an essential drive and will to succeed; his fear was that being Southerners we would be slow, either because of ethos or climate—slow talking, slow thinking, slow acting. But he never put it that way. Instead he would continually exhort us to pay attention, to be energetic. He would frequently say that he always wanted my brother and me "to play heads-up baseball," a favorite expression of his clearly meant as a metaphor for the great game of life, a competition my brother and I would be in danger of losing if we were too Southern.

My mother, on the other hand, tended to be suspicious of these exhortations, suspicious of the assumption that because one was slow talking one was necessarily slow thinking, that because one was slow moving one was necessarily slow to act. For her, all this praise of energy and attention sounded like a hymn to Yankee brusqueness, that businesslike, big-city rudeness that was the opposite of the small-town Southern courtesy she had grown up with. And for her there was always the suspicion that anything Yankee was more than likely "common," to use that most damning word in the vocabulary of a Southern lady of that time and place. Not that she thought my father was common, that gentlest of gentle men. After all, he had had the good sense to come to the South when he was seventeen, and the greater good sense to marry a Texas girl. But still there was a lingering apprehension on her part that there might be some masked Yankee gene that got passed on to her sons that would make them in adulthood care more about winning than about being gentlemen.

This differential opposition between winning and being a gentleman always troubled me as a child, and not just because it implicitly equated being a gentleman with being a loser. I can remember wondering if that had been the reason why the South had lost the Civil War. Were Southerners too gentlemanly to win? Or was it because they weren't energetic enough? Or not attentive enough? For of course what it meant to be a Southerner, what it meant to share in that sense of regional community, was that we were undeniably losers. We shared in the fact and in the aftereffects of a great defeat—the occupation of our territory by an enemy army, a temporary loss of self-rule, and a hundred years of financial and industrial subservience. That was part of the mindset you bought into as a Southerner.

But this regional identification was complicated in my case because I was also a Texan. My mother's maternal grandfather had served in the Army of the Republic of Texas. My mother was a member of the Daughters of the Republic of Texas, and she had wanted to enroll me as a member of the Children of the Republic, though for some reason I never warmed to the idea. In those days Texas was still the biggest state in the Union, and everything in my environment growing up encouraged me in the belief that Texans were not only the biggest but the bravest, the richest, and the best. We were super Americans. As you can see, in those days Texas was not just a state of the Union, it was a state of mind. And this emphasis on being a winner was compounded by the fact that I grew up during the Second World War. The America of my first six years was a country preparing for and then locked in a life-and-death struggle for survival against what everyone on my block agreed were the forces of incarnate evil. To be an American in those years meant one had to win at any cost, simply because the alternative was unthinkable. We were not fighting against gentlemen, and if winning meant that we had temporarily to renounce being gentlemen ourselves, then that's what we had to do. To put it in the words of a football coach who embodied this sentiment in a later decade when its implications had clearly become more problematic, winning wasn't everything, it was the only thing.

I think you can see how for a childish mind a dilemma developed. How could a Texan be a Southerner? How could the winningest of winners be a loser? I can remember one day when I was eleven or twelve having a serious conversation with my mother in which I tried to resolve this problem. I suggested that Texas was really more western than southern, that we were part of the Southwest rather than the deep South. She immediately knew what I was getting at and sternly pronounced, "Texas is the South," no doubt wondering if I had been put up to these speculations by my father or if this was the first hint of that Yankee gene beginning to make its presence felt at the onset of puberty. For she had no illusions that there was any such thing as Southwestern culture beyond Navajo blankets and paintings of steer skulls nailed to fence posts. The only culture she knew was Southern culture, and that was an end to it.

I tell you all this to give you some insight into the mind of an eighteen-year-old college freshman who sat down one Saturday evening in the fall of 1958 to read *The Great Gatsby* and who finished it in one sitting. I was bowled over by Fitzgerald's world. I instantly recognized it not just as a real world but as my real world, a world conceived in terms of many of those oppositions (and their regional alignment) with which I had been raised. For example, though Nick Carraway presents the central geographic polarity in the novel as that between East and West ("I see now," he says at the end, "that this has been a story of the West, after all—Tom and Gatsby, Daisy and Jordan and I, were all Westerners, and perhaps we possessed some deficiency in common which made us subtly unadaptable to Eastern life" [137]), yet it seemed to me that the novel could just as easily be read as the story of three men from the North in pursuit of two women from the South, with Gatsby and Tom vying for Daisy, and Nick laconically wooing Jordan. Of the three men, Tom, the one with the most money, is a boor and a bully; Nick, though clearly raised a gentleman (indeed, it's the very first thing he tells us about himself) is in retreat by the novel's end back to his home in the Middle West, defeated in his plan to make his fortune in New York, having learned just what such monetary success actually amounts to and the price it exacts in terms of one's moral character; and the third, Gatsby, is a kind of natural gentleman without formal training, who possesses those "'good instincts,' honor, courtesy, and courage" Fitzgerald admired but who has compromised these qualities in getting the money to buy his mansion in just three short years, compromised them with fatal results.

The two Southern women are more or less charming trophies to be awarded to whichever of these sons of the North turns out to be most successful. Given their class and time, they would feel that only gentlemen need apply to become their husbands, though their definition of a gentleman would probably be fairly superficial—the right family and school, knowing which fork to use at dinner, speaking correct English, knowing how to dress, and, of course, most important, having enough money to support them in the style to which they were accustomed. Indeed, if this last qualification were in place, any of the other ones could be waived, since their Southern manners could smooth out any of their husbands' rough edges, particularly if those rough edges had been necessary to doing the business that made the money. Neither Daisy nor Jordan requires that there be a necessary link between good manners and a good heart, and if honesty had been one of those qualities included among a gentleman's "good instincts," then from what we know of these two, marrying a gentleman in anything but the most superficial sense of the word would have been downright inconvenient. Their fortune lay in marriage, and it had brought them both north.

There is, of course, another aspect of the novel that suggests its structuring along a symbolic North–South axis, and that is the circumstances under which Gatsby originally met Daisy. Gatsby was an officer in the army during the First World War stationed at a training camp near Daisy's hometown of Louisville. Daisy was "the first 'nice' girl he had ever known." He "had come in contact with such people but always with indiscernible barbed wire between." Gatsby found "excitingly desirable" not only Daisy but also that ambience of inherited privilege epitomized for Gatsby by Daisy's house. But Gatsby knew "he was in Daisy's house by a colossal accident. However glorious might be his future as Jay Gatsby, he was at present a penniless young man without a past, and at any moment the invisible cloak of his uniform might slip from his shoulders" (116). Gatsby felt that he had presented himself "under false pretenses"—not that "he had traded on his phantom millions" but that "he had deliberately . . . let her believe that he was a person from much the same strata as herself—that he was fully able to take care of her. As a matter of fact, he had no such facilities—he had no comfortable family standing behind him" (116).

The class difference between Daisy and Gatsby had been masked when they first met by his officer's uniform, a visible sign that in this emergency the Congress of the United States considered Gatsby a gentleman, even if nobody else did. But it is just this class difference that Tom focuses on in the climactic confrontation at the Plaza, referring to Gatsby as "Mr. Nobody from Nowhere," wondering how Gatsby "got within a mile" of Daisy unless he "brought the groceries to the back door" (101–2) and finally declaring that Gatsby's "presumptuous little flirtation is over" (105). Tom raises doubts in Daisy's mind about Gatsby's background, suggesting that what the reader perceives as Gatsby's heroic work of Platonic self-creation was nothing but the false front of a cheap sharper, a suspicion not relieved in Daisy's mind by Gatsby's pink suit. Yet clearly the circumstances under which Gatsby first met Daisy—the large-scale presence of the U.S. Army in the South during wartime—was meant by Fitzgerald to evoke a previous occasion when this army had been present in the region in force, and the class difference between Lieutenant Gatsby and Southern belle Daisy is further meant to evoke this earlier presence as an incursion of the lower orders into an aristocratic home. Indeed, it was not for nothing that David O. Selznick had had Fitzgerald try his hand at the screenplay of *Gone with the Wind.*

The circumstances of Gatsby's first meeting with Daisy had, of course, a special significance for Fitzgerald, for they were based on his own first meeting with Zelda Sayre. In March 1918 Second Lieutenant Fitzgerald was assigned to the Forty-Fifth Infantry Regiment at Camp Zachary Taylor near Louisville, Kentucky (the same camp where Gatsby had been stationed when he met Daisy). Fitzgerald subsequently moved with his regiment to Camp Sheridan near Montgomery, Alabama, and there he met the eighteen-year-old Zelda at a country club dance in June 1918. (Camp Sheridan was, of course, named for a Union general, a fact whose significance would not have been missed either by Fitzgerald or the natives of Alabama.) Unlike Gatsby and Daisy, Fitzgerald and Zelda were not from different social classes. Zelda's father was a justice of the Alabama Supreme Court, and her maternal grandfather had been a U.S. senator from Kentucky. Fitzgerald was a relative of Francis Scott Key, his maternal grandfather had made a small fortune, and Scott had attended Princeton. (Indeed, Fitzgerald's attending Princeton is perhaps another indication of his Southern leanings, since in his day Princeton was known as the Ivy League school-of-choice for young men from the South, the polar opposite in Fitzgerald's private symbology of Yale, the school for those in pursuit of big-money success.) But Fitzgerald was always aware that his mother's family money was new money and somewhat embarrassed that it had been made in the wholesale grocery business. Tom Buchanan's remark that the only way Gatsby could have ever gotten within a mile of Daisy in the first place is if he had "brought the groceries to the back door" no doubt represents an inside joke about the relationship of Gatsby's case to Fitzgerald's, for though Fitzgerald had not misrepresented his class background in presenting himself as Zelda's suitor, he does seem, like Gatsby, to have given her the impression that he had family money behind him. And when he proposed marriage and it became clear he hadn't the money to support her in style, even though she loved him, she turned him down, something Fitzgerald never forgot.

## 3

Indeed, so absorbed, not to say obsessed, was Fitzgerald with this situation of a Southern belle wooed by a Northern army officer stationed in the South during the First World War that he made it the central episode of his 1928 short story "The Last of the Belles." There, Ailie Calhoun of Tarleton, Georgia, though engaged to one army officer from the North who is a Harvard man and desired by another officer of similar background who narrates the story, becomes involved with yet a third Northern officer who had risen from the ranks and who had been a streetcar conductor in civilian life. The narrator describes Ailie as "the Southern type in all its purity": she possessed "the suggested background of devoted fathers, brothers and admirers stretching back into the South's heroic age, the unfailing coolness acquired in the endless struggle with the heat," as well as "notes in her voice that order slaves around, that withered up Yankee captains, and then soft, wheedling notes that mingled in unfamiliar loveliness with the night" (*Short Stories* 450). And the narrator remarks, after observing her get the better of another young woman in a social contretemps, that it was a case of "Ailie's 'breeding' against the other's 'commonness'" (455). But Ailie had something else about her that caught the narrator's interest: "a winter at school in New York and a prom at Yale had turned her eyes North. She said she didn't think she'd marry a Southern man" (451).

Clearly, Ailie intends to make her fortune by marrying a Northerner, and yet for some reason she becomes attracted to Lieutenant Earl Schoen, an officer from a training camp where "the candidates were from the ranks" and "had queer names without vowels in them" and "you couldn't take it for granted that they came out of any background at all" (454). A character's not knowing how to dress properly is one of Fitzgerald's standard ploys for evoking class difference, but this deficiency is masked in Schoen's case because the only time Ailie sees him out of his officer's uniform (an attire of institutionalized gentlemanliness whose sartorial style is not a matter of personal preference or family upbringing) is at a private swimming party where she is more struck by his physique than by his bathing attire. Yet she immediately remarks that Schoen looks "like a street-car conductor" (454), and when the narrator says that Schoen obviously intends to pursue Ailie, she replies, "He could give me his ticket punch to wear, like a fraternity pin. What fun! If mother ever saw anybody like that come in the house, she'd just lie down and die" (455). Yet Ailie nevertheless becomes involved with Schoen, even though she calls him a "tough" and is alternately intrigued and appalled by his energy and his social obliviousness. The narrator says that Ailie "only knew" Schoen's lower-class origins "with her mind; her ear couldn't distinguish between one Yankee voice and another" (456). Schoen's unit ships out, and he promises to return for Ailie when the war is over. He keeps his promise, and a few months later the narrator, who is also back, runs into Ailie and Schoen on the street in Tarleton:

> I don't think I've ever been so sorry for a couple in my life; though I suppose the same situation was repeating itself in every city where there had been camps. Exteriorly Earl had about everything wrong with him that could be imagined. His hat was green, with a radical feather; his suit was slashed and braided in a grotesque fashion that national advertising and the movies have put an end to. . . . It wasn't as though he had been shiny and poor, but the background of mill-town dance halls and outing clubs flamed out at you—or rather flamed out at Ailie. For she had never quite imagined the reality. (459)

Three days after his arrival, Earl Schoen is back on the train heading North, complaining to the narrator, who had himself just been mustered out, that Ailie is "too much of a highbrow" for him, that "she's got to marry some rich guy that'll give her a great social position," that he has had enough of "this aristocrat stuff," ending finally by pathetically asking, "One thing—how do you suppose she knew I used to command a street car? I never told her that." To which the narrator replies, "Search me" (459).

In "The Ice Palace" (1920), his earlier and more famous story about a Southern girl engaged to a Northerner, Fitzgerald is even more explicit in his regional stereotyping. When it is rumored that Sally Carrol Happer of Tarleton, Georgia, is engaged to a Northern man, her male friends ask her if she has made this choice because she thinks that they as Southerners will "all be failures." Sally Carrol pulls no punches: "Yes. I don't mean only money failures, but just sort of—of ineffectual and sad . . . because you like it" in Tarleton "and never want to change things or think or go ahead" (*Short Stories* 51). But "I want to go places and see people. I want my mind to grow. I want to live where things happen on a big scale" (51). Sally Carrol draws the contrast between the regions about as bluntly as it can be done, and yet when her fiancé Harry Bellamy comes to visit from the North, she tries to make him understand what she is like and what the South means to her by showing him the graves of the Confederate dead, attempts to make him understand, as she says, "that old time that I've tried to have live in me": "they died for the most beautiful thing in the world—the dead South. You see, . . . people have these dreams they fasten onto things, and I've always grown up with that dream. . . . I've tried in a way to live up to those past standards of noblesse oblige—there's just the last remnants of it, you know, like the roses of an old garden dying all round us—streaks of strange courtliness and chivalry in some of those boys an' stories I used to hear from a Confederate soldier who lived next door, and a few old darkies. Oh, Harry, there was something, there was something!" (53–54).

Sally Carrol returns Harry's visit by making a trip in the dead of winter to meet Harry's family in their Northern home, a city very like St. Paul. On the Pullman, heading north through the snowy landscape, Sally Carrol feels "a surging rush of energy" (55), and when Harry meets her, he asks, "Can you feel the pep in the air?" (56). Just as she wanted Harry to understand her South, he wants her to understand his North, and accordingly he has something of a minor revelation for her. Not that he's a streetcar conductor—on the contrary, his family is wealthy and well established—but rather what it means to be well established in a town that, by Southern standards, is not itself well established. "You Southerners," he says,

> put quite an emphasis on family, and all that—not that it isn't quite all right, but you'll find it a little different here. I mean—you'll notice a lot of things that'll seem to you sort of vulgar display at first, Sally Carrol; but just remember that this is a three-generation town. Everybody has a father, and about half of us have grandfathers. Back of that we don't go. . . . Our grandfathers, you see, founded the place, and a lot of them had to take some pretty queer jobs while

they were doing the founding. For instance, there's one woman who at present is about the social model for the town; well, her father was the first public ash man. (56–57)

That the local Emily Post is the daughter of Boffin the golden dustman doesn't particularly bother Sally Carrol; rather, she is affronted by Harry's assumption that she would be so lacking in good manners as to "make remarks about people" and ends up more affronted still when he tells her that "a Southern girl came up here last summer and said some unfortunate things" (57). But the one who seems bent on making remarks about people is Harry. Seeing a man wearing a pair of extremely baggy trousers on the street, Harry remarks jestingly but not in jest, "He must be a Southerner, judging by those trousers." When Sally Carrol objects, he continues, "Those damn Southerners! . . . They're sort of—sort of degenerates—not at all like the old Southerners. They've lived so long down there with all the colored people that they've gotten lazy and shiftless" (62–63). "A Southerner wouldn't talk the way you're talking now," she says. And he replies, "They haven't the energy!" (63).

What interests Fitzgerald here, what provides him with a dramatic situation for staging the war between money and breeding in regional terms, is not so much what Northerners and Southerners are like within their own regions as what each is like in the land of the other and what it is that brings them there—whether it be the Northern officers stationed in the South during the First World War who fall in love with the dream of an old, aristocratic life embodied in a woman or the adventurous Southern belles who head north in search of a rich husband. Of course, these scenarios suggest a major subtext of the stories discussed so far—the sense that the South's devastating defeat in the Civil War represented an emasculation of Southern manhood, that the region's occupation by the enemy's army symbolized Southern men's inability to protect their womenfolk from the depredations or, at least, from the advances, of strangers, or even worse, as is often the case in Faulkner's fiction, their inability to protect their womenfolk from the women's own overheated imaginations. The fictional personification of this sense of inherited emasculation is Faulkner's Quentin Compson, quietly going mad in Cambridge, Massachusetts, as he broods over his own powerlessness to act the man by protecting his sister's virginity, or perhaps to act the man by taking his sister's virginity.

Sally Carrol Happer tells her Southern male friends that they're all fated to be "failures," "ineffectual and sad," but when she visits Harry's hometown, she makes a comment during a conversation with a university professor who is one of Harry's friends that is more revealing still. The professor asks her if she doesn't think that the people at the dinner party they're attending are "a nice-looking crowd," and she replies that they're "canine," explaining that she always thinks "of people as feline or canine, irrespective of sex." She continues, "I'm feline. So are you. So are most Southern men an' most of these girls here." But "Harry's canine distinctly. All the men I've met to-night seem to be canine." The professor asks her if "canine" implies "a certain conscious masculinity as opposed to subtlety" (59), and she says, "Yes."

If "most Southern men," as well as Sally Carrol and the girls at the party, are feline rather than canine, like Harry and the other Northern men there, then does this imply that the psychological or characterological distinction evoked here is ultimately based on some difference in aggressiveness, size, energy, or pugnacity as exhibited in an all-out confrontation, that is, based on the fact that in a fight a dog will usually beat a cat? Which is to ask, does this characterization of Southern men as feline and Northern men as canine result from the fact that the former suffered a devastating defeat at the hands of the latter, a historical defeat that became part of the Southern psyche? Fitzgerald doesn't say this explicitly, but he does make a comment in *Tender Is the Night* about the psychological aftereffects of a humiliating beating. When Dick Diver is in Rome, he gets into a drunken argument with a cab driver and ends up hitting a plainclothes policeman. He is immediately handcuffed and then severely beaten by the Italian police, thrown in jail, and then publicly humiliated in open court, where he is rescued by his wealthy sister-in-law, who will henceforward always have something to hold over him. Here is the way Fitzgerald describes Dick's feelings:

> What had happened to him was so awful that nothing could make any difference unless he could choke it to death, and, as this was unlikely, he was hopeless. He would be a different person henceforward, and in his raw state he had bizarre feelings of what the new self would be. The matter had about it the impersonal quality of an act of God. No mature Aryan is able to profit by a humiliation; when he forgives it has become part of his life, he has identified himself with the thing which has humiliated him. (263)

Similarly, the South had taken a devastating beating and undergone a humiliating occupation in the Civil War, events that would affect the Southern male psyche for generations to come, for those who survive an all-out struggle that they end up losing in which they hold nothing back, keep nothing in reserve, a struggle for home, family, native land, all that is dearest, emerge from that struggle as different people. Once they have accepted the defeat, it becomes a part of their lives; they have identified themselves with the thing that beat them. And this doesn't just mean that young Southerners in the wake of the war had to seek their fortunes in the North (Fitzgerald's father, the gentlemanly, ineffectual Edward, had done this and still been a miserable failure in business) but also that young Southerners who wanted to succeed had to go to school to the North. For whatever those qualities were that had allowed the North to defeat the South, it was clear that one had to identify oneself with them if one wanted to succeed, one had to learn how to be a winner by getting one's education in the land of the winners.

4

That is the opening premise of one of Fitzgerald's best stories, "The Diamond as Big as the Ritz" (1922). John T. Unger of Hades, Mississippi, "had danced all the latest dances from New York before he put on long trousers," and by the time he was sixteen his parents had decided that "Hades was too small to hold their darling and gifted son," so with their provincial "respect for a New England education," they sent him to "St. Midas' School near Boston, . . . the most expensive and the most exclusive boys' preparatory school in the world" (*Short Stories* 182–83). The fathers of all the boys at St. Midas's were "money-kings," and John's parents had clearly sacrificed a great deal to put him in this environment, an environment for which John seems destined, for as he tells a friend, "I like very rich people. The richer a fella is, the better I like him" (184). In the middle of John's second year at St. Midas's, a new boy enrolls named Percy Washington who chooses John as his only friend and who invites John to spend the summer with his family out West. On the Pullman heading for Montana, Percy casually announces that his father is by far the richest man in the world and that he has a diamond bigger than the Ritz-Carlton Hotel. When the two boys finally arrive at the Washingtons' palatial home, Fitzgerald springs the trap in the plot, for John T. Unger, who has left the South to learn how to be a financial success in the North, discovers that, unknown to everyone, the richest man in the world is a Southerner.

As Percy Washington tells John, his grandfather Fitz-Norman Culpepper Washington, "a direct descendant of George Washington, and Lord Baltimore," found himself at end of the Civil War "a twenty-five-year-old Colonel with a played-out plantation" (192). He gave the Virginia plantation to his younger brother and headed west with two dozen of his most faithful former slaves to establish a cattle ranch. But instead he stumbled upon a mountain in Montana that was one solid diamond. Very quickly he learned that he must market his diamonds in secret, for if the world learned of this mountain "not only would the bottom fall out of the market" for diamonds but "there would not be enough gold in the world to buy a tenth part of it." A "panic, in gold as well as in jewels," would surely result from the secret becoming known, and the government "might take over the claim immediately and institute a monopoly" (193). So Fitz-Norman decided on his course of action. He sent for his younger brother in Virginia and put him in charge of the blacks he had brought with him, "who had never realized that slavery was abolished. To make sure of this, he read them a proclamation he had composed, which announced that General Forrest had reorganized the shattered Southern armies and defeated the North in one pitched battle. The negroes . . . passed a vote declaring it a good thing and held revival services immediately" (193). Fitz-Norman then set out on a two-year journey around the world to market his diamonds clandestinely, accumulating incalculable wealth. He married a woman from Virginia, had an only son, Braddock, and "was compelled . . . to murder his brother," whose drinking habit "had several times endangered their safety" (194). His son, who continued his father's policies, finally sealed the mine but still had to keep the mountain's existence a secret lest in the panic attendant on its discovery "he should be reduced with all the property-holders in the world to utter poverty" (195).

Fitzgerald gives his regional coding of the money versus breeding theme a twist in this fantasy by imagining, in effect, what would have happened if the South had won the war, if the country's wealth had ended up in the pockets not of Northern industrialists but of a former plantation owner from Virginia. Not only does Fitz-Norman issue a proclamation of a surprise Southern victory to his former slaves, but he effectively secedes the diamond mountain and its valley from the Union. Percy explains to John that this part of the Montana Rockies is "the only five square miles of land in the country that's never been surveyed" (187), his father and grandfather having either corrupted or tinkered with the surveying process on three separate occasions to insure that their land did not appear on any map of the United States. What Fitzgerald questions in this story is how well Southern breeding (and having both George Washington and Lord Baltimore as ancestors is some breeding) stands up to the corrosive force not of poverty but of the greatest imaginable wealth. (Fitzgerald is, of course, relying here on his readers' knowledge of American history to underline his point, their knowledge that General George Washington, the father of our country, was a slaveholder and the richest man in America and that the brilliant Confederate cavalry general, Nathan Bedford Forrest, who in Fitz-Norman's proclamation reorganizes the Southern armies and defeats the North in one pitched battle, was, as one of the founders of the Ku Klux Klan and the first grand wizard of the Invisible Empire, someone actively involved in trying to undo the results of the Civil War by reorganizing Confederate veterans.)

In seeking to protect his wealth, Fitz-Norman reenslaves his black retainers and kills his own brother, while his son Braddock comes across as Tom Buchanan with a drawl. Further, John finds that Percy and his sisters "seemed to have inherited the arrogant attitude in all its harsh magnificence from their father. A chaste and consistent selfishness ran like a pattern through their every idea" (202). This arrogance and harsh magnificence finds its physical expression in the architecture and decor of the Washington estate. When John asks Percy who designed the estate, he says that his father brought in "a landscape gardener, an architect, a designer of stage settings, and a French decadent poet left over from the last century," but after they all went mad one day "trying to agree upon the location of a fountain," the job ended up getting done by "a moving-picture fella. He was the only man we found who was used to playing with an unlimited amount of money, though he did tuck his napkin in his collar and couldn't read or write" (203).

The irony of the story is not just that John T. Unger (which rhymes with hunger) has come north to learn how to become a money king only to find that the paradigm of the type is a Southerner but also that he has journeyed from Hades, Mississippi, a town so called because it is hot as hell (and probably "boring as hell" too, as Fitzgerald once remarked of his native St. Paul) to the realm of the real Hades, that lord of the underworld who is also the god of wealth because, as the Greeks believed, all wealth, whether gold or golden-haired grain or jewels, comes from beneath the earth. And in that realm he is confronted with a grotesque parody of the notion of Southern "breeding," for in reenslaving their black retainers, the Washingtons in effect treat human beings as if they were animals, and part of that involves, of course, determining who may mate with whom and which offspring survive. What particularly appalls John, however, is that this practice also extends to potential marriage partners for the Washington family. During the course of his visit, John falls in love with Percy's younger sister and wants to marry her, but his ardor cools considerably when she tells him that if her father knew they were in love, he'd have John poisoned. Nor is his mood much improved when she explains that in any case at the end of his summer visit, John, like all the other visitors from school that they'd ever had, was "going to be put away" (205) in order to protect the secret of the diamond mountain.

As Fitzgerald repeatedly emphasizes in the story, a widespread knowledge of the diamond mountain's existence would effectively disintegrate the world's traditional system of material values by making that conventional, single most valuable commodity (part of whose value depends on its scarcity) so plentiful as to be worthless. And certainly part of what Fitzgerald means to evoke by projecting the general collapse of material values in the sudden devaluation of the world's most precious substance is the way that all human values are in danger of collapsing when money becomes the single most precious thing in people's lives. When Braddock Washington is faced with the prospect of losing his wealth, he offers a bribe to God to intervene on his behalf, offers it not in supplication but in a spirit of arrogant complicity, one tycoon to another, and when the bribe is refused, he blows up the diamond mountain, along with himself, his wife, and son. For as any American knows, it is one thing to die rich, but it is quite another thing to escape with one's life at the cost of being poor.

Scott Fitzgerald understood that in the twentieth century, when America would become the richest and most powerful nation in the world, the struggle between money and breeding, between the arrogance of wealth and the reticence of good instincts, between greed and human values, would become the deepest, most serious theme of the American novel of manners. And to the extent that he saw that struggle as a subtext of the Civil War's encounter between the economic forces of industry and trade, on the one hand, and agriculture on the other—a struggle that was passed on to him not as some abstract historical event but as a dual familial inheritance—he tended in much of his fiction to code that struggle as an encounter between Northern money and Southern breeding. A cynical reading of "The Diamond as Big as the Ritz" might argue that whether or not Fitzgerald felt that Southerners were inherently more gentlemanly than Northerners and that this had in some measure contributed to their losing the war, he clearly felt that after their loss they didn't have enough money to tempt them to be anything else, because if they had, more of them would have turned out like Braddock Washington.

In his 1929 short story "The Swimmers" Fitzgerald rings a further change on this theme. At the tale's start Henry Clay Marston, a "Virginian of the kind who are prouder of being Virginians than of being Americans" (*Short*

*Stories* 498), lives and works in France with his French wife, Choupette, and their two sons. An elderly friend, Judge Waterbury, offers Marston a job in Richmond, Virginia, at almost double his present salary and introduces him to his "halfway" business partner, Charles Wiese, "one of the richest men in the South." Marston finds Wiese's voice "rather too deliberately Southern"; he "recognized and detested the type—the prosperous sweater, presumably evolved from a cross between carpet-bagger and poor white" (496). Marston declines Waterbury's offer, restraining himself "from stating his frank opinion upon existence at home" and feeling that "the questions . . . [his] life propounded could be answered only in France" (496). Later that same day, Marston returns home and confronts his wife and her adulterous lover. Under the emotional stress of this discovery, he suffers a nervous breakdown. After a month's recuperation and a stay at the seashore during which he meets an eighteen-year-old girl from Virginia who teaches him to swim, Marston decides to take up Waterbury's offer and return to America with his wife and sons.

He has been working for Waterbury for almost three years when he announces one day that he wants to quit his job in Richmond and take the place of their representative in France. Later that afternoon he returns home to find Choupette and Charles Wiese together; he confronts them, telling them that he has known "for about a year" about their affair but that he let it "drift . . . while I got my financial affairs in shape. But this last brilliant idea of yours makes me feel a little uncomfortable, a little sordid. . . . On my last trip to New York you had me shadowed. I presume it was with the intention of getting divorce evidence against me. It wasn't a success" (504). Saying that his "emotions aren't sufficiently involved," he proposes that he and Choupette divorce and that she marry Wiese, adding that he won't contest the divorce but that he does intend to have "entire legal custody" of their two sons: "I'd rather apprentice them to a trade than have them brought up in the sort of home yours and Choupette's is going to be" (504–5). At another meeting the next day, Wiese initiates a counterattack, telling Marston, "I'm one of the richest men in Virginia" and "Money is power. . . . I repeat, suh, money is power. . . . Yesterday you took us by surprise and I was unprepared for your brutality to Choupette. But this morning I received a letter from Paris. . . . It is a statement by a specialist in mental diseases, declaring you to be of unsound mind, and unfit to have the custody of children. The specialist is the one who attended you in your nervous breakdown four years ago" (507–8). Marston realizes that it is Choupette who has given Wiese this information and that

Wiese "by some extraordinary bribe . . . had obtained such a document and fully intended to use it" (508).

The story ends with a *Saturday Evening Post* deus-ex-machina twist in which Marston by quick thinking and near heroic action defeats Wiese, forcing him to write out a document relinquishing "all lien on the children thence and forever for himself and Choupette" and having them both sign it and then demanding that Wiese turn over "the certificate from the doctor" and "write across the bottom that you paid so much for it, and sign your name" (510–11). With custody of his sons assured, Marston departs for France, discovering that the young Virginia girl who'd taught him to swim four years earlier is also a passenger on the ocean liner. As Marston watches the receding shore from the deck of the ship,

> he had a sense of overwhelming gratitude and of gladness that America was there, that under the ugly débris of industry the rich land still pushed up, incorrigibly lavish and fertile, and that in the heart of the leaderless people the old generosities and devotions fought on, breaking out sometimes in fanaticism and excess, but indomitable and undefeated[,] . . . and all his old feeling that America was a bizarre accident, a sort of historical sport, was gone forever. The best of America was the best of the world. . . .
>
> France was a land, England was a people, but America, having about it still that quality of the idea, was harder to utter—it was the graves at Shiloh and the tired, drawn, nervous faces of its great men, and the country boys dying in the Argonne for a phrase that was empty before their bodies withered. It was a willingness of the heart. (512)

Though Bruccoli describes "The Swimmers" as "one of a significant group of stories in which Fitzgerald contrasts America with Europe, as in the elegant concluding analysis of American idealism" (*Short Stories* 495), I would suggest that "The Swimmers" belongs to an even more significant group of stories in which Fitzgerald contrasts the industrial North and the agricultural South, money and breeding, or as he phrases it in "The Swimmers," "the ugly débris of industry" and "the rich land" that "still pushed up, incorrigibly lavish and fertile" where "the old generosities and devotions fought on . . . , indomitable and undefeated." In "The Diamond as Big as the Ritz" Fitzgerald personifies the defeat of the South by the North, of breeding (good instincts, reticences, obligations) by money, in the fantasized figure of Braddock Washington, the richest man in the world, a descendant of aristocratic Southerners whose limitless wealth (along with the concomitant actions and attitudes necessary to protect that wealth) had turned him into a monster of selfishness. And in "The Swimmers" Fitzgerald produces a more realistic version of this fantasized figure in the person of Charles Wiese, "one of the richest men in the South"—a type evolved from a "cross" between a Northern "carpet bagger" and a Southern "poor white." Yet in 1929 when Fitzgerald wrote this story, he could still imagine that a man with good instincts—a father determined to see that his sons were raised with a sense of morality, "that series of reticences and obligations"—might be able to defeat a rich scoundrel whose mantra was "money is power." But "The Swimmers" was published in the *Saturday Evening Post* in October 1929, the same month as the stock market crash that ushered in both the Great Depression and a decade of increasing depression in Fitzgerald's personal and professional life.

5

Certainly, Fitzgerald was fascinated by and in awe of the rich, something that Hemingway constantly threw up to him. But Fitzgerald knew that the very rich were not only different from you and me but very different from him as well, knew that no matter how successful he was as a writer he would probably never be able to hold on to the money he made. And by the last decade of his life, when he was getting deeper in debt to his publisher and his agent to pay for Zelda's psychiatric care and to keep Scottie in private schools, when he was battling against alcoholism, a series of nervous collapses, a heart condition, and an overwhelming sense of guilt that he had contributed to Zelda's illness while at the same time trying to earn enough money by writing for the movies or doing short fiction for *Collier's* or *Esquire* to allow him to work on *The Last Tycoon*, he knew that he was going to be an even bigger financial failure than his father. Fitzgerald's final years, as he struggled to support his family and practice his art, represent a kind of personal domestic heroism, a gentleman's sense of loyalty to his obligations, that shows he had never lost respect for those "good instincts" his father had tried to instill in him, had never lost the ability when sober to be ashamed of his frequent lapses of conduct when drunk nor the determination to do better. In the 1930s as Fitzgerald came more and more to seem to himself and to others both an economic and an artistic failure, he came, I think, to identify himself increasingly with his Southern father (an identification poignantly evoked in the scene from *Tender Is the Night* where Dick Diver returns his father's body from the North to Virginia to bury him with his ancestors, bidding him farewell with the words "Good-bye, my father—good-bye, all my fathers" [233]) and, correspondingly, came more and more in the fiction of the '30s, his very best fiction of all, to sing of human unsuccess with what he called "the authority of failure" (Bruccoli, *Grandeur* 425). I would suggest, then, that Fitzgerald, consciously or not, is a Southern writer not only because in the thematized struggle between money and breeding in his writing his deepest loyalty is to the latter but because he came to believe that in this century breeding, good instincts, reticences, and obligations, call it what you will, was going to lose this struggle, so that his loyalty, in true Southern fashion, was to a lost cause and to the past.

# CHAPTER THREE

# The Importance of "Repose"

E VER SINCE I WAS A CHILD, I've loved American popular songs, particularly those of the "golden age" of American music: the songs of the 1920s, '30s, and '40s—that favored period when jazz and popular music ran for a time in the same channel before separating in the late 1940s and '50s. My liking for this music was clearly something I inherited from my parents: in 1928 they made their first trip as a married couple to New York City, my father's hometown, where they saw the original, Florenz Ziegfeld production of Kern and Hammerstein's musical *Show Boat*. In later years, as it became clear from two successful film versions of *Show Boat* just how long lasting was the work's appeal, my parents' reminiscences of seeing the original production of this watershed event in American musical theater assumed for me as a child a near legendary quality: it had been summer, the theater wasn't air-conditioned, but there were large ceiling fans close above where my parents were seated in almost the last row of the balcony, and still every word, both spoken and sung, of the performance was (in those pre-miked days) "clear as a bell." I don't recall my parents saying anything about the show's actual content, perhaps because my Southern mother might have been put off by the element of miscegenation in its plot, but over the years they shared their other memories of Broadway, recalling the 1930 production of Kay Swift's *Fine and Dandy*, my father's favorite show, with a libretto by Donald Ogden Stewart and starring my father's favorite comedian, Joe Cook—as well as their mutual admiration for the dancing of the wonderful Marilyn Miller. At any rate, that early sense from my parents that popular songs were something worthwhile and deserving of attention—plus the fact that at any party my parents ever gave the guests would always end up standing around the piano singing the old songs—initiated my lifelong love for this genre. And this shared taste was one of the things that first attracted me to Fitzgerald's fiction. So pervasive is his citing the names of, or quoting lines from, songs of the 1910s, '20s, and '30s as a way of evoking a period or of setting a mood that it is an unmistakable part of his style, making his stories and novels for me, in the words of those old sing-along shorts in the movies, a continuing walk down memory lane; for I knew both the melody and lyrics of every song he mentioned, having heard them either sung by my elders or sung them myself. No wonder that in his early years Fitzgerald considered writing song lyrics as a possible career path, or that he was an admirer of the best American lyricists of his day, or that he met and became a friend of one of the greatest American songwriters.

2

On October 26, 1934, Cole Porter, accompanying himself on the piano, recorded the song "You're the Top" from his new musical *Anything Goes* (its book by Guy Bolton and P. G. Wodehouse, revised by Howard Lindsay and Russel Crouse), a show that would open for its tryout in Boston on November 5, 1934, and on Broadway on November 21, and run for 420 performances. *Anything Goes* was not only one of the great musical comedies of the 1930s but a high point in the history of American musical theater. Five of the show's numbers became popular song standards: along with "You're the Top," there was "I Get a Kick Out of You," "All through the Night," "Anything Goes," and "Blow, Gabriel, Blow." The musical was filmed twice in the twentieth century, once in black and white, once in color, each time starring Bing Crosby, and it has been revived numerous times on stage. Like Porter's earlier hit "Let's Do It" and like "Anything Goes," "You're the Top" is a "list" song, in effect an imaginative enumeration of persons, places, and things that are tops in their fields (to which the loved one is compared), its wit deriving in part from the heterogeneity of the items linked by the rhymes—serious with trivial, ancient with modern, sublime with ridiculous. In the printed version of refrain 4, Porter compares the beloved to a rose (Porter 170).

The only difficulty is that when Porter sang this in his 1934 recording he changed the phrase "a rose" to the word "repose." Part of the song's cleverness is the topicality of its references: among other things Porter cites as "the top" in their fields were the recently perfected cellophane, the toothpaste Pepsodent, Mickey Mouse, Greta Garbo's salary (reputedly at one point the highest of any star in Hollywood), and a ballad by Irving Berlin. Porter's citing Fred Astaire's dancing as an example of "topness" would clearly have had a personal resonance for the composer: Astaire had starred in Porter's 1932

Broadway show *Gay Divorce*, introducing in it what is perhaps Porter's best-known song, "Night and Day." In 1934 Astaire was again to sing "Night and Day" and to dance it with Ginger Rogers in the film *The Gay Divorcée*, making Porter's 1934 reference to Astaire's dancing an allusion with a nationwide, not just a Broadway, currency. And just as the mention of Fred Astaire had a personal resonance, so too, I would argue, had the mention of "repose" in Porter's recording. For most of 1934 Porter had worked on the musical *Anything Goes*, which opened that fall, while Fitzgerald's *Tender Is the Night* had been serialized in four installments of *Scribner's Magazine* between January and April that same year, with the book appearing in April. In book 1, chapter 12, of the novel the notion of repose figures in a memorable scene so crucial to the subject of this chapter that it is worth quoting at length:

> They were at Voisins waiting for Nicole, six of them, Rosemary, the Norths, Dick Diver and two young French musicians. They were looking over the other patrons of the restaurant to see if they had repose—Dick said no American men had any repose, except himself, and they were seeking an example to confront him with. Things looked black for them—not a man had come into the restaurant for ten minutes without raising his hand to his face.
>
> "We ought never to have given up waxed mustaches," said Abe. "Nevertheless Dick isn't the *only* man with repose—"
>
> "Oh, yes, I am."
>
> "—but he may be the only sober man with repose."
>
> A well-dressed American had come in with two women who swooped and fluttered unself-consciously around a table. Suddenly, he perceived that he was being watched—whereupon his hand rose spasmodically and arranged a phantom bulge in his necktie. In another unseated party a man endlessly patted his shaven cheek with his palm, and his companion mechanically raised and lowered the stub of a cold cigar. The luckier ones fingered eyeglasses and facial hair, the unequipped stroked blank mouths, or even pulled desperately at the lobes of their ears.
>
> A well-known general came in, and Abe, counting on the man's first year at West Point—that year during which no cadet can resign and from which none ever recovers—made a bet with Dick of five dollars.
>
> His hands hanging naturally at his sides, the general waited to be seated. Once his arms swung suddenly backward like a jumper's and Dick said, "Ah!" supposing he had lost control, but the general recovered and they breathed again—the agony was nearly over, the garçon was pulling out his chair . . .

With a touch of fury the conqueror shot up his hand and scratched his gray immaculate head.

"You see," said Dick smugly, "I'm the only one."

Rosemary was quite sure of it and Dick, realizing that he never had a better audience, made the group into so bright a unit that Rosemary felt an impatient disregard for all who were not at their table. (62–63)

But if this scene (from a novel published six months before the opening of *Anything Goes*) is what Porter's mention of repose alludes to, what would have been the scene's personal resonance for the composer? Fitzgerald had never concealed the fact that he created the characters of Dick and Nicole Diver in *Tender Is the Night* by combining traits and biographical details of two different couples—Scott and Zelda Fitzgerald and their friends Gerald and Sara Murphy. Cole Porter and Gerald Murphy had been friends ever since they were undergraduates at Yale, remaining close their entire lives, and Cole and Linda Porter, like the Fitzgeralds, were very much a part of the set the Murphys gathered around themselves in the 1920s and early '30s at their home Villa America in Cap d'Antibes. (Indeed, it was the Porters who had first introduced the Murphys to Cap d'Antibes, when in the summer of 1922 Gerald and Sara visited the Porters in their rented villa there. The Murphys were so taken with the locale that they decided to relocate there permanently.)

The Murphys' set of friends would have recognized the world of Dick and Nicole Diver at Villa Diana in Cap d'Antibes as modeled on that of Gerald and Sara. And Porter, knowing both Gerald and Scott, would have known that the quality of repose Dick Diver attributed to himself would likely have been drawn from the character of his friend, the wealthy, talented, socially well-connected Gerald Murphy, rather than from Scott Fitzgerald. Recall that Fitzgerald had described himself in a July 1933 letter to John O'Hara as having developed at an early age "a two-cylinder inferiority complex" because "the black Irish half" of his family who "had the money . . . looked down upon the Maryland side of the family" who had the "breeding": "So if I were elected King of Scotland tomorrow after graduating from Eton, Magdalene to Guards, with an embryonic history which tied me to the Plantagenets, I would still be a parvenu. I spent my youth in alternately crawling in front of the kitchen maids and insulting the great" (*Letters* 503). Clearly, Fitzgerald felt that what he'd inherited was a sense of social inferiority from his under-bred Irish mother and of economic inferiority from his unsuccessful Southern father, but not in any case that unselfconscious self-assurance in social situations that characterizes Dick Diver's understanding of repose.

Whether Cole Porter's use of repose in his recorded version of "You're the Top" represented an earlier version of the lyric that was then changed to "a rose" in the published version or whether (which seems more likely) Porter interpolated the word "repose" on the recording as a nod to his friend Gerald Murphy and as an acknowledgment to Fitzgerald that Porter recognized their mutual friend in Dick Diver's self-proclaimed possession of this quality, we may never know. If "repose" represented an earlier stage of the lyric, then his decision to change it in the printed version may have been due to *Tender Is the Night's* being neither a critical nor popular success in the early days following its publication, Porter perhaps thinking that an allusion to the word's use in the novel wouldn't have sufficient currency to be generally understood by the public. But certainly other images in refrain 4 suggest that Fitzgerald's fiction was on Porter's mind at the time. The first instance of excellence Porter cites in this refrain is an Arrow collar, and most contemporary readers of *The Great Gatsby* would have recognized Daisy's remark to Gatsby ("You always look so cool. . . . You resemble the advertisement of the man. . . . You know the advertisement of the man" [92–93]) as a reference to the young men with highly chiseled features in J. C. Leyendecker's drawings for Arrow collar ads (and indeed Bruccoli's Cambridge University Press edition of *Gatsby* so identifies it). Moreover, though the printed lyric's "a rose" would seem appropriate to the next line's mention of the poet Dante (given the image of the mystical rose formed by the souls of the blessed that Dante sees near the end of the *Paradiso*), yet calling someone a rose also recalls the moment in *Gatsby* when Daisy turns to Nick during her first dinner party for him and says,

> "I love to see you at my table, Nick. You remind me of a—of a rose, an absolute rose. Doesn't he?" She turned to Miss Baker for confirmation. "An absolute rose?"
>
> This was untrue. I am not even faintly like a rose. (15)

If the inspiration for Porter's "You're repose" came from *Tender Is the Night*, this would not be the only instance in which Porter used a phrase borrowed from Fitzgerald in one of his songs. In his Fitzgerald biography, Jeffrey Meyers, listing the authors and works influenced by Scott's fiction, notes that "Cole Porter, who met Fitzgerald on the French Riviera, lifted a phrase from the first sentence of 'Absolution'—'in the still of the night'—and in 1937 turned it into one of his best songs" (339), part of the score Porter wrote for the 1937 MGM musical *Rosalie* and sung in the film by Nelson Eddy.

Perhaps the most conclusive evidence that Fitzgerald recognized Porter's use of "repose" as an allusion to *Tender* and recognized further that Porter would have seen this self-proclaimed quality of Dick Diver's as something borrowed from their mutual friend Gerald Murphy is a letter dated August 15, 1935, that Fitzgerald wrote to Sara Murphy, trying to console her over the death of her elder son, Baoth, the previous March. He begins the letter by recalling Sara's objection to his use of the Murphys' lives in creating the Divers: Admitting that "I used you again and again in *Tender*," he goes on to explain that "I tried to evoke not *you* but the effect you produce on men." Speaking of her "*dauntless courage*," he assures her "that not one thing you've done has been for nothing" because of the good effect she has had on "the people whose lives you've touched directly or indirectly," adding "I know that you & Gerald are one & it is hard to separate one of you from the other, in such a matter for example as the love & encouragement you chose to give to people." And he closes the letter by noting, "it's odd that when I read over this letter it seems to convey no particular point, yet I'm going to send it. Like Cole's eloquent little song. 'I think it'll tell you how *great* you are.' From your everlasting friend, Scott" (Vaill 264–65). Cole's eloquent little song is, of course, "You're the Top," and the line Fitzgerald cites is the last line of the song's opening verse, which Porter sings on the recording (Porter 169).

Yet we should not conclude that the current of influence ran only in one direction (from novelist to popular song writer) or that Fitzgerald didn't appreciate Porter's achievement as a lyricist. Fitzgerald was clearly a devotee of American popular music and recognized its power to set a mood or evoke a moment in time. In *Gatsby*, for example, he quotes four lines from the 1921 song "The Sheik of Araby" and seven lines from another 1921 tune "Ain't We Got Fun?," and he mentions the 1920 song "The Love Nest" (a melody best known in the 1930s, '40s, and '50s as the theme song of the George Burns and Gracie Allen show on radio and television), the 1921 waltz "Three O'Clock in the Morning," W. C. Handy's 1916 "Beale Street Blues" (popularized by Gilda Gray [whom Fitzgerald mentions elsewhere in the novel] when she sang it in the 1919 musical revue *Schubert's Gaieties*), and the 1898 song "The Rosary." In *Tender Is the Night* Nicole plays the latest recordings from America for Dick one night at the sanatorium, which is described in a paragraph constructed almost wholly out of song titles and lines, evoking, for example, "I'm Sorry I Made You Cry," "Darktown Strutters Ball," "Smiles," "Hindustan," and "After You've Gone":

> They were in America now, even Franz with his conception of Dick as an irresistible Lothario would never have guessed that they had gone so far away. They were so sorry, dear; they went down to meet each other in a taxi, honey; they had preferences in smiles and had met in Hindustan, and shortly afterward they must have quarrelled, for nobody knew and nobody seemed to care—yet finally one of them had gone and left the other crying, only to feel blue, to feel sad. (156)

In the 1930 *Saturday Evening Post* story "The Bridal Party" he mentions "Among My Souvenirs" and "The Wedding of the Painted Doll"; in the 1931 story "Indecision" it's Cole Porter's "I'm Getting Myself Ready for You," while in his 1934 *Post* story "No Flowers" he includes references to "Smoke Gets in Your Eyes," "Boulevard of Broken Dreams," "The Carioca," "Coffee in the Morning," and "Orchids in the Moonlight." And in his 1936 *Esquire* story "Three Acts of Music," Fitzgerald manages in the space of five pages to mention or quote lines from Vincent Youmans's "Tea for Two," Irving Berlin's "All Alone," "Remember," "Always," "Blue Skies," and "How About Me," and Jerome Kern and Dorothy Fields's "Smoke Gets in Your Eyes" and "Lovely to Look At," while in the unfinished *Last Tycoon* he names seven different songs and quotes a line from "Smoke Gets in Your Eyes."

Fitzgerald clearly respected the light verse tradition represented by Porter and the best popular song lyrics of his era (a tradition whose great nineteenth-century practitioner in English had been Sir W. S. Gilbert, whom Fitzgerald mentions in a February 1939 letter to his daughter, Scottie, recommending in the course of commenting on a poem she'd sent him that she "read W. S. Gilbert because his is at least the *best*—Cole Porter knows it by heart" [*Correspondence* 527]). In a December 1939 letter to his Baltimore friend Marguerite Ridgely, he expresses the hope that Scottie's friend Marjorie Ridgely "will turn out to have what Cole Porter called 'listening in advance.' He had an instinct about his music. In writing what he himself wants to hear he anticipates other peoples wants" (*Correspondence* 569). Indeed, in "The Lost Decade," published in *Esquire* in December 1939, Fitzgerald has one character remark, "Just a matter of rhythm—Cole Porter came back to the States in 1928 because he felt that there were new rhythms around" (*Short Stories* 749). But perhaps the most significant mention of Porter in Fitzgerald's correspondence is in November 1939 letter to his daughter inquiring about the part she played in a college show at Vassar: "Again let me repeat that if you start any kind of a career following the footsteps of Cole Porter and Rodgers and Hart, it might be an excellent try. Sometimes I wish I had gone along with that gang, but I guess I am too much a moralist at heart and really want to preach at people in some acceptable form rather than to entertain them" (*Letters* 63). In his biography André Le Vot notes this "sad letter" was written "from Hollywood," where Fitzgerald "was turning out scripts that were every bit as lightweight as his college musicals" (52), and he links Fitzgerald's sometimes wishing he had gone along with the gang of Cole Porter and Rodgers and Hart (which is to say, gone along from writing college musicals to writing Broadway shows) to memories of what had been one of, if not the, high point of Fitzgerald's Princeton career: his writing the first draft of the libretto and the song lyrics for the Princeton Triangle Club's 1914 musical comedy *Fie! Fie! Fi-Fi*. The show, which toured various cities during the Christmas vacation, received glowing reviews, and though Fitzgerald was prevented from going on the tour because of academic ineligibility, many of these reviews, such as the one in the *Baltimore Sun*, singled out Fitzgerald's work: "The lyrics of the songs were written by F. S. Fitzgerald, who could take his place right now with the brightest writers of witty lyrics in America" (Bruccoli, *Grandeur* 55). Le Vot notes that "the Brooklyn *Citizen* compared 'this delicious little vehicle' with Broadway musicals that had 'less vivacity, less sparkling humor and less genuine music'" and that Fitzgerald apparently received inquiries from Broadway producers about his availability (52). Fitzgerald was to go on to write the lyrics for the 1915 Triangle Club show *The Evil Eye* and the 1916 show *Safety First*.

In mentioning Cole Porter and Lorenz Hart to Scottie, Fitzgerald was invoking two writers particularly known for witty lyrics, and in the February '39 letter criticizing her poem, he'd said, "When you send me doggerel such as your last *have some wit in your closing lines*" (*Correspondence* 527). But there is probably another reason Fitzgerald singled out Porter and Hart in the November letter to Scottie, for both had, like him, attended Ivy League schools (Porter had gone to Yale and Hart to the Columbia School of Journalism, and Hart's collaborator Rodgers had also been a Columbia undergraduate) and both had written student shows that served as apprenticeships for their subsequent work on Broadway. In citing these two lyricists, Fitzgerald clearly had in mind the time in his own undergraduate life when, after the success of

*Fie! Fie! Fi-Fi!*, he could have made a similar move from college musicals to Broadway.

Apparently Fitzgerald looked back on that moment as a kind of a crossroads in his career: a choice between working in the theater or writing prose fiction. And in light of the attraction as the road not taken that writing for dramatic performance (on stage or screen) held for Fitzgerald throughout his life, we can appreciate the significance of the alternative Porter lyric with which we began. For I would argue that the allusion contained in Porter's word "repose," an allusion by a successful American songwriter (who was about to have his biggest Broadway hit yet) to a much anticipated American novel that on its publication turned out to be neither a critical nor popular success, underlines a central crux of Fitzgerald's life as a writer, a crux that, once Fitzgerald had found a way to thematize it in his fiction, became the backbone of his best writing.

### 3

Fitzgerald began publishing fiction in his school magazine in 1909 at the age of thirteen, but between 1911 and 1914 he also wrote four plays that were performed by the Elizabethan Dramatic Club in St. Paul, and three of these—*The Captured Shadow*, *"Coward,"* and *Assorted Spirits*—were marked by ever-increasing dramatic craft. As Fitzgerald biographer Matthew Bruccoli notes, " '*Coward*' was warmly received by the local press at its performance at the St. Paul Y.W.C.A. . . . on 29 August 1913, and a second performance was given 'upon urgent demand' at the White Bear Yacht Club on 2 September. Fitzgerald captioned the reviews in his scrapbook: THE GREAT EVENT and ENTER SUCCESS!" (*Grandeur* 39). Clearly it was Fitzgerald's experience writing these plays (in which he had leading roles) and participating in their staging that gave his draft of *Fie! Fie! Fi-Fi!* (entered in the Triangle Club's competition to select the Christmas show for 1914) greater polish than those of his fellow undergraduates. The success of his St. Paul plays and his Triangle Club lyrics must have left the young Fitzgerald with the sense that whether he chose to write fiction or plays, either was a sure path to fame and that perhaps he could manage successful careers in both fields.

What one notices about his first novel, *This Side of Paradise*, is that most of one entire chapter (book 2, chapter 1, "The Debutante") is written as a play, its format consisting of only the characters' names, dialogue, and stage direc-

tions. The chapter (which serves to introduce the character of Rosalind Con-
nage) is partly an adaptation of a dramatic sketch Fitzgerald had published
in January 1917 in Princeton's *Nassau Literary Magazine*. One explanation of
Fitzgerald's opting for a dramatic format in this chapter may be that it was
one more variation on his goal of exhibiting his fiction's experimental mo-
dernity by mixing modes (prose narrative, poetry, epistolary chapters). But
there are other indications in the book that there is something more at work.
For one thing he gives his protagonist Amory Blaine the central event from
his own Princeton career—his participation in the Triangle Club Christmas
show. Amory's "vague desire to do immortal acting with the English Dramatic Association faded out when he found that the most ingenious brains
and talents were concentrated upon the Triangle Club, a musical comedy
organization that every year took a great Christmas trip" (49). And part of
one chapter is devoted to a description of the rehearsals and performance of
a Triangle Club show called "Ha-Ha Hortense!"

Even more significantly, Fitzgerald invokes images of theatricality throughout the book to characterize the social behavior of the novel's principal figures. He tells us that Amory Blaine used his friends "simply as mirrors of
himself, audiences before which he might do that posing absolutely essential
to him" (33). And when Amory and Isabelle first meet at the Minnehaha Club,
Fitzgerald describes Isabelle's entrance to the club dining room as being like
that of "leading ladies on opening nights" as she pauses at the top of a broad
staircase: "She should have descended to a burst of drums or a discordant
blend of themes from 'Thaïs' and 'Carmen'" (63). When Amory's first words
to her are "You're my dinner partner, you know. We're all coached for each
other," Isabelle "gasped—this was rather right in line. But really she felt as if
a good speech had been taken from the star and given to a minor character. . . . She mustn't lose the leadership a bit" (67). One of the stage directions
of "The Debutante" contrasts Rosalind's "*vivid, instant personality*" to "*that
conscious, theatrical quality that* AMORY *had found in* ISABELLE" (161). And
indeed, a stage direction in parenthesis and italics can pop up anywhere in
the prose narrative, as in chapter 4, "Narcissus Off Duty," where the direction
"*(Enter a floor-walker—silence till he moves forward, smirking)*" (136) irrupts
into a conversation among sales clerks.

The notion of theatricality as an ongoing allusive background that can be
used to characterize social interactions becomes even more explicit near the
novel's end after Amory has become involved with Eleanor: "The night and

the scarred trees were like scenery in a play, and to be there with Eleanor, shadowy and unreal, seemed oddly familiar" (216), like a role he had played before. In a subsequent scene when Eleanor says that "just one person in fifty has any glimmer of what sex is," adding "I'm hipped on Freud and all that, but it's rotten that every bit of *real* love in the world is ninety-nine per cent passion and one little soupçon of jealousy," Amory replies, "It's a rather unpleasant overpowering force that's part of the machinery under everything. It's like an actor that let's you see his mechanics" (220). In the novel's final chapter Amory stands beneath the portcullis of a New York theater as a matinee is letting out. Not unexpectedly, within one more page a conversation begins in Amory's mind in which one voice "acted alike as questioner and answerer" (238), the interior dialogue being presented in dramatic form. As Amory walks on in the rain, he "looked futilely back at the stream of his life" (240): "Probably more than any concrete vice or failing Amory despised his own personality—he loathed knowing that tomorrow and the thousand days after, he would swell pompously at a compliment and sulk at an ill word like a third-rate musician or a first-class actor" (241). The "pageantry" of Amory's "disillusion took shape" in terms of those men whose "dreams, personalities, and creeds had in turn thrown colored lights on his soul; . . . each had depended after all on the set stage and the convention of the theatre" (243). Amory's narcissism, his inclination to treat other people as "audiences before which he might do that posing absolutely essential to him," accounts for his attraction to women who exhibit a "theatrical quality" like Isabelle and for his sense that all *successful* social gestures involve at bottom some form of acting—the ability to deliver a "line" when one first meets an attractive woman, the ability to create an intriguing persona, or the ability to pull off the sort of actor's trick that Nick Carraway identifies in Daisy's tone of voice: "I've heard it said that Daisy's murmur was only to make people lean toward her" (*Gatsby* 11).

In his second novel *The Beautiful and Damned* Fitzgerald's use of theatricality as a template for depicting social behavior, particularly in high society, expands to include screen acting as well. At no less than five points in the novel Fitzgerald interrupts the prose narrative with conversations cast in a dramatic format of character name, dialogue, and stage direction, and in the second of these (titled "A Flash-Back in Paradise") there is conversation between Beauty and the Voice in which Beauty asks where she will journey next and the Voice replies, "To a new country—a land you have never seen before" (30). When Beauty asks "What will I be" there?, the Voice says, "At first it was thought that you would go this time as an actress in the motion-pictures but, after all, it's not advisable. You will be disguised during your fifteen years as what is called a 'susciety gurl.'" When Beauty asks, "What's that?," the Voice replies, "It's a sort of bogus aristocrat" (31). And so the society girl Gloria Patch actually tries near the end of the novel to become a film actress to rescue her and Anthony's finances. Just shy of her twenty-ninth birthday, Gloria "grew supremely conscious that she and beauty were going to make use of these next three months. . . . It cheered her that in some manner the illusion of beauty could be sustained, or preserved perhaps in celluloid after the reality had vanished" (325). Using her father's business connection with Joseph Bloekman, vice president of Films Par Excellence, she gets a screen test and then spends an agonizing three days waiting to learn the result. When she gets a note from Bloekman saying that the film's director felt he needed a younger woman for the starring role but that there was a "*small character part supposed to be a very haughty rich widow that he thought you might*" be right for, she gazes in a mirror and intones, "Oh, my pretty face! Oh, I don't want to live without my pretty face! Oh, what *happened*?" (333).

As with his first novel, Fitzgerald keeps up a steady stream of theatrical images and comparisons. For example, Anthony Patch early in the book feels that his well-planned day was "marching along surely, even jauntily, toward a climax, as a play should, as a day should" (51). And at another moment when he and Gloria are becoming involved, they are "stars on this stage, each playing to an audience of two: the passion of their pretense created the actuality. Here, finally, was the quintessence of self-expression" (116). Later Anthony critiques New York City for the out-of-towner Gloria as if it were a Broadway show: "It's really a transparent, artificial sort of spectacle. It's got it's press-agented stars and its flimsy, unending stage-settings and, I'll admit, the greatest army of supers ever assembled. . . . Technically excellent, perhaps, but not convincing" (119). Gloria replies that when they're married she'd "like to go on the stage sometime—say for about a year." To which Anthony says, "You bet. I'll write a play for you" (119).

At first, however, Gloria believes that the real stage for her acting will be their marriage: "Marriage was created not to be a background but to need one. Mine is going to be outstanding. It can't, shan't be the setting—it's going to be the performance, the live, lovely, glamourous performance, and the world shall be the scenery" (127). But once they're wed, and Joseph Bloekman, who is obviously attracted to Gloria, offers to get her a screen test, Anthony objects, telling her she won't want to hang around "a studio all day with a lot of cheap chorus people," and he concludes with an amateur's denunciation of a professional, "I hate actors" (181)—with the result that when Gloria decides near the novel's end to have the screen test, she doesn't tell Anthony.

If Fitzgerald's use of a dramatic format for one chapter in his first novel was meant to exhibit his modernist experimentalism, his continued use of this technique in *The Beautiful and Damned* suggests that he also probably meant it to advertise his playwriting ability for any prospective producer who might consider commissioning either an original work or a stage or screen adaptation of his fiction. Fitzgerald, whose lifestyle (once he'd married Zelda) always had him more or less in debt, was tempted by the larger and more immediate monetary rewards of playwriting. In "How to Live on $36,000 a Year" Fitzgerald says: "We knew what colossal sums were earned on play royalties, and just to be sure, we asked several playwrights what was the maximum that could be earned on a year's run. . . . I took a sum halfway between the maximum and the minimum, and put that down as what we could fairly count on its earning, I think my figures came to about $100,000" (*Lost* 31). Consequently, after completing *The Beautiful and Damned*, Fitzgerald turned in the spring and summer of 1922 to writing a play. For several months the manuscript of *The Vegetable* made the rounds of Broadway producers without finding any takers, so Fitzgerald had Scribner's publish it as a small book in April 1923. But then George M. Cohan's partner Sam Harris agreed to produce it, and it seemed that Fitzgerald's Broadway career had been launched. Watching the play in rehearsals, Fitzgerald recalls thinking it "was magnificent; my estimate had been too low. I could almost hear the people scrambling for seats, hear the ghostly voices of the movie magnates as they bid against one another for the pictures rights"; it was sure "to be the success of the year" (*Lost* 33). Then the play opened for its tryout in Atlantic City in November 1923, and as Fitzgerald tells it, "It was a colossal frost. People left their seats and walked out, people rustled their programs and talked audibly in bored impatient whispers. After the second act I wanted to stop the show and say it was all a mistake but the actors struggled heroically on" (*Lost* 33).

*The Vegetable* tells the story of Jerry Frost, a railroad clerk, who longs to become a postman but who gets drunk and in an extended dream-sequence comprising the entire second act, imagines he's the president of the United States. Not the worst play ever written, but certainly one of the worst ever written by a major writer, *The Vegetable* is meant to be a satiric comedy, except that it forgets to be funny and the satire is sophomoric. Clearly at this point in his career Fitzgerald's sense of what would play well on the Broadway stage hadn't progressed much past the sort of thing he'd written for the Triangle Club shows. But there can be no doubt about the effect that the failure of his play had on Fitzgerald. As biographer André Le Vot phrases it, "Fitzgerald's play was his swan song to his early manner; its failure wrecked his theatrical ambitions, which, from his boyhood efforts in St. Paul to his Princeton musicals, had seemed to him an alternative to novel writing and a shortcut to glory. With this illusion dissolved, he could devote himself entirely to completing his third novel" (132). Writing in August 1924 to his Princeton classmate Ludlow Fowler (who was the model for Anson Hunter in Fitzgerald's "The Rich Boy"), Fitzgerald says, "I remember our last conversation and it makes me sad. I feel old too, this summer—I have ever since the failure of my play a year ago. Thats the whole burden of this novel [*The Great Gatsby*]—the loss of those illusions that give such color to the world so that you don't care whether things are true or false as long as they partake of the magical glory" (*Correspondence* 145). And in a December 1924 letter to his editor Maxwell Perkins, Fitzgerald, knowing how good the novel he was currently revising really was, could refer to his previous disillusion about his talents as a playwright from a position of renewed strength: "Anyhow I think (for the first time since The Vegetable failed) that I'm a wonderful writer + its your always wonderful letters that help me to go on believing in myself" (Bruccoli, *Grandeur* 216).

4

Critics have noted the way Fitzgerald's abortive venture into Broadway theater with *The Vegetable* may have enabled his achievement in *The Great Gatsby*, and not simply by giving him a vivid taste of that disillusion of youthful dreams that is the core of Gatsby's story. His time spent working with theater professionals readying *The Vegetable* for Broadway probably accounts for the tighter structure of *The Great Gatsby*, accounts for the novel's being written in a series of discrete memorable scenes—the first dinner party at Tom and Daisy's home, the drunken party at Myrtle's apartment, Nick's first attendance at one of Gatsby's parties, Nick and Gatsby's lunch with Meyer Wolfshiem, Daisy's visit to Nick's where she meets Gatsby again and tours Gatsby's home, the confrontation scene at the Plaza hotel, the hit-and-run scene at

George Wilson's garage and its aftermath, Nick's visit to Wolfshiem, Gatsby's funeral.

It is this structure in scenes that has always made *Gatsby* seem a natural vehicle for stage or screen adaptation, and dramatic versions began to appear almost immediately, first with Owen Davis's stage adaptation (directed by George Cukor) that opened on Broadway in February 1926 and then with Paramount Pictures' screen version (based on Davis's play) that opened in November 1926. The silent film (in which the actor William Powell, the embodiment of suave sophistication in so many MGM films of the '30s and '40s, was strangely cast as George Wilson) has not survived. The first sound version of *Gatsby* (1949), directed by Elliott Nugent and starring Alan Ladd, was also made by Paramount, using Davis's adaptation as the basis for the script. The second sound version, released in 1974 and directed by Jack Clayton, starred Robert Redford as Gatsby. I have never seen the silent film, but the two talkies are disappointing, and the Redford film is ruined by miscasting in some of the supporting roles, its only redeeming features being Sam Waterston's performance as Nick Carraway and Howard Da Silva's as Meyer Wolfshiem. As I write this, a new film version of *Gatsby* starring Leonardo DiCaprio has just been released, and it's totally disappointing. The film is filled with the sort of things that Hollywood calls "production values" (color, 3D, special effects, lavish sets, and a soundtrack that mixes recordings of the 1920s with contemporary hip-hop), things that are felt to be necessary when the filmmakers or the studio have lost faith in the story's human value to move us. It's not an ignorant movie (the director Baz Luhrmann and his coscript writer Craig Pearce seem to know something about Fitzgerald's fiction), but it's a movie so full of stupid moments in which the director has made vulgar, incredibly wrong-headed choices that the experience of viewing the film leaves one feeling intellectually and emotionally soiled. But let Fitzgerald have the last word. In "Boil Some Water—Lots of It," the down-at-heels screenwriter Pat Hobby describes his sense of outrage when, in the studio commissary, an extra presumes to sit down at the lunch table reserved for the studio big shots: "It was as if someone had crayoned Donald Duck into 'The Last Supper.'"

More significant for our purposes than the theatrical structuring of the novel in a series of dramatic scenes is the way Fitzgerald makes the notion of theatricality and acting (which had been simply an allusive background for characterizing certain types of social behavior in his first two novels) integral to his third novel's theme. In *Gatsby* theatricality in its various shades of

meaning is evoked as part of a mutually constitutive opposition with the notion of high society, an opposition embodied in the connection between West
Egg and East Egg. The former location, as Nick tells us, is "the less fashionable
of the two, though this is a most superficial tag to express the bizarre and not
a little sinister contrast between them" (8). West Egg was modeled on Great
Neck, Long Island, where the Fitzgeralds lived from the fall of 1922 to the
spring of 1924. At the start of this period Fitzgerald was working on readying
*The Vegetable* for Broadway, and after the play's failure, he used the latter part
of his stay there preparing to write *Gatsby*. When Fitzgerald describes West
Egg as "this unprecedented 'place' that Broadway had begotten upon a Long
Island fishing village" (84), he is literally describing the Great Neck of his day.
It was a town of the newly affluent and particularly of those whose money
came from working in show business (as the protagonist of Fitzgerald's 1927
story "Jacob's Ladder" says to the young woman he's driving back to Manhattan from Long Island, "This is Great Neck . . . that we're passing through. A
lot of moving-picture stars live here" [*Short Stories* 354]).

John Held Jr.'s map of Great Neck and Manhasset (East Egg) published in
the *New Yorker* in 1927 illustrates the concentration of theater and film people in the area. Its residents included Broadway producer Florenz Ziegfeld;
songwriter, producer, director Gene Buck, who wrote the book and lyrics for
many of the Ziegfeld *Follies*; actor and songwriter George M. Cohan; Cohan's partner Sam Harris, who produced *The Vegetable*; Edgar Selwyn, who
ran Goldwyn Productions with his partner Sam Goldfish (who, after chang-
ing his name to Goldwyn, became the G in MGM); actors Lillian Russell,
Basil Rathbone, Leslie Howard, and Ernest Truex (who played the lead role
in *The Vegetable*); and comedians Ed Wynn, Groucho Marx, Eddie Cantor,
and Lew Fields. As Le Vot notes, "the area had been taken over by theater
people, newspapermen, songwriters, and musicians, along with a few rich
bootleggers" (120). Among the newspapermen were Fitzgerald's friends Ring
Lardner and Herbert Bayard Swope. Another resident was Edward Fuller, a
stock swindler who ran "bucket shops" (fraudulent stock brokerage offices)
and was tried several times in the 1920s for fraud and who was a reputed business associate of Arnold Rothstein, the model for *Gatsby*'s Meyer Wolfshiem.
Fuller and Fitzgerald's bootlegger, one Max Gerlach or von Gerlach, provided
the models for Gatsby's shady activities. As opposed to Great Neck, the more
fashionable Manhasset was home to people of old money—money made
from business, finance, and industry—and social position: O. H. P. Belmont,

Dan Guggenheim, Will Guggenheim, Solomon Guggenheim, and Vincent Astor, to name a few.

If East Egg represents high society, a haute monde of inherited wealth and position that endows its possessors with a certain level of visibility or celebrity, then West Egg in some sense represents its reciprocal, the demimonde of show business, that half-world of people who are still in the process of making their fortunes through stage or screen visibility. In effect, wealth creates high society and social visibility in East Egg, while in West Egg theatrical visibility creates affluence and a "less fashionable" society in the making. In Fitzgerald's day the half-world of show-business people shaded off into the underworld of bootleggers, stock swindlers, and gamblers precisely because nightclub and cabaret performers often worked in speakeasies and thus were subject to arrest as lawbreakers just like any other employee of an illegal liquor establishment. This connection often led to underworld figures being secret backers of Broadway shows in order to gain entrée to entertainers for their nightclubs and access to chorus girls. In his 1926 story "The Rich Boy" Fitzgerald says of its protagonist Anson Hunter that "he plunged vigorously into all the movement and glitter of post-bellum New York . . . , moving in three worlds—his own world, the world of young Yale graduates, and that section of the half-world which rests one end on Broadway" (*Short Stories* 325).

This mixture of the half-world of show business with the underworld of bootlegging in the town on which West Egg is modeled suggests what Fitzgerald has in mind in locating Gatsby and Nick next to each other there. Nick is in West Egg because as a young bond salesman he doesn't have much money, and so he goes in with a fellow worker to rent "a weatherbeaten cardboard bungalow at eighty a month," but at the last minute the firm orders the other young man to Washington, and so Nick goes "out to the country alone" (7). Nick is there because, like many of its show-business residents, he is still in the process of working to become successful. He buys "a dozen volumes on banking and credit and investment securities" that promise to "unfold the shining secrets that only Midas and Morgan and Maecenas knew" (7) and is like those "young Englishmen" he notices when he first attends one of Gatsby's parties: they were "all well dressed, all looking a little hungry and all talking in low earnest voices to solid and prosperous Americans. I was sure that they were selling something: bonds or insurance or automobiles. They were, at least, agonizingly aware of the easy money in the vicinity and convinced that it was theirs for a few words in the right key" (35).

As the "vicinity" of "easy money," West Egg represents two career paths (show business and the underworld) a young man can take to get rich quick. Nick knows his path to affluence won't be via the former, but on at least one occasion he is clearly tempted by the latter: when Gatsby, in gratitude for Nick's arranging a meeting with Daisy and knowing that Nick is a bond sales-man, offers to set Nick up with a business deal, "a rather confidential sort of thing," that wouldn't take up much of his time but through which he "might pick up a nice bit of money," Nick refuses, "because the offer was obviously and tactlessly for a service to be rendered." But he realizes in retrospect "that under different circumstances that conversation might have been one of the crises of my life" (65). Apparently the business deal would have involved sto-len bonds, to judge from the long distance phone call Nick receives after Gatsby's death. Thinking he's speaking with Gatsby, the caller says, "Young Parke's in trouble. . . . They picked him up when he handed the bonds over the counter. They got a circular from New York giving 'em the numbers just five minutes before" (129). Of course, the irony of Nick's refusal of Gatsby's offer (along with his subsequent understanding that it would have involved a shady form of payment for a service to be rendered) is that the service he does render—the conveyance of a woman to a man for sexual purposes—is usually thought to be a shady enough, evoking the words "pander" and "pimp."

As a young man trying to make it, Nick belongs in West Egg among people whose success, like Gatsby's, is self-made. And Gatsby, with his shady connec-tions, would have felt at home in West Egg precisely because the half-world of show business seemed to "rest one of its ends" on the underworld. But Gatsby would have also fit in there because Fitzgerald (and this is crucial to our un-derstanding of an element that structures this novel and his two subsequent novels) in some sense thought of Gatsby not so much as an impostor or a parvenu but as the producer, director, writer, and actor in a theatrical perfor-mance, one meant to convince Daisy that they belonged to the same social class and that she should have waited for him. Fitzgerald's sense of Gatsby as an actor is suggested by a passage in his 1924 short story "Absolution" (origi-nally planned, as already noted, as part of *The Great Gatsby* depicting James Gatz's childhood but cut from the novel and published separately), in which the protagonist Rudolph Miller (the young James Gatz) says that when he grows up, he wants to be either "an actor or a Navy officer" (*Short Stories* 270).

Fitzgerald had, of course, used the scenario of a young man staging an elaborate dramatic performance for a young woman in three earlier short stories—"Myra Meets His Family" (March 1920), "The Offshore Pirate" (May 1920) and "Rags Martin-Jones and the Pr-nce of W-les" (July 1924)—but in each case the performance is a trick and the man and woman are both from the same social class. In "Myra Meets His Family" a wealthy young man becomes engaged without his parents' consent to a woman he begins to suspect is a fortune hunter, so he invites his fiancée to meet his family but hires a group of actors to play his parents and behave so outrageously that the young woman will break the engagement. The plan backfires, and the story ends with the woman getting her revenge. On the other hand, in "The Offshore Pirate" a wealthy young man, Toby Moreland, stages an elaborate ruse to win the affection of Ardita Farnam, a rich, bored young woman hungry for adventure. Moreland, claiming to be the leader of a jazz band called Curtis Carlyle and His Six Black Buddies, boards Ardita's uncle's yacht with his band off the Florida coast and pretends to pirate the ship, carrying off Ardita to a deserted island. The excitement of the adventure ultimately captures Ardita's imagination and her heart. When the ruse is revealed, Toby fears she'll be angry at being tricked, but Ardita only asks if he'll swear the whole plan "was entirely a product of your own brain." When he says yes, she replies, "What an imagination! . . . I want you to lie to me just as sweetly as you know how for the rest of my life" (*Short Stories* 95–96).

The most significant aspect of "The Offshore Pirate" for our purposes is that, though Toby and Ardita are both rich, the story that Toby, playing the role of Curtis Carlyle, tells Ardita about his background sounds like a trial run for Gatsby's story. He says that "he began life as a poor kid in a Tennessee town, . . . so poor that his people were the only white family in their street." This close association with black folk "diverted a rather unusual musical gift into a strange channel," and he came under the tutelage of "a colored woman named Belle Pope Calhoun who played the piano at parties given for . . . nice white children that would have passed Curtis Carlyle with a sniff. But the ragged little 'poh white' used to sit beside her piano by the hour and try to get in an alto with one of those kazoos that boys hum through." Curtis then began playing ragtime on the violin, and eight years later when "the ragtime craze hit the country," he organized a band and almost before he knew it, "was on Broadway, with offers of engagements on all sides, and more money than he had ever dreamed of" (79). With success, Curtis began to raise his sights: "He wanted to have a lot of money and time, . . . and the sort of men and women round him that he could never have—the kind who, if they thought of him at all, would have considered him rather contemptible; in short he wanted all those things which he was beginning to lump under the general head of aristocracy, an aristocracy which it seemed almost any money could buy except money made as he was making it" (80), that is, money made in the demimonde of show business. Curtis says he finally became so fed up with entertaining the upper classes that one night in Palm Beach when his band was playing a high society party, he and the other band members put away their instruments, whipped out automatics, and held up the crowd—the half-world of show business giving way to the underworld of armed robbery. When Ardita asks what he intends to do now, Curtis says he plans to go to India and "be a rajah, . . . buy up a palace and a reputation, and then after about five years appear in England with a foreign accent and a mysterious past. . . . Then . . . comes aristocracy" (84). (Curtis's plan to be a rajah recalls Gatsby's remark to Nick during their car ride into Manhattan: "I lived like a young rajah in all the capitals of Europe" [52].) Ardita calls Curtis "an idealistic boy with a lot of caste nonsense in his head," and says, "Perhaps if I were just a little bit older and a little more bored I'd go with you. As it is, I think I'll go back and marry—that other man" (91).

Similarly, in "Rags Martin-Jones and the Pr-nce of W-les" wealthy John M. Chestnut tries to capture the imagination of the rich, spoiled Rags Martin-Jones, whom he has been in love with for five years, by staging a wildly exciting performance. The heiress Rags has just returned from France and tells Chestnut she's going back soon and won't marry him because he hasn't "any imagination. . . . No Americans have any imagination. Paris is the only large city where a civilized woman can breathe." Rags adds, "Last spring in Sorrento I almost eloped with an Indian rajah, but he was half a shade too dark," though "he was the third richest subject of the British Empire" (*Short Stories* 277). Sensing that Rags is impressed by British royalty, Chestnut that same night puts on an elaborate ruse for Rags at a Manhattan rooftop nightclub; he has hired someone who resembles the Prince of Wales (at the time the world's most eligible bachelor) to be part of a scenario in which the police will raid the nightclub and arrest Chestnut for murder. Rags tries to help Chestnut escape by convincing the bogus Prince of Wales to take her and Chestnut over the Canadian border in his limousine, saying that "it's a runaway marriage" (285). When the theatrical performance is revealed, Rags asks, "Was the whole thing just *mine*? . . . Was it a perfectly gorgeous, useless thing, just for me?" (287); needless to say, Rags marries Chestnut. For our purposes, the story's most interesting moment takes place in the nightclub during the floor show when the spotlight is turned on Rags seated at her table, a moment that anticipates the restaurant scene in *Tender Is the Night* where Dick Diver claims that he's the only American with repose. As part of his act, the nightclub comedian, Sheik B. Smith, indicates that he wants the spotlight to focus on this strikingly beautiful young woman, and he begins to make fun of her: "Instinctively she had composed her face at the first shock of the light and now she smiled. It was a gesture of rare self-possession. Into this smile she insinuated a vast impersonality, as if she were unconscious of the light, unconscious of his attempt to play upon her loveliness—but amused at an infinitely removed *him*, whose darts might have been thrown just as success-fully at the moon. . . . Rags stripped her attitude to a sheer consciousness of her own impervious beauty, sat there glittering until the comedian began to feel alone as he had never felt alone before. At a signal from him the spot-light was switched suddenly out. The moment was over" (281).

As Toby Moreland in "The Offshore Pirate" mounts a production in which he pretends to be the Gatsby-like, rags-to-riches figure Curtis Carlyle, so Gatsby mounts one in which he pretends to be a Toby-like figure, the scion of inherited wealth. Fitzgerald's sense of Gatsby's mansion and his extrava-gant hospitality as a stage setting is established at the first party Nick attends. When Nick and Jordan come upon Owl Eyes in Gatsby's library, the drunken man shows them one of the books and says, "It's a bona fide piece of printed matter. It fooled me. This fella's a regular Belasco. It's a triumph. What thor-oughness! What realism!" (38). The legendary Broadway producer, director, playwright, and theater owner David Belasco (1853–1931) was known in his own day for the realism of his stage sets, though he is probably best remem-bered today for his 1900 play *Madame Butterfly* (which he had dramatized from John Luther Long's short story of the same name and which Puccini had used as the libretto for his 1904 opera *Madama Butterfly*) and also for his 1905 play *The Girl of the Golden West* (which Puccini used as the libretto for his 1910 opera *La fanciulla del West* and which also served as the libretto for the 1938 Nelson Eddy and Jeanette MacDonald film *The Girl of the Golden West* with music by Sigmund Romberg and lyrics by Gus Kahn).

And if Gatsby is evoked as the theatrical producer of his parties, then it seems only natural that many of his guests on that set should be from show business, like "Newton Orchid, who controlled Films Par Excellence [the same company of which Joseph Bloekman is vice president in *The Beautiful and Damned*], and Eckhaust and Clyde Cohen and Don S. Schwartze (the son) and Arthur McCarty, all connected with the movies in one way or another" (50) or "the moving picture director and his Star" seated beneath "the white plum tree" (83) in Gatsby's garden at the party Daisy and Tom attend, or the young woman who starts the dancing at the first party Nick goes to and who is erroneously rumored to be "Gilda Gray's understudy from the 'Follies'" (34), or the two "girls in yellow" who had met Jordan Baker at a previous Gatsby party and who turned out to be "a pair of stage 'twins'" and "did a baby act in costume" (39). Of course, any professional entertainer invited to a party would have been expected to do a bit of entertaining, indeed, would have been disappointed if they hadn't at least been asked. Moreover, anyone invited to a party in the 1920s, unlike today, would have expected the guests to entertain themselves, even if nothing more than gathering around a piano to sing the old songs or sing current popular songs to the accompaniment of a ukulele. And there would have been other party goers who could be counted on to perform their characteristic "party piece"—a song, a dance, a skit—like the routine my uncle and aunt, who were young people in the 1920s, performed at parties to the songs "My Grandfather's Clock" and "When I Get You Alone Tonight." Consequently, at Gatsby's party, "a celebrated tenor had sung in Italian and a notorious contralto had sung in jazz, and between the numbers people were doing 'stunts' all over the garden" (39).

To the extent that Gatsby's mansion and parties are theatrical productions, he is the playwright of the role he enacts there, a role he originated when James Gatz became Jay Gatsby. The first time that he tries to tell Nick something about his life (because he doesn't want Nick "to get a wrong idea" of him "from all these stories you hear"), he says, "I am the son of some wealthy people in the middle-west. . . . My family all died and I came into a good deal of money" (52). As Thorstein Veblen notes in *The Theory of the Leisure Class* (1899) (a favorite book of Fitzgerald's), from the notion of wealth as "intrinsically" conferring "honour on its possessor," a "further refinement" occurs in which "wealth acquired passively by transmission from ancestors or other antecedents . . . becomes even more honorific than wealth acquired by the possessor's own effort" (19)—a sentiment with which Gatsby apparently agrees. Gatsby adds that he was "brought up in America but educated at Oxford because all my ancestors have been educated there for many years. It is a family tradition." Nick says, "He hurried the phrase 'educated at Oxford,' or swallowed it or choked on it as though it had bothered him before. And with this doubt his whole statement fell to pieces" (52). When Gatsby claims to be the son of wealthy people from the Middle West, he knows Nick would probably have no immediate grounds to doubt this, but when he adds that he was "educated at Oxford," he realizes that Nick, a Yale graduate familiar with the social markers of a college education, is someone who can critique his performance with a knowing eye, and so Gatsby's acting ability falters. He becomes self-conscious under the gaze of the other, immediately checking to see whether that gaze has registered his discomfort. Nick says that Gatsby "looked at me sideways—and I knew why Jordan had believed he was lying" (52). Made suspicious by the Oxford claim, Nick then questions the claim about his wealthy family in the Middle West and asks, "What part of the middle-west?" To which Gatsby replies, "San Francisco." Nick's only response is "I see" (52). Nick's skepticism grows as Gatsby elaborates his life story: "With an effort I managed to restrain my incredulous laughter. The very phrases were worn so threadbare that they evoked no image except that of a turbaned 'character' leaking sawdust at every pore as he pursued a tiger through the Bois de Boulogne" (52). But when Gatsby, like David Belasco, produces two realistic stage props (the medal of the Order of Danilo from Montenegro and the photograph taken in the Trinity Quad at Oxford with a man who "is now the Earl of Doncaster"), Nick doesn't exclaim like Owl Eyes in the library, "What thoroughness! What realism!" He simply thinks, "Then it was all true. I saw the skins of tigers flaming in his palace on the Grand Canal; I saw him opening a chest of rubies to ease, with their crimson-lighted depths, the gnawings of his broken heart" (53).

To appreciate what is at stake emotionally for Fitzgerald in his evocation of Gatsby as an actor in a social drama, consider a passage in his memoir "Pasting It Together" (one of "The Crack-Up" essays) published in March 1936. Noting the kind of emotional jolts from which "a man does not recover" but rather "becomes a different person" who "finds new things to care about," Fitzgerald talks about the kind of person he turned into when Zelda at first refused to marry him because he was penniless, then consented, once his first book was published and his success seemed assured:

> It was one of those tragic loves doomed for lack of money, and one day the girl closed it out on the basis of common sense. During a long summer of despair I wrote a novel instead of letters, so it came out all right, but it came out all right for a different person. The man with the jingle of money in his pocket

who married the girl a year later would always cherish an abiding distrust, an animosity, toward the leisure class—not the conviction of a revolutionist but the smouldering hatred of a peasant. In the years since then I have never been able to stop wondering where my friends' money came from, nor to stop thinking that at one time a sort of *droit de seigneur* might have been exercised to give one of them my girl.

For sixteen years I lived pretty much as this latter person, distrusting the rich, yet working for money with which to share their mobility and the grace that some of them brought into their lives. (*Lost* 146–47)

Fitzgerald's mother's family had had enough money to send him to a private prep school in the East and then on to Princeton, where many of his classmates and friends would have been the sons of wealthy men, but Fitzgerald was not the son of a wealthy man and had no inherited money waiting to give him his start in life. During those sixteen years (the period from 1920 to 1936), Fitzgerald—who had acquired the education, manners, social connections, and expectations associated with the leisure class but not its capital—wanted nevertheless to move among the wealthy, to share the mobility and grace their money brought, and as a result he seems to have continually felt like an actor playing a role, giving people the social impression (much like that which Gatsby had given Daisy when he first wooed her) not that he had "phantom millions" but that "he was a person from much the same strata" (116). And Fitzgerald's sense that he was acting a role, creating a quasi-theatrical social persona, must have served as a way of explaining to himself (of distancing and defending himself psychologically from) the numerous compromises his social role-playing demanded. In the sentence that immediately follows the passage just quoted from "Pasting It Together," Fitzgerald says, "During this time I had plenty of the usual horses shot from under me—I remember some of their names—*Punctured Pride, Thwarted Expectation, Faithless, Show-off, Hard Hit, Never Again*. And after awhile I wasn't twenty-five, then not even thirty-five, and nothing was quite as good" (*Lost* 147). As social actors Gatsby and Fitzgerald are in a sense reciprocals of one another: Gatsby has the money but not the markers (background, education, social polish, society connections) that go with inherited wealth, while the Princetonian Fitzgerald has the markers but not the money. And in each instance it is the pursuit of a woman—a woman won in Fitzgerald's case but lost in Gatsby's—that precipitates the man's painful awareness of what he lacks.

The automobile ride into New York City, during which Gatsby tells Nick the lie that he is "the son of some wealthy people in the middle-west," brings them to the lunch with Meyer Wolfshiem, and Fitzgerald again evokes a theatrical ambience for this meeting. The restaurant where they lunch is in "a well-fanned Forty-second Street cellar" (55), Forty-Second Street being then as now the heart of the theater district, as the movie musical of the same name makes clear—the place, as the film's title song explains, "where the underworld can meet the elite." After the meal is over and Wolfshiem has left, Gatsby explains, "He's quite a character around New York—a denizen of Broadway." To which Nick replies, "Who is he anyhow—an actor?" And Gatsby says, "No, he's a gambler. . . . He's the man who fixed the World Series back in 1919" (58). Though Wolfshiem may in fact be a gambler, Fitzgerald uses the specific example illustrating this (the fixing of the World Series) to suggest why Wolfshiem is described as "a denizen of Broadway"; for what the gambler has done, in effect, is turn a legitimate sporting event into a quasi-theatrical performance in which certain players for the Chicago White Sox were acting as if they were trying to win when in fact they were throwing the series to the Cincinnati Reds. This was yet one more example for Fitzgerald of how the "section of the half-world which rests one end on Broadway" rested its other end on the underworld. Moreover, Fitzgerald probably knew that the usual spot where Wolfshiem's model, Arnold Rothstein, hung out was a famous restaurant frequented by show people—Lindy's, located in the 1920s on Broadway between Forty-Ninth and Fiftieth. Rothstein called it his favorite "office."

As they're talking, Nick spies Tom Buchanan across the restaurant and says to Gatsby, "Come along with me for a minute, . . . I've got to say hello to someone." Gatsby accompanies Nick, not knowing that the person he's going to greet is Buchanan, and when Nick introduces the two, they shake hands, but Nick notices that "a strained, unfamiliar look of embarrassment came over Gatsby's face." When Tom asks Nick how he happened to come this far uptown to eat, Nick explains that he'd been lunching with Gatsby: "I turned toward Mr. Gatsby, but he was no longer there" (59). Given that Gatsby's assuming the role of an Oxford graduate had faltered earlier under the gaze of a Yale man, he clearly wasn't going to trust, for the second time in the space of a few hours, his performance as a person of inherited wealth in the presence of the real thing.

Yet Gatsby is not the only character in the novel who gives a quasi-

theatrical performance. When Nick first has dinner at the Buchanans', he has
the sense that Daisy is playing a role and that he's the intended audience:
While sitting on the front porch by themselves, Daisy tells Nick, "You see I
think everything's terrible anyhow. . . . Everybody thinks so—the most ad-
vanced people. And I *know*. I've been everywhere and seen everything and
done everything. . . . Sophisticated—God, I'm sophisticated!" But "the instant her voice broke off, ceasing to compel my attention, my belief," Nick

> felt the basic insincerity of what she had said. It made me uneasy, as though the
> whole evening had been a trick of some sort to exact a contributory emotion
> from me. I waited, and sure enough, in a moment she looked at me with an
> absolute smirk on her lovely face as if she had asserted her membership in a
> rather distinguished secret society to which she and Tom belonged. (17)

Which is to say, the sophisticated high society of East Egg. And Nick discovers this same theatrical social behavior in Jordan Baker, but put to a more
sinister purpose. He finds that the "bored haughty face" Jordan "turned to the
world concealed something—most affectations conceal something eventually, even though they don't in the beginning." At a house party Jordan leaves
a borrowed car out in the rain with the top down and then lies about it, and
this jogs Nick's memory, recalling a story he'd heard about her having moved
her ball from a bad lie in her first big golf tournament. Nick judges that Jordan "felt safer on a plane where any divergence from a code would be thought
impossible. She was incurably dishonest. She wasn't able to endure being at a
disadvantage, and given this unwillingness I suppose she had begun dealing
in subterfuges when she was very young in order to keep that cool insolent
smile turned to the world" (47–48). Certainly, Fitzgerald means for us to see,
as instances of postwar moral decline, the implied link between this incident
of a society girl cheating in a sporting event (an incident that was hushed-
up, as Nick remembers) and a gambler fixing a sporting event like the World
Series (an incident that became a national scandal).


## 5

As a reader of Veblen, Fitzgerald would have understood many of the activities of the leisure class as essentially matters of "display"—either of monetary
"waste" or "conspicuous consumption"—the putting on of a social "show" at
parties or debutante balls, at weddings or fundraisers or horse shows or polo

matches, displays of grand houses, yachts, foreign cars, custom-made clothes, or designer gowns. And he saw that these displays required a degree of social stagecraft in their presentation, as well as a certain type of acting ability on the part of people wishing to play a role in this society. Given his sense of the quasi-theatrical activities of East Egg, we can understand the reciprocity Fitzgerald establishes between it and its "less fashionable" counterpart—between the amateur (money "acquired passively by transmission from ancestors" [19]) and the professional (money "acquired by the possessor's own efforts" [19]). This sense of the theatrical aspect of one's being in "society" implicates a whole series of related notions: the gaze, physical sight versus imaginative insight, visibility as power versus visibility as vulnerability, to name a few. We can see, for example, that West Egg's show people, striving to create a society in their "less fashionable" demimonde, have made their money in a business whose very essence, whose capital, is visibility (whether on stage, screen, or a nightclub floor). As professionals they have the training and experience that allow them to stand the gaze of the Other without betraying any self-consciousness at being scrutinized by eyes that may be hostile, indifferent, or uncomprehending, a self-consciousness that might cause them to flub a line, forget a lyric, or miss a step. They know their success as professionals, their ability to make money and be part of the "society" of West Egg, ultimately depends on their self-possession, their continuing power not just to invite but to *attract* the gaze of the Other. As Joel Coles, the young Hollywood writer in Fitzgerald's 1932 story "Crazy Sunday," phrases it on observing the crowd of show-business people at Miles and Stella Calman's party, "he felt happy and friendly toward all the people gathered there, people of bravery and industry, superior to a bourgeoisie that outdid them in ignorance and loose living, risen to a position of the highest prominence in a nation that for a decade had wanted only to be entertained" (*Short Stories* 701). Fitzgerald tells us, predictably enough, that, earlier at the party, when Joel greets his hostess, the movie star Stella Walker Calman, he "drew quickly on the dramatic adequacy inherited from his mother," a famous stage actress, adding that the movie director "Miles Calman's house was built for great emotional moments . . . , as if the far silences of its vistas hid an audience" (699.)

As visibility creates wealth for the show people of West Egg, so wealth creates visibility for the society people of East Egg—the visibility of being "recognized" by their social peers, of having their names or photos appear in the society pages of newspapers and magazines, of being acknowledged as one of "our crowd." But there is also a degree of vulnerability attendant on vis-ibility, of being someone whose name and face are known by a public whose names and faces one does not know or recognize in turn. As we shall see, Fitzgerald deals with this type of vulnerability as it effects show people in his depiction of Rosemary Hoyt, the budding movie star, in *Tender Is the Night*. But in *The Great Gatsby* Fitzgerald subtly evokes the vulnerability attaching to high society's visibility when Tom Buchanan dragoons Nick into meeting his mistress and accompanying them to the Manhattan apartment that is, as the tabloid headlines would say, their "love nest" (recall that one of the songs Klipspringer plays on the piano when Daisy first visits Gatsby's house is "The Love Nest"). And indeed the notion of how a tabloid would have described this hideaway is clearly on Fitzgerald's mind.

When Nick, Tom, and Myrtle Wilson disembark at the train station in Manhattan, Myrtle buys "a copy of 'Town Tattle' and a moving picture maga-zine" (24), and later, at the apartment, Nick notices "several old copies of 'Town Tattle'" (25) on the coffee table. This repeated reference alludes, as Sharon Hamilton has shown, to a New York high society scandal magazine of the day called *Town Topics*. The magazine specialized in reporting upper-class suicides "and extra-marital affairs," and "there were even allusions to homosexuality . . . and cross dressing" in its society columns (Hamilton 35). Moreover, the magazine's owner, Colonel William D'Alton Mann, was not above using the magazine to extort amounts ranging from $2,500 to $10,000 from people whose careers or social standing would have been ruined by the report of an adulterous affair—like that between Tom Buchanan of East Egg and the wife of a garage owner. Indeed, one can only imagine what *Town Topics* would have done with the story of Tom Buchanan's wife running down Tom's mistress in a hit-and-run accident and the subsequent murder, by Myr-tle's husband, of the man who was in the car with Tom's wife (and who was having an affair with her), the bootlegger Jay Gatsby.

Fitzgerald points out how Gatsby's social notoriety had almost risen to the level of celebrity in the incident of the "ambitious young reporter" who shows up "one morning at Gatsby's door." The reporter "had heard Gatsby's name around his office in a connection which he either wouldn't reveal or didn't fully understand" and had come out on his day off hoping to get an in-terview: "Gatsby's notoriety, spread about by the hundreds who had accepted his hospitality and so become authorities upon his past, had increased all summer until he fell just short of being news. Contemporary legends such as the 'underground pipe-line to Canada' attached themselves to him" (76). This kind of visibility, considered as the celebrity or near celebrity that attaches both to the demimonde of show business and to the haute monde of society, clearly lay behind Fitzgerald's remark in *The Beautiful and Damned* about Beauty being reincarnated in modern America either as "an actress in the motion-pictures" or "a 'susciety' gurl, . . . a sort of bogus aristocrat" (31). And in the case of Gatsby, the lavish party giver, and his associate Wolfshiem, the man who fixed the 1919 World Series, this type of near celebrity could extend from the half-world of show business into the underworld.

Given the notion of celebrity as being at once powerful and vulnerable, we can begin to grasp the network of motivations created by locating Jay Gatsby's home in West Egg. In *The Great Gatsby* both protagonist and narrator, as we have observed, each try to keep in view his respective object of desire: Daisy in Gatsby's case and Gatsby in Nick's. The first time Nick catches sight of Gatsby is at night: Gatsby is looking at the green light at the end of Daisy's dock, a gazing that embodies his determination never to lose sight of the woman he loves. Indeed, as Gatsby tells Jordan, he had subscribed to a Chicago newspaper "for years just on the chance of *catching a glimpse* of Daisy's name" (63, italics mine) in the society pages. By relocating to West Egg and giving lavish parties, Gatsby plans to make it possible (indeed, inevitable) for Daisy once again to catch sight of him, either by showing up at one of his parties and realizing that the host was the man she once loved or by hearing his name mentioned by one of his guests, as she does when Jordan Baker drops his name at the dinner party she and Nick attend at the novel's start. But Gatsby's relationship to near-celebrity status requires a delicate balance: he wants visibility enough to attract Daisy and effect their reunion but not so much that he rises to the level of being news, of attracting reporters who would inquire into his background and the source of his wealth. But there is yet a further sense in which Gatsby means to take advantage of the power of celebrity.

In playing the role of someone of inherited wealth, Gatsby means to show Daisy that when he'd first met her he'd indeed been "a person from much the same strata as herself" and that she'd made a mistake in marrying Tom instead of waiting for him. But since Daisy is already married to someone from her own class, Gatsby feels that to win her back he must show her he possesses an added something Tom doesn't have. And here is where Gatsby avails himself of the stage and screen visibility of his West Egg neighbors. When Gatsby first shows Daisy his house and asks her if she likes it, she says,

"I love it, but I don't see how you live there all alone." And he replies, "I keep it always full of interesting people, night and day. People who do interesting things. Celebrated people" (71). Fitzgerald would make the attraction of stage celebrities for society people explicit in his 1933 short story "I Got Shoes": the actress Nell Margery tells her upper-class suitor that "when an actress marries a society man . . . they're both taking a chance for the sake of vanity. He wants to parade her celebrity through his world, and she wants to parade his background through hers" (*Price* 477). Gatsby means for the acclaim of his show business neighbors to rub off on him, which is clearly the reason why, at the party Daisy and Tom attend, he says, "Look around. . . .You must see the faces of many people you've heard about." And when Tom says, "We don't go around very much. . . . In fact I was just thinking I don't know a soul here," Gatsby counters with, "Perhaps you know that lady," pointing out "a gorgeous, scarcely human orchid of a woman who sat in state under a white plum tree": "Tom and Daisy stared, with that peculiarly unreal feeling that accompanies the recognition of a hitherto ghostly celebrity of the movies" (82).

But Gatsby's plan to impress Daisy at his party doesn't work. Nick wonders if Tom's accompanying Daisy hadn't given "the evening its peculiar quality of oppressiveness," but he concludes that the party had "an unpleasantness in the air, a pervading harshness that hadn't been there before," only because he had, from previous parties, "grown to accept West Egg as a world complete in itself, with its own standards and its own great figures, second to nothing because *it had no consciousness of being so*, and now I was looking at it again, through Daisy's eyes" (81, italics mine). Daisy is "offended" by Gatsby's party, Nick theorizes, "because it wasn't a gesture but an emotion. She was appalled by West Egg, this unprecedented 'place' that Broadway had begotten upon a Long island fishing village—appalled by its raw vigor that chafed under the old euphemisms. . . . She saw something awful in the very simplicity she failed to understand" (84). If West Egg represents the realm of "emotion"— the "raw vigor" and enthusiasm of its newly affluent, first-generation strivers trying to create with their earnings a new kind of *arriviste* "society"—then East Egg represents the realm of the "gesture"—the unspoken set of acceptable social performances or behaviors mutually recognized by second- or third-generation possessors of inherited wealth.

Fitzgerald's narrative emphasizes the contrast between these two realms through the event that immediately precedes Tom and Daisy's attendance at Gatsby's party. Having effected the reunion of Gatsby and Daisy, Nick loses touch with Gatsby for several weeks, so he goes over to Gatsby's house one Sunday afternoon. Within minutes "a party of three on horseback" show up— "Tom and a man named Sloane and a pretty woman in a brown riding-habit" (who had attended one of Gatsby's parties). Gatsby rings for drinks and plays host, trying to engage his guests in small talk: "Mr. Sloane didn't enter into the conversation but lounged back haughtily in his chair; the woman said nothing either—until unexpectedly, after two highballs, she became cordial" (79–80). Gatsby invites them all to stay to supper, but the woman counters by inviting Gatsby and Nick to supper at her house: "Gatsby looked at me questioningly. He wanted to go and he didn't see that Mr. Sloane had determined he shouldn't" (80). Nick demurs, but when the woman repeats her invitation, Gatsby, taking it at face value, says he'll follow them in his car and goes to get his topcoat. Tom says to Nick, "My God, I believe the man's coming. . . . Doesn't he know she doesn't want him?" Nick replies, "She says she does want him," and Tom says, "She has a big dinner party and he won't know a soul there" (81), so the three ride off before Gatsby returns. Fitzgerald underlines the link between this scene and the one immediately following (where Tom and Daisy survey the crowd at Gatsby's party) by having Tom remark, "I was just thinking I don't know a soul here" (82). Since Gatsby doesn't understand the type of social playacting that characterizes East Egg's elite, he looks to Nick to see how he should respond to the woman's dinner invitation, but then he doesn't follow Nick's lead in declining because he wants to appear at the same East Egg function Daisy and Tom will be present at so as to show Daisy that he's been accepted by her set. What Gatsby doesn't understand about the woman's dinner invitation is the difference between a more or less perfunctory social "gesture" of politeness (by which the woman has declined Gatsby's offer to stay to supper by making a counteroffer, so that Gatsby will have to do the declining) and the authentic "emotion" of friendship and hospitality.

Fitzgerald directs our attention to the ongoing importance of the gaze and its special relevance to the novel's quasi-theatrical social interactions when he has Nick remark at the Gatsby party Daisy and Tom attend that he was now looking at the world of West Egg "again, through Daisy's eyes." The gaze takes various forms in *Gatsby*, depending on whether one is looking at another or being looked at by another, whether the one being observed is aware of the other's gaze, whether the one being observed is also engaged in the act of gazing, or whether one imagines looking through another's eyes. Although

Nick's role as narrator demands that he keep the protagonist of his story in view, whether through physical sight or imaginative insight, when Nick first catches sight of the subject of his narrative, it is at night, and Gatsby, unaware that he's being observed, is himself gazing at the green light on Daisy's dock. Nick thinks he should introduce himself to his neighbor, but Gatsby "gave a sudden intimation that he was content to be alone—he stretched out his arms toward the dark water in a curious way, and far as I was from him I could have sworn he was trembling" (20). This idea—that when a person is unaware of being looked at, his physical gestures or facial expression display his true character or feelings—is explicitly voiced for Nick at the first Gatsby party he attends. Speculating about Gatsby's background, one of the guests says, "Somebody told me they thought he killed a man once. . . . You look at him sometime when he thinks nobody's looking at him. I'll bet he killed a man" (36–37). And that initial scene of observing a gazer who is unaware of being looked at is repeated for Nick during the drive into New York on that fatal Sunday. Tom, driving Gatsby's yellow roadster with Nick and Jordan as passengers, pulls into George Wilson's service station for gas, and Nick, who says that this "locality was always vaguely disquieting," now turns his head as though he "had been warned of something behind":

> Over the ashheaps the giant eyes of Doctor T. J. Eckleburg kept their vigil but I perceived, after a moment, that other eyes were regarding us with peculiar intensity from less than twenty feet away.
>
> In one of the windows over the garage the curtains had been moved aside a little and Myrtle Wilson was peering down at the car. So engrossed was she that she had no consciousness of being observed and one emotion after another crept into her face like objects into a slowly developing picture. (97)

Nick says that "her expression was curiously familiar" from his having seen it on the faces of other women, but Myrtle's look of "jealous terror" had seemed at first "inexplicable" until he realized that her eyes "were fixed not on Tom but on Jordan Baker, whom she took to be his wife" (97). (Fitzgerald will produce a variant of this scene in *Tender Is the Night* when Nicole goes to see Abe North off at the Gare Saint Lazare, and Abe "watched her" from a distance: "she was self-revelatory in her little expressions as people seem to someone waiting for them, who as yet is himself unobserved. She was frowning, thinking of her children, less gloating over them than merely animally counting them—a cat checking her cubs with a paw" [93].)

Unaware that she is being observed, Myrtle makes no attempt to keep her feelings from showing, but later when Tom, during the confrontation scene at the Plaza, tells Daisy, Nick, and Jordan what he's learned about Gatsby's shady dealings, Gatsby is unable to hide his emotions. Nick says, "That unfamiliar yet recognizable look was back again in Gatsby's face" (105), a look that Nick had seen earlier in the day at the Buchanans' house when Tom had remarked "you can buy anything at a drug store nowadays": "an indefinable expression, at once definitely unfamiliar and vaguely recognizable, as if I had only heard it described in words, passed over Gatsby's face" (94). And on the second occasion when Nick sees that expression, he remembers what he had heard described: "He looked—and this is said in all contempt for the babbled slander of his garden—as if he had 'killed a man'" (105). And of course, in some sense Gatsby has killed a man—James Gatz.

In staging his performance as a person of inherited wealth, Gatsby continually finds himself caught in a dilemma. On the one hand, he wants, as we said, to become visible enough in West Egg to attract the attention of Daisy across the "courtesy bay" in East Egg. But, on the other hand, he doesn't want to become so visible that he turns into news and thus attracts the attention of inquiring reporters. Similarly, in his confrontation with Tom at the Plaza, Gatsby, who has chosen to stage his quasi-theatrical social performance in West Egg among a community of theater people, doesn't, on the one hand, possess a professional actor's training or experience, the kind of stagecraft that would allow him to continue convincingly playing the role of inherited wealth after Tom has exposed the source of Gatsby's money. Nor does he, on the other hand, possess the sophisticated social "theatricality" of East Egg, the sangfroid or "repose" (to use Dick Diver's word) not to betray his self-conscious discomfort when faced with Tom's scorn at his presumption in trying to associate with people of Tom and Daisy's class. It seems clear that Gatsby must have realized Daisy would discover sooner or later the kind of business he was in and thus be led to wonder whether he had been lying, when he first made love to her in Louisville, in giving her the impression he was "a person from much the same strata as herself." Yet one can imagine Gatsby had already prepared a story to answer any such doubts. Having told Nick that he was the son of wealthy people in the Middle West who had left him "a good deal of money," Gatsby, on the day he has Nick invite Daisy to tea, stands looking at his house and says, "My house looks well, doesn't it? . . . It took me just three years to earn the money that bought it." And Nick says,

"I thought you inherited your money."

"I did, old sport," he said automatically, "but I lost most of it in the big panic—the panic of the war."

I think he hardly knew what he was saying, for when I asked him what business he was in he answered, "That's my affair," before he realized that it wasn't an appropriate reply. (70–71)

That Gatsby would have eventually explained the source of his money to Daisy by saying that he'd lost his inherited wealth in the "panic of the war" and then been forced to go into a questionable line of work to recoup his fortune can be inferred from his response to Tom's accusation at the Plaza that Gatsby "and this Wolfshiem bought up a lot of side-street drug stores here and in Chicago and sold grain alcohol over the counter. . . . I picked him for a bootlegger the first time I saw him" (104). To which Gatsby says, "What about it? . . . I guess your friend Walter Chase wasn't too proud to come in on it" (104). In pointing out that a personal friend from Tom's social class had thrown in with him and Wolfshiem, Gatsby implies in Daisy's presence that his way of making money is not déclassé enough to be beneath someone from East Egg, someone of inherited wealth who had fallen on hard times, not déclassé enough to be an impediment to their ultimate marriage. Or as a character in Fitzgerald's 1931 short story "A Change of Class" says when her husband objects to attending a party at the home of a reputed bootlegger, "Lots of nice people are bootleggers now—society people even." And she adds, "They have a beautiful home, and they're more refined than most of the people we know" (*Price* 356). Indeed, in recent American history, we have an example of someone who started out as a reputed bootlegger, then owned a movie studio, became ambassador to England, and had a son who became president of the United States.

If society people can be bootleggers, then bootleggers can be society people, especially if they have a beautiful home. But of course what Fitzgerald means for the reader to recall is that the type of inherited wealth represented by the residents of East Egg would have come from fortunes originally amassed two or three generations earlier by individuals whose business dealings made bootlegging and trafficking in stolen bonds seem like child's play. Indeed, the only real persons of extreme wealth mentioned by name in *Gatsby* are J. P. Morgan and John D. Rockefeller. Nick says he bought a dozen volumes on banking that promised to "unfold the shining secrets that only

Midas and Morgan and Maecenas knew" (7), and he notes that the old man who sells Myrtle a puppy outside the Manhattan train station bears "an absurd resemblance to John D. Rockefeller" (24). Recall that J. P. Morgan's first successful business venture had involved buying defective muskets from the U.S. Army on the East Coast during the Civil War and then shipping these same muskets out to the West and reselling them to the Army as new, while Rockefeller's business practices in founding the Standard Oil Trust had continually wavered between the unethical and the illegal. If, as the saying goes, at the origin of every great fortune is a great crime, then the American corollary of this is that the stain of a great crime can always be washed off a family name by the waters of time and the detergent of philanthropy.

Fitzgerald enunciates a three-generation rule for this transformation in his 1920 short story "The Ice Palace" (and not the one about shirt sleeves to shirt sleeves in three generations). Recall that in explaining his Northern hometown to his Southern fiancée, Harry Bellamy says he knows "Southerners put quite an emphasis on family" but if she notices in the town

> things that'll seem to you sort of vulgar display at first, . . . just remember that this is a three-generation town. Everybody has a father, and about half of us have grandfathers. Back of that we don't go. . . . Our grandfathers, you see, founded the place, and a lot of them had to take some pretty queer jobs while they were doing the founding. For instance, there's one woman who at present is about the social model for the town; well, her father was the first public ash man—things like that. (*Short Stories* 56–57)

And Nick invokes the three-generation rule as well when he first introduces himself at the start of the novel: "My family have been prominent, well-to-do people in this middle-western city for three generations," explaining that "the actual founder of my line was my grandfather's brother who came here in fifty-one, sent a substitute to the Civil War and started the wholesale hardware business that my father carries on today" (6). (Recall that J. P. Morgan had also sent a paid substitute to the Civil War and that Fitzgerald's maternal grandfather, Philip McQuillan, had come to St. Paul in 1857 and founded the wholesale grocery business that was the source of the family's wealth.) Gatsby, with his self-made riches, clearly has the means to found a family that would grant his grandson all the advantages in terms of education, social connections, sophistication, and inherited wealth that Gatsby tries unsuccessfully to procure. And Fitzgerald specifically invokes the notion of founding a family when Nick tells us that "there was a story" about the brewer who'd originally built Gatsby's mansion that "he'd agreed to pay five years' taxes on all the neighboring cottages if the owners would have their roofs thatched with straw. Perhaps their refusal took the heart out of his plan to Found a Family—he went into an immediate decline. . . . Americans, while occasionally willing to be serfs, have always been obstinate about being peasantry" (69). Although we usually think of Gatsby's problem as involving a past that can't be repeated, we could just as easily phrase it as a problem with the future: that the person he really wants to be is his own grandson.

Earlier we mentioned how the theatrical aspect of society implicates the notion of the gaze, and certainly *Gatsby* is a novel obsessed with gazing— from the moment near its beginning when Nick says, "life is much more successfully looked at from a single window, after all" (7), to Nick's watching Gatsby gazing at the green light on Daisy's dock, to Nick's imagining during the drunken party at Myrtle and Tom's apartment that he is a "casual watcher in the darkening streets" outside looking up at its lighted windows, at once "within and without, simultaneously enchanted and repelled by the inexhaustible variety of life" (30), to Gatsby's inviting Tom and Daisy at the party they attend to "look around. . . . You must see the faces of many people you've heard about" (82), to Nick's observing Myrtle as she gazes from her window in "jealous terror" at Jordan Baker (an observation made while Nick himself is under the unseeing gaze of Dr. T. J. Eckleburg), on to the moment after the hit-and-run accident when Nick sneaks up to the window in Tom and Daisy's house to see the couple sitting at the kitchen table, noting that "they weren't happy . . . and yet they weren't unhappy either. There was an unmistakable air of natural intimacy about the picture" (113), and finally to that moment at the very end when Nick imagines looking through "Dutch sailors' eyes" at "the old island, . . . a fresh, green breast of the new world" and then looking through Gatsby's eyes "when he first picked out the green light at the end of Daisy's dock" (140–41). Again, one of the crucial aspects of the gaze is whether or not the person looked at is aware of being observed, and the resulting difference such awareness or its lack has on the person's behavior. If the eyes of Dr. T. J. Eckleburg evoke the gaze of the all-seeing Father, the God who sees not just the visible things a person does (no matter how secret) but also what the person intends (the hidden contents of the human heart)—and that is certainly the way George Wilson interprets Eckleburg's gaze for his wife—then the fact that Eckleburg's eyes don't represent a real observing but only its painted image suggests Fitzgerald's sense, on the one hand, of the modern loss of belief in an absolute consciousness that sees, judges, and enforces the moral law, and on the other hand, his sense of the prior state as one in which the illusory (i.e., painted) gaze of the nonexistent all-seeing Father had been introjected, becoming an individual's conscience: the notion that a child (of whatever age) is always under the paternal eye that assigns reward or punishment.

The extent to which civilized human existence depends simply on the *image* (in effect, the painted, unseeing eyes) of an all-seeing gaze is one of the ongoing motifs in *Gatsby*. For the purposes of this discussion let me make a distinction here between two English words with roughly the same meaning but whose etymological roots lie in two different classical languages: "*ethics*" and "*morality*." Their roots are respectively the Greek "*ethos*" and the Latin "*mores*." Both words refer to the customs or practices of a country or a people, to the customary, accepted behavior in a culture that determines the difference between praise and blame, right and wrong. In order to speak more exactly about the transformation that occurs in *The Great Gatsby*'s narrator through his involvement with its protagonist, I use the words "*ethics*" or "*ethical*" to refer only to the kind of knowledge of people's actions and intentions that can be achieved by a limited, purely human agency and only to the kind of judgments (with their resulting sanctions or rewards) that can be enacted in *this* world, and I use the words "*morality*" or "*moral*" to refer only to the kind of knowledge possessed by an absolute consciousness and to the otherworldly judgment of a soul after death, with its accompanying sanction or reward.

Recall that Nick starts out as a limited, first-person narrator, confining himself to recounting things he'd actually seen or been told, but becomes by the end an omniscient, third-person narrator, able to imagine things Gatsby saw and felt when Nick wasn't present. And recall Fitzgerald's comment about this same progression in *The Last Tycoon*, in which by making the narrating character "an intelligent and observant woman," he planned to grant himself "the privilege, as Conrad did, of letting her imagine the actions of the characters," adding that he thus hoped "to get the verisimilitude of a first person narrative, combined with a Godlike knowledge of all events that happen to my characters" (*Correspondence* 547). At the very start of the novel Nick tells us, "When I came back from the East last autumn I felt that I wanted the world to be in uniform and at a sort of *moral* attention forever; I wanted no more riotous excursions with *privileged* glimpses into the human heart" (5, italics mine). Nick has seen how little the ethical, the merely human, system of knowledge and legal judgment has been able to discover about the deaths of Myrtle Wilson, Gatsby, and George Wilson (and thus, of course, about their lives) compared to how much he has come to know from his privileged position as narrator. At the coroner's inquest Nick fears that once Michaelis mentions "Wilson's suspicions of his wife," the "whole tale would shortly be served up in racy pasquinade," but when Myrtle's sister Catherine swears that Myrtle "had never seen Gatsby, that her sister was completely happy with her husband," then the inquest's judgment reduced Wilson to "a man 'deranged by grief'" in order that the case might remain in its simplest form. And it rested there" (127).

Nick ends up knowing more of the facts and motivations surrounding these deaths than anyone else in the novel: more than Gatsby and Daisy (e.g., that Myrtle was Tom's mistress), more than Tom (e.g., that Daisy was driving the car), and more than Jordan (e.g. that Myrtle was Tom's mistress and that Daisy was driving the car). The revulsion that Nick feels on his return from the East stems not only from his having seen how limited the merely human agency for discovering the truth has been but even more from his having seen how that ethical judgment had ultimately been subordinated to a social purpose by the reduction of the case to "its simplest form," keeping a further pursuit of the inquiry from becoming more socially disruptive by involving more people, like Nick's relative Daisy. But if the unseeing, painted eyes of Dr. T. J. Eckleburg symbolize a modern loss of belief in an absolute consciousness that empowered the moral law, then Nick's revulsion also reflects his sense of the personal cost incurred by his having, in that moral vacuum, to step into the Godlike role of third-person, omniscient narrator, in effect, by his having to make moral determinations based on his knowledge of the intertwined lives of Gatsby, Daisy, Tom, and Myrtle—an act he performs with his next-to-last words to Gatsby: "'They're a rotten crowd,' I shouted, across the lawn. 'You're worth the whole damn bunch put together'" (120).

Part of Nick's moral revulsion at his involvement with this "whole damn bunch" stems from his sense of how much, at significant moments in the novel, he has compromised his own moral values for social reasons by caring more for good manners than for good conduct. If, as Nick claims, "Everyone suspects himself of at least one of the cardinal virtues, and this is mine: I am one of the few honest people that I have ever known" (48), then at least Nick honestly records those moments in which he sacrifices morality to manners—the most obvious of these being when Nick runs into Tom on a Manhattan street near the novel's end. Tom asks, "What's the matter, Nick?

Do you object to shaking hands with me?" and Nick says, "Yes. You know what I think of you" (139). When Tom admits that it was he who sent Wilson to Gatsby's house in the belief that Gatsby had run down Myrtle, Nick thinks, "There was nothing I could say, except the one unutterable fact that it wasn't true" (139). Whatever Nick's motives for not telling Tom who was really driving (whether out of loyalty to Gatsby's wish to shield Daisy or his own wish to protect his cousin), Nick's avoidance of the truth here seems very much of a piece with his evident relief at Myrtle's sister lying at the coroner's inquest to keep the case to "its simplest form," thus avoiding further social and/or legal complications in which he might be called to testify. After Nick's final conversation with Tom, the most damning judgment he's willing to make is that Tom and Daisy are "careless people," and he says, "I shook hands with him; it seemed silly not to, for I felt suddenly as though I were talking to a child" (139–40)—that last statement being Nick's excuse for his allowing a social gesture to trump a moral stance, a stance he had originally taken immediately after the accident when Tom drove Nick and Jordan back to his house and Nick had refused to go in even though it meant alienating Jordan.

What Nick's situation as narrator suggests is the way that the observer, the wielder of the gaze, becomes implicated in what he observes, for if Nick ultimately ends up knowing more of the story than anyone else in the novel, achieving what Fitzgerald called a "Godlike knowledge" that allows him to make moral judgments, Nick, as a human being who assumes that role, is still subject to the demands of social life, demands that lead him not to correct the false judgments arrived at by the inquest or by Tom Buchanan. Fitzgerald suggests this division in Nick when he has Nick, immediately after telling Gatsby that he's "worth the whole damned bunch put together," say, "I've always been glad I said that. It was the only compliment I ever gave him, because I disapproved of him from beginning to end" (120). Clearly, Nick's disapproval is a social judgment by which he qualifies the preceding moral one.

If knowing the truth but being unwilling for social reasons to speak it publicly suggests the compromising effect on the gazer of what he observes, then the reverse of that—the effect of the gaze on something observed or on someone who knows she's being observed—is also a recurring motif in the novel. The power of Daisy's gaze is made explicit when Gatsby gives her and Nick a tour of his house: "He hadn't once ceased looking at Daisy and I think he revalued everything in his house according to the measure of response it drew from her well-loved eyes. Sometimes, too, he stared around at his possessions in a dazed way as though in her actual and astounding presence none of it was any longer real" (72). Nick's sense that the feeling of unpleasantness pervading the party Tom and Daisy attended was due to Nick's now "looking at it again, through Daisy's eyes" and that it was "invariably saddening to look through new eyes at things upon which you have expended your own powers of adjustment" (81), is matched by Gatsby, who brings his lavish entertaining abruptly to an end after learning that Daisy hadn't had a good time at the party: "So the whole caravansary had fallen in like a card house at the disapproval in her eyes" (88).

6

Of course, the most significant impact of the other's gaze in the novel is on Gatsby's sense of himself, and Sartre's discussion in *Being and Nothingness* of the gaze's effect on the constitution of the self seems particularly relevant here, as Mitchell Breitwieser has suggested. Sartre distinguishes between individual consciousness as being-for-itself and the world of objects as being-in-itself, and he says that although we see other people as objects in the world and intuit their subjectivity, we still can never actually know their subjectivity or prove their existence but must accept them as a *"factual necessity"* (367). He continues, "If the Other-as-object is defined in connection with the world as the object which sees what I see, then my fundamental connection with the Other-as-subject must be able to be referred back to my permanent possibility of *being seen* by the Other. It is in and through the revelation of my being-as-object for the Other that I must be able to apprehend the presence of his being-as-subject" so that " 'being-seen-by-the-Other' is the *truth* of 'seeing-the-Other' " (344–45). The self must accept the "permanent possibility" of being seen and the sense that "at each instant the Other *is looking at me*" (345). Sartre sees individual consciousness as subjective, interior, and free, and he posits that the for-itself enacts two negations, or what he calls "nihilations," that define it: the for-itself sees both that the world (the in-itself) is *not me* and that the Other is *not me.*

The Other's gaze, what Sartre calls the look, can take many forms: "Of course what *most often* manifests a look is the convergence of two ocular globes in my direction. But the look will be given just as well on occasion when there is a rustling of branches, or the sound of a footstep followed by silence, or the slight opening of a shutter, or a light movement of a curtain. . . . It is obvious that the object thus constituted still manifests the look as being probable" (346). Distinguishing between the unreflective consciousness (which is "a consciousness *of* the world") and the reflective consciousness (which "has the self directly for an object"), Sartre argues that "I see *myself* because *somebody* sees me," that, in effect, "the person is presented to consciousness *in so far as the person is an object for the Other*" (349). The self's "being-for-others" means that the for-itself knows that the external aspect of its being exists as an image in the Other's subjectivity but also that, since the Other's subjectivity is unknowable, "this being which I am preserves a certain indetermination, a certain unpredictability, . . . the Other's freedom is revealed to me across the uneasy indetermination of the being which I am for him" (351). The difference between what the for-itself knows itself to be internally and the uncertain image of its external being-for-others means that I have to "accept and wish that others should confer upon me a being which I recognize" (351). Of one's being-for-others he says, "I do not reject it as a strange image, but it is present to me as a self which I *am* without *knowing* it; for I discover it in shame and, in other instances, in pride. . . . Now shame . . . is shame of *self*; it is the *recognition* of the fact that I *am* indeed that object which the Other is looking at and judging. I can be ashamed only as my freedom escapes me in order to become a *given* object" (350).

Sartre discusses the various reactions the self manifests to its sense of possessing a being-for-others—shame, pride, anguish, fear—and he notes that "to be looked at is to apprehend oneself as the unknown object of unknowable appraisals—in particular, of value judgments. But at the same time that in shame or pride I recognize the justice of these appraisals, I do not cease to take them for what they are. . . . A judgment is the transcendental act of a free being. Thus being-seen constitutes me as a defenseless being for a freedom which is not my freedom. It is in this sense that we can consider ourselves as 'slaves' in so far as we appear to the Other" (358). Adding that "there is no one who has not at some time been surprised in an attitude which was guilty or simply ridiculous," Sartre say that being-for-others "suddenly pushes me into a new dimension of existence—the dimension of the *unrevealed*," producing a me that is "outside my reach, outside my action, outside my knowledge" (358–59). The Other is then "the one who looks at me and at whom I am not yet looking, the one who delivers me to myself as *unrevealed* but without revealing himself" (360). The "fact of the Other . . . touches me to the heart. I realize him through *uneasiness*; through him I am perpetually *in danger* in a world which is *this* world and which nevertheless I can only glimpse" (367).

In a comment that recalls the eyes of Dr. T. J. Eckleburg, Sartre says that it is "never eyes which look at us; it is the Other-as-subject" (369); further, "it is not sure that those eyes which are fixed on me are eyes; they could be only 'artificial ones' resembling real eyes" (368). Discussing Kafka's *The Trial*, he remarks that "without doubt Kafka is trying here to express the transcendence of the divine; it is for the divine that the human act is constituted in truth. But God here is only the concept of the Other pushed to the limit" (356).

Sartre's distinction between individual consciousness as a being-for-itself and as a being-for-others becomes particularly complex when applied to Gatsby, for "Jay Gatsby" has come into existence precisely through a conscious choice by the teenage James Gatz to recreate himself as an external persona, an image in the eyes of others. Whatever James Gatz's subjective sense of self had been prior to his introducing himself to Dan Cody under a new name, one aspect of it is clear: an already developed sense of the gap or opposition between what Whitman calls "the real I myself, / An image, an eidolon" and his being-for-others as objectified by the youthful Gatz's surroundings and background. Fitzgerald evokes this gap between an interior "real me" and an exterior "perceived me" with the qualification (and thus distinction) Nick inserts in his claim that "James Gatz . . . was *really, or at least legally,* his name" (76, italics mine). Because Gatz's "parents were shiftless and unsuccessful farm people . . . his imagination had never really accepted them as his parents at all" (76).

In "Absolution," Rudolph Miller tells Father Schwartz in confession that he has committed the sin of "not believing I was the son of my parents." When the priest says, "Why not?" Rudolph replies, "Oh, just pride"—which Father Schwartz takes to "mean you thought you were too good to be the son of your parents" (*Short Stories* 262). Like James Gatz, Rudolph possesses a "real," interior self (named Blatchford Sarnemington) that is the imaginative opposite of his perceived, outer one, and as he leaves the confessional, aware that in telling the priest that he never tells lies he has told a lie, he keeps repeating the name of his imaginary persona: "Blatchford Sarnemington was himself, and these words were in effect a lyric. When he became Blatchford Sarnemington a suave nobility flowed from him. Blatchford Sarnemington lived in great sweeping triumphs. When Rudolph half closed his eyes it meant that Blatchford had established dominance over him and, as he went by, there were envious mutters in the air: 'Blatchford Sarnemington! There goes Blatchford Sarnemington'" (263–64).

With that last sentence Fitzgerald suggests that the imagined interior self needs the Other's gaze in order to actualize its unrevealed, subjective self as an objective being-for-others, a requirement that also explains why Fitzgerald introduces the subject of Rudolph's imaginary self in connection with the boy's having just been to confession. Confession is the sacrament in which a self reveals its interior secrets to another human being who represents the absolute consciousness, secrets that are a matter of shame because they are sins against God. And significantly, the secret Rudolph reveals is the sin of pride in believing that he is too good to be the son of his parents, a pride that has made him ashamed of his real father, Carl Miller, "the local freight-agent" (264). As Rudolph walks home from church, the mantra of Blatchford Sarnemington gradually begins to lose power, and "the horror of his lie" in confession starts to dawn on him when he realizes that his father will expect him to receive communion the next day. Indeed, in repeating the name of his imaginary self on his walk—a self whose very name (in being different from his own) reemphasizes his belief that he's not his father's son—Rudolph in effect recommits the sin he has just confessed, and, contemplating his lie, he thinks, "God, of course, already knew of it—but Rudolph reserved a corner of his mind where he was safe from God, where he prepared the subterfuges with which he often tricked God. Hiding now in this corner he considered how he could best avoid the consequences of his mistatement" (264). But none of Rudolph's subterfuges work, and he is forced under the eye of his stern father to receive communion with what he feels is a mortal sin on his soul. Fearing that he will be damned to eternal punishment, Rudolph returns to Father Schwartz to confess what has happened, but he finds the priest in the throes of a nervous breakdown, and as Father Schwartz begins to babble, Rudolph thinks, "This man is crazy . . . and I'm scared of him. He wants me to help him out some way, and I don't want to" (270). What Father Schwartz is babbling about is the heartbreaking beauty of a world whose "heat and . . . sweat and . . . life" (271) represent a dangerous temptation to his otherworldly belief, and the image he evokes for Rudolph of that worldly beauty is an amusement park seen at night:

> "It's a thing like a fair, only much more glittering. . . . You'll see a big wheel made of lights turning in the air, and a long slide shooting boats down into the water. A band playing somewhere, and a smell of peanuts—and everything will twinkle." . . .
>
> All this talking seemed particularly strange and awful to Rudolph, because

this man was a priest. . . . But underneath his terror he felt that his own inner convictions were confirmed. There was something ineffably gorgeous somewhere that had nothing to do with God. (271)

As Father Schwartz, "muttering inarticulate and heart-broken words," collapses on his knees, Rudolph runs "in panic from the house" (271–72), but his climactic realization that there is an imaginative beauty wholly separate from God has already begun to free him from his stern, religious father, from this emotionally crippled, priestly father, and perhaps ultimately from a belief in an all-knowing Father. In *Gatsby* Fitzgerald again uses this imagery of an amusement park at a fair to evoke the sort of vulgar beauty Gatsby's imagination prizes: Nick says that the uninvited guests at Gatsby's parties "conducted themselves according to the rules of behavior associated with amusement parks" (34). And when Nick returns home one night to see all the lights on in Gatsby's house, he remarks to his neighbor, "Your place looks like the world's fair." To which Gatsby replies, "I have been glancing into some of the rooms. Let's go to Coney Island, old sport. In my car" (64). The dust jacket of the first edition of *Gatsby* highlighted this imagery by showing the disembodied face of a woman superimposed on a view of a lighted Ferris wheel in an amusement park at night.

The difference between Rudolph Miller and James Gatz is, of course, that the former is eleven years old in "Absolution" whereas the latter is seventeen at the point when Nick first starts to imagine Gatsby's past, and thus the further difference is that though we don't know whether the interior persona "Blatchford" ever develops into anything more in Rudolph's life than a psychological defense mechanism (like the secret life of Walter Mitty), James Gatz's interior persona becomes objectified in the world at the moment he introduces himself to Dan Cody. Significantly, the image of fatherhood and of father substitutes (in regard to the protagonist's not believing in his parentage) carries over from "Absolution" to *Gatsby* when Nick describes James Gatz's act of self-naming:

The truth was that Jay Gatsby, of West Egg, Long Island, sprang from his Platonic conception of himself. He was a son of God—a phrase which, if it means anything, means just that—and he must be about His Father's Business, the service of a vast, vulgar and meretricious beauty. So he invented just the sort of Jay Gatsby that a seventeen year old boy would be likely to invent, and to this conception he was faithful to the end. (76–77)

Since James Gatz, like Rudolph, has elevated his own imagination to the highest level of value (in effect, to a personal absolute), it is not surprising that his imaginative re-creation of himself is compared to deific autogenesis. (If what Gatsby really wanted to be was his own grandson, the preceding passage suggests that in some sense he is his own son as well.) And if "Jay Gatsby" is the mental son, the Logos, of James Gatz's imagination, then when that mental son is incarnated through Gatz's first using his new name to introduce himself, Cody becomes his human stepfather (à la St. Joseph)—the successful, millionaire miner substituting for the shiftless, unsuccessful farmer. Cody's yacht represented for Gatsby "all the beauty and glamor in the world," and Nick adds, "I suppose he smiled at Cody—he had probably discovered that people liked him when he smiled. At any rate Cody asked him a few questions (one of them elicited the brand new name) and found that he was quick, and extravagantly ambitious" (78), so when Cody's yacht left, Gatsby went with it, serving over the next five years as "steward, mate, skipper, secretary, and even jailor" for the drunken Cody. And "it was from Cody that he inherited money—a legacy of twenty-five thousand dollars. He didn't get it. He never understood the legal device that was used against him," but "he was left with his singularly appropriate education; the vague contour of Jay Gatsby had filled out to the substantiality of a man" (78–79).

This legacy suggests the way that Gatsby created the falsified story of his past he first tells Nick, created it not out of whole cloth but from shreds of truth. The award for bravery from Montenegro is real, and he has the inscribed medal to prove it; however, the story about his being educated at Oxford because it was "a family tradition" is a lie but built around the truth that he spent five months there in 1919 after the war (an admission made during the confrontation scene at the Plaza that elicits from Nick "one of those renewals of complete faith in him that I'd experienced before" [101]). Similarly, the story of his being the son of wealthy people in the Midwest who left him "a good deal of money" suggests that the unreceived legacy from Dan Cody had been the thread of truth from which he wove this fiction, a detail made explicit in the earlier *Trimalchio* version of the novel when Nick says to Gatsby, "I suppose it was from him [Cody] that you inherited money" (119). And certainly $25,000 pre–World War I dollars—the equivalent buying power of $250,000 today—would not have been an insignificant inheritance. All of which raises the question of why Nick ultimately doesn't judge Gatsby to be simply a compulsive liar, for certainly Gatsby has told lies (both to Nick and to Daisy) and has lied by omission in concealing his shady dealings. Yet we can see that just as Rudolph Miller excuses his lie in confession once he realizes there exists a beauty having nothing to with God, excuses it precisely because "he no longer thought that God was angry at him . . . because He must have understood that Rudolph had done it to make things finer in the confessional, brightening up the dinginess of his admissions by saying a thing radiant and proud" (271), so Nick excuses Gatsby on the same aesthetic grounds, understanding Gatsby's imaginative flights not so much as lies as "a satisfactory hint of the unreality of reality, a promise that the rock of the world was founded securely on a fairy's wing" (77). For John Keats there may have been an essential equivalence of beauty and truth, but for Jay Gatsby and Rudolph Miller the weight would have all been on the beauty side of the equation, while Nick Carraway, with his self-proclaimed honesty, is at least open to the sort of argument Gatsby and Rudolph would have made.

As James Gatz's ideal self, "Jay Gatsby" is an interior image that represents the antithesis of what young Gatz feels must be his being-for-others given his background and surroundings, and, as we saw, Nick specifically evokes Gatsby's imaginative self-creation in terms of a Platonic ideal form. And since Plato's otherworld of ideal forms was in part the model for Christianity's imagining of an otherworld of pure spirits, it is a short intellectual step from Nick's image of Gatsby springing "from his Platonic conception of himself" to his statement that Gatsby "was a son of God"—a step validated by St. Thomas Aquinas's explanation of the procession of persons within the Trinity. Noting that there are two faculties of the spirit—the intellect and the will—and that the function proper to each, respectively, is to know and to love, St. Thomas says that as a pure spirit, God the Father's first object of knowledge is himself. He creates a mental image of himself, and since he is perfect, he knows himself perfectly, putting himself so completely into that image that it become a second person, God the Son, the Logos or mental word—the procession of knowledge. The Father and Son then look at each other, and seeing that each is perfect, they love each other absolutely, putting themselves so completely into their love for each other that it becomes a third person, the Holy Spirit. This is the procession of love. Since the great codifier of Christian theological orthodoxy specifically figures the relationship of the Father to the Son as that of a being to his mental image of himself, we can see how the notion of springing from a Platonic conception of oneself leads almost inevitably to the phrase "a son of God." And this image of Gatsby implicitly evokes the second person's incarnation as an allusive background to James Gatz's objectification of his inner self through the act of *speaking* his new name to the man who will be a substitute father figure.

I will come back to the notion of incarnation in examining Fitzgerald's explicit use of the image at the end of chapter 6 of *Gatsby*, but for the present I need only remark that Nick's image of Gatsby as "a son of God" evokes the reciprocity, not to say doubling, between the novel's protagonist and its narrator. Nick paints Gatsby in these deific terms at the beginning of chapter 6, when Nick first begins to recount the backstory of Gatsby's earlier life as James Gatz, which is to say, begins to narrate incidents that Nick as a first-person narrator did not see but was only told about, and within that passage Nick begins the transition from first-person limited to third-person omniscient narration by not only recounting these incidents but also imagining Gatsby's emotions and motivations during them, in effect, creating one of those "privileged glimpses into the human heart" (5) that Fitzgerald described as the technique of combining the "verisimilitude" of first-person narration with that third-person "Godlike knowledge of all events that happen to my characters." And it is precisely at the moment that Nick exercises this Godlike knowledge of Gatsby's inner life that he pronounces Gatsby "a son of God"—like mirroring like—for if Gatsby is the mental image of James Gatz's ideal self, a mental image incarnated in a new name and life, then *The Great Gatsby* is Nick's mental image of Gatz/Gatsby's life incarnated in the words of his narrative. So when Nick pronounces Gatsby a son of God, he is implicitly asserting that the Gatsby of his narrative is in some sense the offspring of Nick's own Godlike imagination.

Earlier we cited Sartre's statement that to possess a being-for others "suddenly pushes me into a new dimension of existence—the dimension of the *unrevealed*," creating a me "outside my reach, outside my action, outside my knowledge," and he adds that I have to "accept and wish that others confer upon me a being which I recognize." The question of how the for-itself determines whether its external being-for-others more or less corresponds to its interior sense of its self, of whether its image in the Other's consciousness is one "which I recognize," comes up at crucial moments in *The Great Gatsby*. The young James Gatz chooses to change his being-for-others by objectifying his interior sense of himself, by rendering an imagined and imaginative self real—an ongoing work of objectification that turns out in Gatsby's case to be largely a matter of acquiring *objects*, ones that bespeak a new social status. The work begins when he gains access to a millionaire's yacht and acquires a new set of clothes, trading in his "torn green jersey and a pair of canvas pants" (76) for the "blue coat, six pairs of white duck trousers and a yachting cap" (78) that Dan Cody buys him. And the work continues during the next five years as he sails on the yacht and acquires ever-increasing levels of responsibility in Cody's employ. During World War I he would add a further aspect to his external appearance, trading his yachting clothes for the status garment of a military officer's uniform and a commission by which Congress declared him a "gentleman." And it is under the deceptive cloak of a uniform attesting to his status that he first meets and woos Daisy.

Since Dan Cody had been the first person to whom Gatsby introduced himself with his new name, the millionaire miner constituted the original embodiment of the Other's gaze directed at "Gatsby." And Nick implies that the effect of Cody's acceptance of the Gatsby persona only confirmed and exacerbated the essential vulgarity of Gatz's adolescent notions of beauty and class—that seventeen-year-old boy's conception of himself to which "he was faithful to the end" (77). Nick makes this opinion clear when he describes Cody's portrait in Gatsby's bedroom: "a grey, florid man with a hard empty face—the pioneer debauchee who during one phase of American life brought back to the eastern seaboard the savage violence of the frontier brothel and saloon." Nick goes on to note that during the "gay parties" on Cody's yacht, women "used to rub champagne into his [Gatsby's] hair" (78)—festivities that must have made the hijinks at Gatsby's parties seem refined by comparison.

If Cody's yacht is the object that gives James Gatz his first real glimpse of the higher lifestyle to which he aspires, then the object associated with Daisy that raises the level of his aspirations is her house in Louisville. Gatsby first visits her home with other officers from the army camp, and Nick records the impression it made on him:

> He had never been in such a beautiful house before. . . . There was a ripe mystery about it, a hint of bedrooms upstairs more beautiful and cool than other bedrooms, of gay and radiant activities taking place through its corridors, and of romances that were not musty and laid away already in lavender but fresh and breathing and redolent of this year's shining motor cars and of dances whose flowers were scarcely withered. (116)

And the thing that most impressed Gatsby was that Daisy's house "was as casual a thing to her as his tent out at the camp was to him" (116), which is to say, that her house and all it represented was something Daisy had been born into and took for granted, becoming for Gatsby a symbol of inherited wealth and privilege. And clearly this is the reason Gatsby wants to re-woo Daisy by way of another symbolic house. As Jordan explains to Nick, Gatsby wants Nick to invite him and Daisy over for tea because "he wants her to see his house. . . . And your house is right next door" (63).

Dan Cody's is the first gaze to which James Gatz's new persona is presented, but Daisy's, among the many subsequent gazes cast on him, is clearly for Gatsby the most important. And it is in this connection that Sartre's notion of the unrevealed dimension of one's being-for-others becomes particularly relevant, for what Gatsby desires from the woman he loves is a gaze that not only approves of Jay Gatsby but also selectively penetrates his being-for-others so as to reveal the meaning of "Jay Gatsby." Fitzgerald makes clear what such a gaze would amount to when he has Nick describe his reaction to Gatsby's smile on their first being introduced:

> He smiled understandingly—much more than understandingly. It was one of those rare smiles with a quality of eternal reassurance in it, that you may come across four of five times in life. It faced—or seemed to face—the whole external world for an instant, and then concentrated on *you* with an irresistible prejudice in your favor. It understood you just so far as you wanted to be understood, believed in you as you would like to believe in yourself and assured you that it had precisely the impression of you that, at your best, you hoped to convey. (40)

If that's what Gatsby's smile was like, no wonder Nick remarks that at an early age James Gatz had "discovered that people liked him when he smiled" (78). And certainly what Gatsby wanted from Daisy's gaze was the assurance that she had precisely the impression of him at his best that he tried to convey. But he wanted much more: that she should be able to understand what had led James Gatz to become Jay Gatsby, be able to penetrate his exterior being-for-others and share in his subjectivity, to understand and share his quest for "all the beauty and glamor in the world" (78). When Daisy attends Gatsby's party and is put off by its vulgarity, its being not a perfected social "gesture" but "an emotion" (84), Gatsby complains afterward to Nick that she doesn't understand Gatsby's need for her not just to renounce her mistake in marrying Tom but to obliterate her years with Tom and any love she might have felt for him: "'And she doesn't understand,' he said despairingly. 'She used to be able to understand. We'd sit for hours—'" (86). They had sat for hours talking of the future, of which Gatsby says to Nick later, "What was the use of doing great things if I could have a better time telling her what I was going to do?" (117).

If the symbolic object first associated with Daisy was her house in Louisville, by the end of his time there the symbolic object had become Daisy herself. At the conclusion of chapter 6 Nick evokes her objectification in an image of incarnation, imagery that resonates with the chapter's beginning and Nick's claim that Gatsby was "a son of God":

> He knew that when he kissed this girl, and forever wed his unutterable visions to her perishable breath, his mind would never romp again like the mind of God. So he waited, listening for a moment longer to the tuning fork that had been struck upon a star. Then he kissed her. At his lips' touch she blossomed for him like a flower and the incarnation was complete. (86–87)

The ultimate meaning of all this son-of-God, mind-of-God, incarnation imagery is to suggest that what Gatsby really wants in Daisy (as his object of desire) is an object, an other, capable of comprehending (which is to say, of entering wholly into as if from within) his own subjectivity and responding sympathetically—the sort of total comprehension of an individual's subjectivity that we feel is possible only to God. And thus we grasp the meaning of two cognate moments in "Absolution" and *Gatsby*—Rudolph Miller's going to confession and Nick's giving Gatsby conditional unconditional absolution when he tells him at the end of their final meeting, "They're a rotten crowd. . . . You're worth the whole damn bunch put together," then mentally adding the condition, "I've always been glad I said that. It was the only compliment I ever gave him, because I disapproved of him from beginning to end." Nick says Gatsby "first . . . nodded politely, and then his face broke into that radiant and understanding smile, as if we'd been in ecstatic cahoots on that fact all the time" (120). Gatsby's "understanding smile" here is a moment of mirroring meant to convey Gatsby's understanding of Nick's interior subjectivity at the precise moment that the other's subjectivity comprehends Gatsby's inner self, an understanding (as Nick had said earlier on the first occasion when Gatsby had smiled at him "understandingly—much more than understandingly") that the other "believed in you as you would like to believe in yourself, and assured you . . . it had precisely the impression of you that, at your best, you hoped to convey."

In the sacrament of confession one engages in self-revelation, theoretically to an all-knowing deity who doesn't need the revelation because it is omniscient but practically to another human being who acts as God's surrogate, and this revelation of some portion of an individual's inner subjectivity to the other is meant to gain the Other's understanding and sympathy in the form of forgiveness. But when Rudolph Miller confesses to Father Schwartz his sin of pride in believing that he's too good to be his parents' son and that he never tells lies, the ultimate understanding and forgiveness comes not from the priest but from Rudolph himself, comes at the moment when Rudolph makes his own imagination his personal absolute and sees that what others might call lying is really for him an aesthetic sacrament of high imagination by which he improves on God's world. And at that same moment Rudolph, who had previously "reserved a corner of his mind where he was safe from God, where he prepared the subterfuges with which he often tricked God," suddenly enters the mind of God, thinking that God was no longer "angry at him about the original lie, because He must have understood that Rudolph had done it to make things finer in the confessional, brightening up the dinginess of his admissions by saying a thing radiant and proud." And once Rudolph's imagination has entered into God's mind, it takes the place of God's mind. If Rudolph's confession to Father Schwartz is an act of self-revelation, a revelation of his interior subjectivity to another human being, then its equivalent in *Gatsby* is the late night conversation Gatsby has with Nick in the wake of the confrontation at the Plaza and the death of Myrtle Wilson, a conversation in which Gatsby makes a full confession about his previous life and intentions and receives final absolution. And one sees the further reciprocity between the two confessional moments in "Absolution" and *Gatsby* in the effect the hearing of each confession has on the individual occupying the priestly office: where Father Schwartz is left in the throes of a nervous breakdown, babbling incoherently as Rudolph runs in terror from his study, Nick returns to the Midwest wanting "the world to be in uniform and at a sort of moral attention forever" and wanting "no more riotous excursions with privileged glimpses into the human heart." For Fitzgerald hearing another's confession exacts a high cost.

In this regard we can see one reason why the film versions of *Gatsby* ultimately seem so unsatisfying. Though Gatsby is the novel's protagonist and Nick its narrator, Gatsby is no more the main character of *The Great Gatsby* than Kurtz is the main character of Conrad's *Heart of Darkness* (the work from which Fitzgerald likely learned the technique of letting a narrator progress from first-person limited to third-person omniscient over the course of a narrative; recall that Conrad's is the name Fitzgerald mentions in connection with this technique in his comment about *The Last Tycoon*). As the narrator Marlow is the main character in Conrad's story, so Nick is in Fitzgerald's, with the whole emotional point of *Gatsby* being the impact Nick's imaginative participation in Gatsby's life and subjectivity has had on the tale's teller. Indeed, in a letter to Mencken written in 1925 after the appearance of *Gatsby*, Fitzgerald listed some of the writers who were "imitators" of Conrad: significantly, "O'Neill in *Emperor Jones*," who was influenced by "*Heart of Darkness*," and "me in *Gatsby* (God! I've learned a lot from him)" (*Letters* 482).

The influence of *Heart of Darkness* on *Gatsby* can perhaps be seen most clearly in two structurally cognate moments in which the tales' narrators know an essential truth about the subjects of their narratives but either tell a lie or fail to contradict an untruth. When Marlow returns from the Congo and goes to see Kurtz's fiancée, she tells him what a good and great man Kurtz was, saying "I am proud to know I understood him better than any one on earth—he told me so himself" (160). Marlow doesn't contradict what he calls her "great and saving illusion" (161), even going so far as to lie to her: instead of telling her that Kurtz's final words were "The horror! The horror!" (162), he tells her that "the last word" he "pronounced was—your name" (163). (One can guess what might have suggested the narrative technique of *Heart of Darkness* for use in *The Great Gatsby* from a detail that Marlow records about the woman's fiancé: "Her engagement with Kurtz had been disapproved by her people. He wasn't rich enough or something" [160]—the implication being that it was the attempt to make his fortune which had driven Kurtz to the perilous adventure in the Congo that ruined him morally and physically.) The equivalent moment of concealing the truth in *Gatsby* is Nick's accidental meeting with Tom Buchanan on a Manhattan street at the novel's end. Tom says that Gatsby "had it coming to him. He threw dust into your eyes just like he did in Daisy's but he was a tough one. He ran over Myrtle like you'd run over a dog and never even stopped his car" (139)—a statement Nick doesn't contradict and even seems to sanction in agreeing to shake hands with Tom. Thus one main reason the film versions of *Gatsby* seem so unsatisfying is the filmmakers' misunderstanding about who the story's main character is, a misunderstanding that leads them to cast the starring actor in the role of Gatsby and a second lead or supporting actor as Nick.

What Gatsby ultimately wants most from Daisy—that she should participate in the interior life of James Gatz / Jay Gatsby as if from the inside, have the impression of him, at his best, that he hopes to convey—he doesn't get. Daisy is too shallow, too lacking in perception and empathy to gain a privileged

glimpse into another's heart—something Nick emphasizes when, after apply-
ing the "privileged glimpse" image to his knowledge of Gatsby, he remarks, "I
had no sight into Daisy's heart" (9). But what Gatsby doesn't get from Daisy
as his object of desire, he gets from Nick once he becomes the subject of Nick
narrative, that is to say, once he becomes, as its protagonist, its narrator's object of desire. At their final meeting, when Nick gives Gatsby absolution and
Gatsby waves good-bye, Nick makes his insight into Gatsby's inner life, his
penetration of his friend's being-for-others, explicit in the contrast between
those who had attended Gatsby's parties and "guessed at his corruption" and
his sense of Gatsby, standing on the steps of his home, "concealing his incorruptible dream, as he waved them goodbye" (120). Since Gatsby dies that day,
his revelation of himself to Nick in effect takes the place of a last confession,
and since Nick has given him absolution, this imagery of corruption and the
incorruptible echoes the New Testament imagery in the burial service taken
from Corinthians 15:42: "So also is the resurrection of the dead. It is sown in
corruption; it is raised in incorruption." Gatsby's incorruptible dream will be
restored to life in Nick's narrative.

# CHAPTER FOUR

# "An Almost Theatrical Innocence"

J AY GATSBY, as James Gatz's Platonic "ideal self," must, I have suggested, be objectified for others, must, in effect, be performed in order for it to become actual. And having invoked Sartre's *Being and Nothingness* to examine the existential aspect of the self as a being-for-others created by the Other's gaze, I now want to turn to the sociologist Erving Goffman's *The Presentation of Self in Everyday Life* to examine the notion of a self that must be continually performed. Remarking that "life itself is a dramatically enacted thing" (72), Goffman understands any social interaction as in some sense a performance of self, and he defines performance as referring to "all the activity of an individual which occurs during a period marked by his continuous presence before a particular set of observers and which has some influence on the observers" (22). Goffman distinguishes between sincere performers and cynical ones, the former being those "who believe in the impression fostered by their own performance," while the latter have no belief in their "own act and no ultimate concern with the beliefs" of their audience (18). By this definition, Gatsby is clearly a sincere performer. And though he is involved in shady dealings, he is certainly no confidence man, which is to say, "Jay Gatsby" is not an alias adopted for the purpose of perpetrating a fraud.

Interestingly enough, in distinguishing between "real, sincere, or honest performances" and false ones, Goffman describes the latter as those "that thorough fabricators assemble for us, whether meant to be taken unseriously, as in the work of stage actors, or seriously, as in the work of confidence men" (70). This grouping together of actors and con men as purveyors of false performances distinguished from one another only by whether they are meant to be taken unseriously or seriously gives a further resonance to Gatsby's living in a community largely populated by theater and movie people and thus to Gatsby's remark to Nick after the confrontation at the Plaza: that Tom had told Daisy what he discovered about Gatsby "in a way that frightened her— that made it look as if I was some kind of cheap sharper" (118–19). Gatsby objects to the performance of his ideal self being characterized as that of a swindler or cheating gambler (the dictionary definition of "sharper"), yet it's not clear whether Gatsby objects more to the implication of the word "sharper" or the word "cheap," that is, to the implication that he'd be unable to support Daisy in the style to which she is accustomed. Since Gatsby's money ultimately comes from his association with Meyer Wolfshiem—a man he describes to Nick as "a gambler" who fixed the World Series, that is, a cheating gambler—Gatsby realizes that this could easily be construed as making him a "sharper" by association—just not a cheap one.

Since the performance Gatsby means to give, as we said, is of a person of inherited wealth, someone of much the same social stratum as Daisy, Goffman's remarks about performing in a higher social class are relevant: "A status, a position, a social place is not a material thing, to be possessed and then displayed; it is a pattern of appropriate conduct, coherent, embellished, and well articulated. Performed with ease or clumsiness, awareness or not, guile or good faith, it is none the less something that must be enacted and portrayed, something that must be realized" (75), and he cites a passage from Sartre's *Being and Nothingness* to illustrate this. Yet Gatsby understands status as being very much a matter of material things (clothes and cars and a hydroplane) and understands social place as a matter of physical setting (a mansion on Long Island). Gatsby can handle the material objects and physical settings associated with social status; it's the "pattern of appropriate conduct, coherent, embellished, and well articulated" and *"performed with ease"* (italics mine) that gives him problems. At their first meeting Nick observes a certain unease in Gatsby's manner, noting that his "elaborate formality of speech just missed being absurd. Some time before he introduced himself I'd got a strong impression that he was picking his words with care" (40). Recall that in the schedule of self-improvement the young James Gatz had written out for himself and that his father shows Nick, he includes "Practice elocution, poise and how to attain it" (135). But how to achieve social ease or poise or repose? Goffman quotes Adam Smith from *The Theory of Moral Sentiments* about the highest form of social ease (that of a "young nobleman") and the way it is learned:

> Is it by knowledge, by industry, by patience, by self-denial, or by virtue of any kind? As all his words, as all his motions are attended to, he learns a habitual regard to every circumstance of ordinary behavior, and studies to perform all those small duties with the most exact propriety. As he is conscious of how

much he is observed, and how much mankind are disposed to favor all his inclinations, he acts, upon the most indifferent occasions, with that freedom and elevation which the thought of this naturally inspires. His air, his manner, his deportment, all mark that elegant, and graceful sense of his own superiority, which those who are born to inferior stations can hardly ever arrive at. (34)

The young nobleman's consciousness of "how much he is observed" suggests the degree to which his elegant "and graceful sense of his own superiority" is a function of his continual performance of an expected self under the gaze of others. This example from English nobility recalls the moment in "The Offshore Pirate" when Toby Moreland, playing the role of the ur-Gatsby Curtis Carlyle, tells Ardita Farnam that after he had begun to make money, "he wanted all those things which he was beginning to lump under the general head of aristocracy" (*Short Stories* 80) and recalls as well John M. Chestnut's use of a bogus Prince of Wales to win the heart of Rags Martin-Jones.

At one point near the end of *Gatsby* Nick, trying to account for his decision to return to the Middle West, says, "I see now that this has been a story of the West, after all—Tom and Gatsby, Daisy and Jordan and I, were all Westerners, and perhaps we possessed some deficiency in common which made us subtly unadaptable to Eastern life" (137). In Fitzgerald's symbolic geography (and in the American mind) the older, higher culture (and by implication, the older, higher class) always lies to the east: if one is from the West, it's on the East Coast; if one is from the East Coast, then it's in England. But since the historical development of the United States was from east to west, Nick and his fellow Westerners, by coming to live in the East, have set their "boats against the current" of historical time, with the result at the novel's end that Nick, in deciding to return home, is "borne back . . . into" his own "past" (141). If, as Nick says, he and his fellow Westerners shared "some deficiency in common" that made them "subtly unadaptable to Eastern life," it could only be because they were all born and raised in a more recent place than the East Coast (in a place less developed in terms of culture and manners, in terms of social expectations and what goes without saying). If they have a deficiency, it's their sense of inferiority at having to play catch-up, once they have come east in their teens or twenties, their feeling of deficiency in having to acquire those things that would have been theirs from birth had they been born there. And it is precisely this higher-culture-to-the-east mindset that Gatsby tries to use for a bit of one-upmanship with his fellow Westerners: though admitting to Nick he's from the Middle West, he claims to have operated in and been accepted by a culture even farther to the east than Long Island, a culture of aristocracy implied by his claim of an Oxford education, his friendship with a man who "is now the Earl of Doncaster" (53), and his having "a man in England who buys" Gatsby clothes, which he sends over "at the beginning of each season, spring and fall" (72).

Gatsby's leapfrogging the American East Coast to England as a fictive background for an implied move back to the West (one that would explain his presence on the East Coast) recalls Curtis Carlyle's similar plan to go even farther east to an older culture than England (India, where he will become "a rajah" and "buy up a palace and a reputation") and then return to the West, taking his next step to "aristocracy" by appearing "in England with a foreign accent and a mysterious past" (*Short Stories* 84). So in the American mind it's not just that old money is classier than new money (or, as Veblen says, that inherited money is classier than money you've earned yourself); it's that older (more socially and culturally developed) places are classier than newer ones, and by that rubric Nick suggests that all the novel's Westerners are more or less deficient in the high society of New York and Long Island, all operating in a society they weren't born into, whose ways they've each (to a greater or lesser degree) had to learn. Nick says, "Even when the East excited me most, even when I was most keenly aware of its superiority to the bored, sprawling, swollen towns beyond the Ohio, . . . even then it had always for me a quality of distortion" (137), a distortion represented in his "more fantastic dreams . . . as a night scene by El Greco" (137), the famously astigmatic painter. In returning to the Middle West, Nick expresses his sense that though the older place is clearly superior in terms of society and culture, the price of this superiority has been a certain moral decadence (a price Nick is unwilling to pay), the East's having outgrown the pioneer virtues of the newer place. And given that this older place is one that none of the novel's main characters belong to by right of birth, Gatsby becomes, in effect, the most obvious, the most single-mindedly energetic representative of those Westerners engaged in that learning process required to operate successfully in the East.

In *The Presentation of Self in Everyday Life* Goffman distinguishes between two kinds of "bounded regions" in relation to the performance of self: "front regions where a particular performance is or may be in progress, and back regions where action occurs that is related to the performance but inconsistent with the appearance fostered by the performance" (134), and he notes that realizations about oneself and illusions about others is one of the important dynamics and disappointments of social mobility. . . . In attempting to escape from the two-faced world of front region and back region behavior, individuals may feel that in the new position they are attempting to acquire they will be the character projected by individuals in that position and not at the same time a performer. When they arrive, of course, they find their new situation has un-anticipated similarities with their old one; both involve a presentation of front to an audience and both involve the presenter in the grubby, gossipy business of staging a show. (132–33)

Making a further distinction between performances given by a single indi-vidual and those given by a team of individuals, Goffman notes that "the object of a performer is to sustain a particular definition of the situation, this representing, as it were, his claim to what reality is" (85). One could char-acterize a Gatsby party, then, as a show in which his team (i.e., himself, his servants, the hired caterers, the orchestra, etc.) stages a performance of the host's self as a wealthy, hospitable individual of a higher social class (higher, at least, than many of those who've been invited or who've simply shown up uninvited) for an audience (the team of guests).

At the first party he attends, Nick, like the audience, is an observer of the performance of Gatsby's team, but he is self-conscious about whether he will be accepted as a member of the audience's team: he says that as soon as he arrived, he tried to find the host but that the people he asked about Gatsby "stared at" him "in such an amazed way and denied so vehemently any knowledge of his movements" that finally he "slunk off in the direction of the cocktail table—the only place in the garden where a single man could linger without looking purposeless and alone." He was on his way to getting "roaring drunk from sheer embarrassment when Jordan Baker came out of the house." Finding it "necessary to attach" himself "to someone" before he began "to address cordial remarks to passers-by," he accosts her: "'Hello!' I roared, advancing toward her" (35).

Because at the start of that first party Nick knows no one present, he real-izes that he is, in his turn, not known by anyone there. As a result, he becomes self-consciously aware of his own being as solely a matter of his external ap-pearance in the Other's gaze, aware that the other audience members don't possess the kind of knowledge of his family and background that Nick gives the reader at the start of the novel and that thus his being-for-others will be simply that of "a single man . . . looking purposeless and alone," a social wallflower or perhaps even a minor show business or underworld figure or a party crasher. Just as Nick later in the novel describes Gatsby's "indefinable expression" (in response to Tom's remark, "You can buy anything at a drug store nowadays") as being "at once definitely unfamiliar and vaguely recognizable, as if I had only heard it described in words" (94), so the reader should recognize that when Tom tells Nick that Gatsby "won't know a soul" at the "big dinner party" (81) in East Egg to which the woman accompanying Sloane had invited him, the sense of social isolation this conveys has already been "described in words" by Nick during his initial moments at Gatsby's party. Nick is ultimately rescued from his isolation by the arrival of Jordan, an attendee at previous Gatsby parties, who in recognizing Nick, vets him, as it were, incorporating him into the audience's team.

Nick, having attended two of Gatsby's parties and having subsequently "mounted in his hydroplane, and, at his urgent invitation, made frequent use of his beach" (51), remains part of the audience's team until that "morning late in July" when Nick drives into Manhattan with Gatsby to lunch with Meyer Wolfshiem. When Gatsby tells Nick about his wealthy family in the Middle West and his Oxford education, he is performing his idealized self for an audience of one, but performing it with the intention of making Nick a part of Gatsby's team. From that moment on, Nick's relationship to Gatsby begins to shift; he becomes what Goffman would term a kind of "training specialist" (Goffman 158) and ultimately a "confidant" (159). Goffman defines a training specialist as someone who has "the complicated task of teaching the performer how to build up a desirable impression while at the same time taking the part of the future audience and illustrating by punishments the consequences of improprieties" (158). Already knowing that Nick is Daisy's cousin (and thus from much the same social stratum as she), Gatsby uses the occasion of their drive into Manhattan to try out his invented past on someone who represents the future audience (Daisy and Daisy's social set) to see how well it plays, a sort of dress rehearsal. And quite clearly Gatsby comes to think of Nick as someone able to school him in the finer points of social behavior, to tip him off to those signs and hints (the things that go without saying) within a certain social class that indicate the reality of a situation: as when Nick indicates the correct social response to a gesture not sincerely meant by declining the invitation to dinner extended by the woman who had been horseback riding with Tom and Sloane, but Gatsby, allowing an "emotion" to trump a "gesture," fails to take the hint and goes to get his topcoat. In his 1932 story "What a Handsome Pair!" Fitzgerald makes explicit the role of the training specialist. The tale's protagonist, Stuart Oldhorne, is an upper-class young man who has lost his fortune and is offered a job managing racing stables by his friend Gus Myers. Oldhorne's wife asks him, "But with Gus Myers, isn't there a string attached? Wouldn't he expect a boost up?" and Oldhorne replies, "He probably would . . . and if I can help him socially, I will. As a matter of fact, he wants me at a stag dinner tonight" (*Short Stories* 687). But at the stag dinner Gus Myers makes a social gaffe, and Oldhorne corrects him:

> "When you made that little speech, you mentioned me as if you had some-how bought me, as if I was a sort of employee in your office. Now, in the sporting world that doesn't go; things are more—more democratic. I grew up with all these men here tonight, and they didn't like it any better than I did."
>
> "I see," Mr. Myers reflected carefully—"I see." Suddenly he clapped Stuart on the back. "That is exactly the sort of thing I like to be told; it helps me. From now on I won't mention you as if you were in my—as if we had a business arrangement. Is that all right?" (689)

By *The Great Gatsby's* close Nick has moved from the role of training specialist to that of "confidant"—"a type of person," according to Goffman,

> who is not a performer yet has access to back regions and destructive information. . . . Confidants are persons to whom the performer confesses his sins, freely detailing the sense in which the impression given during a performance was merely an impression. Typically, confidants are located outside and participate only vicariously in back and front region activity. . . .
>
> A person in whom another confides, unlike the service specialist [lawyers, doctors, trainers, etc.] does not make a business of receiving such confidences; he accepts the information without accepting a fee, as an expression of the friendship, trust, and regard the informant feels for him. We find, however, that clients often attempt to transform their service specialists into confidants (perhaps as a means of ensuring discretion), especially when the work of the specialist is merely to listen and talk, as is the case with priests and psychotherapists. (159)

At the Gatsby party Tom and Daisy attend, Gatsby's team has been enlarged: it includes not just the host, his servants, the hired caters, the orchestra, but all the guests at the party, for now this larger team is giving a performance of Gatsby's idealized self as not just a wealthy man of high class and social generosity but also as someone who keeps his mansion "full of interesting people, night and day," "celebrated people" (71), as he'd boasted to Daisy. And they are giving this performance for an audience of two (Daisy and Tom)—for Daisy, to make good on his boast, and for Tom, to show him that Gatsby has something Tom doesn't. At this party, Nick finds himself in an ambiguous position: no longer a member of the guests' team (considered simply as audience) nor of that group of "celebrated people" who've been incorporated into Gatsby's team, Nick (midway in his movement from training specialist to confidant) looks at the party through Daisy's eyes and sees why she'd be put off by its vulgarity, by the fact that although some of the guests are celebrities, most are either wannabes or party crashers.

Particularly relevant to Gatsby's situation is Goffman's emphasis on the necessity of "dramaturgical discipline" in the enactment of a successful performance: a discipline that focuses on "the management of one's face and voice"—"the crucial test of one's ability as a performer. Actual affective response must be concealed and an appropriate affective response must be displayed" (217), which is to say, that emotion must be hidden and gesture must take its place. The climactic moment of the novel occurs, of course, at the Plaza when Tom confronts Gatsby with what he's learned of his background and business, the two verbally squaring off in front of Daisy in order to demonstrate which is the better man, a demonstration that will turn on who gives the better performance of himself. Gatsby loses this encounter when he's unable to control his face and voice on seeing Daisy "staring terrified between Gatsby and her husband." It's at that moment that Nick reports his being "startled" by Gatsby's expression: he looked "as if he had 'killed a man'" (105). Gatsby "began to talk excitedly to Daisy, denying everything, defending his name against accusations that had not been made. But with every word she was drawing further and further into herself, so he gave up" (105). In "What a Handsome Pair!" Fitzgerald characterizes the social/psychological dynamics of a situation in which two men vie for the same woman's affection in her presence: "The two men regarded each other with a curious impotence of expression; there can be no communication between men in that position, for their relation is indirect and consists in how much each of them has possessed or will possess of the woman in question, so that their emotions pass through her divided self as through a bad telephone connection" (*Short Stories* 682). Fitzgerald would again use this passage almost verbatim in *Tender Is The Night* in the scene where Dick and Tommy Barban confront each other in Nicole's presence at a sidewalk café in Cap d'Antibes (344).

Another comment of Goffman's seems particularly apt in regard to Gatsby's facial expression in the Plaza scene:

> Whether the character that is being presented is sober or carefree, of high station or low, the individual who performs the character will be seen for what he largely is, a solitary player involved in a harried concern for his production. Behind many masks and many characters, each performer tends to wear a single look, a naked unsocialized look, a look of concentration, a look of one who is privately engaged in a difficult, treacherous task. (235)

In their confrontation Tom delivers the final fillip when Daisy asks him to take her home, and he contemptuously replies that Gatsby can drive her: "He won't annoy you. I think he realizes that his presumptuous little flirtation is over" (105). What Gatsby has lacked in Daisy's eyes at this crucial moment of performing his idealized self battling with Tom is self-possession, the quality Dick Diver calls "repose"—an absolute composure of manner under the Other's gaze. And Daisy understands that, lacking this trait, Gatsby could never move in the society she moves in, that he could never face down someone who might challenge him for his right to be there. Whatever Tom may be, he's quite sure of being the thing he thinks he is; while whatever Gatsby may seem, he's not quite sure he is that thing—a difference in appearance that recalls the one Nick observed between Tom and George Wilson when they had stopped by Wilson's gas station on their way to the Plaza: noting that each man "had made a parallel discovery less than an hour before" about their wives' infidelity, Nick thinks, "there was no difference between men, in intelligence or race, so profound as the difference between the sick and the well. Wilson was so sick he looked guilty, unforgivably guilty—as if he just got some poor girl with child" (96–97). Possessing neither East Egg's inherent (i.e., inherited) training in the gestures of amateur (social) theatricality nor West Egg's acquired training in professional performance, Gatsby has neither "repose" by right of birth nor the dramaturgical discipline to act it.

Yet if Gatsby's failure in self-assurance amounts in effect to a lack of theatrical skill, it nonetheless recalls that in his original conception of Gatsby's character Fitzgerald seems to have entertained the notion of his being attracted to show business. In chapter 7 of *The Great Gatsby: A Facsimile of the Manuscript* (the late night conversation with Gatsby after the hit-and-run accident) Nick says:

> The part of his life he told me about began when he was fifteen, when the popular songs of those days began to assume for him a melancholy and romantic

beauty. He attached them to reveries as transitory as themselves and attributed deep significance to melodies and phrases set down cynicly [*sic*] in tin-pan alley. "I'm going to Maximes [*sic*]" and the Stein Song from the Prince of Pilsen carried him effectually to a world of shining boots and furred dolmans—when their romantic possibilities were finally exhausted he made up his own song and sang it to himself with infinite satisfaction in the images it evoked for his eyes. For awhile these reveries provided an outlet for his vitality, reflecting with their contemporary glamor the gaudy universe in which he believed, they were a satisfactory hint of the unreality of reality, a promise that the rock of the world was founded securely on a fairy's wing. (217)

And earlier, in chapter 6, Gatsby tells Nick about his first falling in love with Daisy and hints that the ideal that Daisy had been for him for years had begun to fade since their reunion:

"Why,—Daisy's all I've got left from a world that was so wonderful that when I think of it I feel sick all over." He looked around with wild regret. "Let me sing you a song—I want to sing you a song!"

He began to sing a song in a low unmusical baritone. The tune seemed to be a vague compendium of all the tunes of twenty years ago. It went about like this:

"We hear the tinkle of the gay guitars
We see the shining Southern moon;
Where the fire-flies flit
And the June bugs sit
Drones the crickets single tune.
We hear the lapping of the wavelets
Where the lonesome nightbirds sing
And the soft warm breeze
Tell the tall palm trees
The Dreaming Song of Spring"

"I made it up when I was fourteen," he said eagerly, "and the sound of it makes me perfectly happy. But I don't sing it often now because I'm afraid I'll use it up." (162–63)

As Fitzgerald had written song lyrics in his teenage years, so had Gatsby; and as Tin Pan Alley songs, with their "melancholy and romantic beauty," had attached themselves to Gatsby's "reveries," so apparently had they attached themselves to Fitzgerald's imagination, to judge by the sheer number of song titles and lines from popular songs pervading his fiction from the start to the end of his career. From Gatsby's attraction to popular songs and his having written the one he sings to Nick, we get the sense that when Fitzgerald originally imagined the Gatsby character some of what got swept into it was the fictive biography of Curtis Carlyle from "The Offshore Pirate," the lower-class young man who wins fame and fortune in show business leading a ragtime band but who then, because the kind of money he's earned himself in this demimonde would never allow him to achieve "aristocracy," turns to crime and holds up a party of swells. One also senses that once Fitzgerald eliminated from the final version of the novel the details of Gatsby's attraction to popular songs and his performing one of his own lyrics for Nick, all that was left of the two career paths by which a young man could get rich quick—show business and the underworld—was the two types of residents of West Egg. And I would argue further that just as the two possible careers the young Fitzgerald had imagined for himself (fiction writing and play writing) are paralleled by the two possible careers that seem to have been part of the early conception of Gatsby, so in 1923, once Fitzgerald's play *The Vegetable* had failed and he began his novel about "the loss of those illusions that give such color to the world" (*Correspondence* 145), Fitzgerald's own loss of illusion about a playwriting career is paralleled in the novel by his excising from the earlier conception of Gatsby's character (in the transition from manuscript to finished novel) any sense of the character's possible show business career. Gatsby thus ends up as a wealthy underworld figure who gives lavish parties whose guests are mostly show people, precisely because Fitzgerald becomes not a successful playwright but a fiction writer for whom theatricality (both social and professional, with all the ramifications thereof) would become the framework on which *Gatsby* and his subsequent novels were to be constructed.

2

What Fitzgerald had at stake psychologically, then, in deploying this framework in his fiction was that it represented a way of symbolically recuperating a lost illusion (a road not taken), which is to say, that if he couldn't write successfully for the theater at least he could write successful fiction about the pervasiveness of theatricality in people's lives—express his sense that, like Fitzgerald in Great Neck and Gatsby in West Egg, we all live, one way or another, surrounded by show people. And certainly this was not an unprecedented move in the tradition of the American novel of manners that immediately preceded him. Henry James too had had this same twin ambition to be both a successful novelist and a playwright. And as the failure of *The Vegetable* in 1923 had sent Fitzgerald back to fiction writing, so the failure of James's 1895 play *Guy Domville* ultimately sent James back to writing the novels of his last great period, novels built on a classical, scene-by-scene structure reminiscent of French drama. Fitzgerald turned to writing *The Vegetable* because his second novel, *The Beautiful and Damned*, had not matched the commercial success of his first, and similarly, James had, in the wake of the commercial failure of his 1890 novel *The Tragic Muse*, turned to playwriting "in the hope," as Leon Edel notes, "of recouping a waning fame and diminishing royalties." *The Tragic Muse*, "his novel about the stage," was "the prelude to his 'dramatic years,'" the five years in which he devoted his efforts mainly to play writing (viii).

As Edel has shown, one can hardly overrate in terms of James's life and career the importance of his love of the theater and his ambition to be a successful playwright or the devastating psychological impact of the disastrous opening night of *Guy Domville* at London's St. James's Theatre on January 5, 1895. James had been so nervous on opening night that he hadn't stayed to see the first performance but had walked to the Haymarket Theatre a short distance away to see Oscar Wilde's *The Ideal Husband* while his own play was running. *Guy Domville*'s first act went well, but with the second act the play began to falter, and it was downhill from there. In the meantime Wilde's play at the Haymarket had ended, and James, who was not an admirer of Wilde, found the play, as Edel notes, "helpless, crude, clumsy, feeble, vulgar. . . . And yet it had been accepted by the audience, accepted with eagerness, with laughter, with unstinted applause. Its success, it seemed to Henry James, could only be an ill omen for *Guy Domville*" (*Plays* 476). When James reentered the St. James's Theatre by the stage door, his own play was in the final minutes of the third act, and after the curtain fell and the actors had been applauded during curtain calls, the cry of "author, author" went up and the lead actor and manager of the theater, George Alexander, led James on stage by the hand, and pandemonium erupted. As James recalled it, "all the forces of civilization in the house waged a battle of the most gallant, prolonged and sustained applause with the hoots and jeers and catcalls of the roughs, whose roars (like those of a cage of beasts at some infernal 'zoo') were only exacerbated . . . by the conflict." As "a nervous, sensitive, author" faced with this public humiliation, James says he no sooner found himself "in the presence of those yelling barbarians . . . and learned what could be the savagery of their disappointment . . . than the dream and delusion of my having made a successful appeal to the . . . British imagination . . . dropped from me in the twinkling of an eye" (*Plays* 477).

The event sent James into a year-long depression from which he eventually recovered by a return to the novel, specifically, a return to writing a type of fiction that restored James's sense of the value of those five years spent on drama by making him realize that his long apprenticeship constructing plays on a scene-by-scene basis had enabled, as Edel notes, "the ultimate integration, in his work, of Picture and Scene" (*Plays* 64). As James himself wrote, henceforth "the *scenic* method is my absolute, my imperative, my *only* salvation" (*Plays* 64); or as he was to say in 1910, "I come back yet again and again, to my only seeing it in the dramatic way—as I can only see everything and anything now" (*Plays* 19). James's reaction to the fiasco of *Domville*'s premiere recalls Fitzgerald's feelings on the opening night of *The Vegetable*'s tryout in Atlantic City when during the performance people "walked out, . . . rustled their programs and talked audibly in bored impatient whispers": "After the second act I wanted to stop the show and say it was all a mistake but the actors struggled heroically on" (*Lost* 33). Yet Fitzgerald's public humiliation had, at least, occurred out of town, whereas James's had taken place in London before a brilliant first-night audience that included among others Sir Edward Burne-Jones, George du Maurier, John Singer Sargent, Edmund Gosse, Mrs. Humphry Ward, George Bernard Shaw, the young H. G. Wells, and Arnold Bennett. Certainly, this was not the outcome James had expected when he turned to writing *for the stage* from writing *about the stage* in *The Tragic Muse*.

In that novel James had combined two themes that he "was to call 'my theatrical case' and 'my political case'" (Edel ix)—the former embodied in the budding career of a brilliant, young actress named Miriam Rooth and the latter in the unsatisfying career of Nick Dormer, a young member of Parliament. Though everything in Dormer's family history (his father was a distinguished MP), as well as the wishes of all those closest to him, push him toward the political arena, he is deeply inclined toward the world of visual art and feels his real talent lies in portrait painting. After considerable inner turmoil, Dormer opts for an artistic career and gives up his seat in Parliament, resulting in a temporary estrangement from his mother and the end of his engagement to his wealthy cousin Julia Dallow, a widow, who had had unlimited political ambitions for her fiancé. The cases of Miriam Rooth and Nick Dormer become entwined because Julia Dallow's brother, the rising young diplomat Peter Sherringham, a devoted connoisseur of the theater, becomes involved in advancing Miriam Rooth's career and ultimately falls in love with her.

Playing on two senses of "representation"—one political, one theatrical— James draws a parallel between the artistic commitments of Miriam Rooth and Nick Dormer. A young woman with a striking physical appearance and a fierce determination to succeed but little formal training as an actress, Miriam begins her rise to fame when Peter Sherringham introduces her to the aging French actress Madame Carré, who gives Miriam informal lessons. Miriam's ultimate success results not just from her innate talent but from her unwavering commitment to the highest professional standards, to emulating the best style of acting performed in the best dramatic literature. Her ideal is always to give the truest, most moving theatrical "representation" of any character she plays. In contrast, Nick Dormer, as a member of Parliament, must pursue the political "representation" of his constituents, but he finds that this also involves a form of theatricality. Nick's political talent, his electability, is a function of his personal attractiveness and his cleverness as a public speaker. But his speaking engagements often demand that he act out, before his constituents or fellow party members, enthusiasms he doesn't share with them, demand that he play a role in which he must talk a lot of "rubbish," as he says, in order to portray a coincidence of interests and opinions with his electors. Where Miriam's acting fulfills and energizes her through its commitment to the aesthetic truth of dramatic representation, Nick's pretended enthusiasms for policies and constituents he doesn't truly care about amounts to a kind of acting that continually puts him in what he feels is a false, debilitating position. So he quits political life to pursue his own form of aesthetic truth: the visual representation of a person's true character in oil paint on canvas, as opposed to Miriam's theatrical representation of character in grease paint on stage. And appropriately enough, Nick's first portrait exhibiting his talent for this type of representation is of Miriam Rooth, the leading actress.

James also uses the parallel between Miriam and Nick to contrast the form their commitment to the aesthetic life takes. When we first meet Miriam, she and her mother have been traveling around Europe living from hand to mouth by selling off their possessions while trying to get Miriam started on an acting career. Once Peter Sherringham sponsors Miriam, her career begins to take off, but there is never any sense that her unwavering commitment to her art has required her to give up other possibilities in her life. Yet with

Nick Dormer, who has just been elected for the second time to a seat in Parliament, the decision to become a painter requires that he sacrifice a brilliant political future, as well his engagement to Julia Dallow and the inheritance old Mr. Carteret would have settled on him with Nick's marriage to Julia. Nick's opting for painting over politics replicates, in Edel's words, James's "deeply rooted belief that an artist must make a choice between art and 'the world'" (*Plays* 47): James himself had made a similar choice as a young man at Harvard Law School, that "crucial decision of his life—renunciation of Law for Letters" (*Plays* 465–66). In *The Tragic Muse* James represents Nick's decision as a braver one than Miriam's—not just because unlike Nick, Miriam has nothing to lose by an all-out commitment to her art but also because Miriam's talent and determination lead to her almost immediate success as an actress, while Nick, who makes his decision at an older age than does Miriam, realizes that he is getting started late and has much to learn and that his success as a painter, if there is to be any, may lie years off. For all of these reasons, James implies, Nick's is the nobler commitment. The subject of James's ill-fated play *Guy Domville* was, as Edel notes, "a reiteration of the problems presented in *The Tragic Muse*": the conflict of "the worldly life versus the dedicated life, compromise with 'success' versus renunciation" (*Plays* 465).

The sense of the theatrical world as a demimonde that we have noted in *Gatsby* is also present in *The Tragic Muse*. From Miriam's repeated avowals that though she is an actress, she is still "a good girl," to the novel's several references to actors as "mountebanks," and on to Peter Sherringham's inner struggle over the social acceptability of his falling in love with Miriam, this sense of theatrical people as déclassé culminates in the scene where Peter proposes marriage to Miriam if she will only give up professional acting and Miriam counters by saying she'll marry him if he gives up his diplomatic career to manage her career on the stage. As Miriam expects, Peter refuses, leaving for a diplomatic post in Central America, and Miriam subsequently marries Basil Dashwood, a fellow actor of limited ability who will become her manager. Peter loses Miriam by opting for diplomacy over art, while Nick loses Julia Dallow by choosing art over politics, though at the novel's end there is a hint that Julia's objection to Nick's artistic career as something trivial and unserious has softened somewhat when she agrees to have Nick paint her portrait.

If James in *The Tragic Muse* contrasts the aesthetic theatricality of the stage with the worldly theatricality of politics and Fitzgerald in *Gatsby* contrasts the professional theatricality of Broadway and the movies with the amateur theatricality of upper-class manners and social display, then the link between these two in a genealogy of influence is James's friend and admirer Edith Wharton, to whom Fitzgerald sent a copy of *The Great Gatsby* when it appeared. In her 1905 novel *The House of Mirth*, for example, Wharton makes Lily Bart's friend Lawrence Selden the character who is at once most aware and most critical of the theatrical quality of high society: He tells Lily, "The queer thing about society is that the people who regard it as an end are those who are in it, and not the critics on the fence. It's just the other way with most shows—the audience may be under the illusion, but the actors know that real life is on the other side of the footlights. The people who take society as an escape from work are putting it to its proper use; but when it becomes the thing worked for it distorts all the relations of life" (73). And later, attending a party hosted by Wellington and Louisa Bry, a couple determined to rise in society on the wings of wealth and lavish entertaining, Selden muses on the way that the amateur theatricality of a series of *tableaux vivants*, in one of which Lily Bart appears, seems to blend almost imperceptibly into the theatricality of the party itself and the Brys' mansion. Selden

> enjoyed spectacular effects, and was not insensible to the part money plays in their production: all he asked was that the very rich should live up to their calling as stage-managers, and not spend their money in a dull way. This the Brys could certainly not be charged with doing. Their recently built house, whatever it might lack as a frame for domesticity, was almost as well-designed for the display of a festal assemblage as one of those airy pleasure-halls which the Italian architects improvised to set off the hospitality of their princes. The air of improvisation was in fact strikingly present: so recent, so rapidly-evoked was the whole *mise-en-scène* that one had to touch the marble columns to learn they were not of cardboard, to seat one's self in one of the damask-and-gold arm-chairs to be sure it was not painted against the wall. (139)

The inherent theatricality of Lily's quest to capture a rich husband forces her to seek dramatic opportunities for displaying her beauty, such as appearing in the Brys' *tableaux vivants*. Lily's "dramatic instinct was roused by the choice of subjects, and the gorgeous reproductions of historic dress stirred an imagination which only visual impressions could reach. But keenest of all was the exhilaration of displaying her own beauty under a new aspect: of showing that her loveliness was no mere fixed quality, but an element shaping all emotions to fresh forms of grace" (138). Early in the novel Lily sets her cap for Percy Gryce, a wealthy young man interested in religion, and she feigns a similar interest in order to exhibit her suitability as a mate. During a country-house visit, Gryce is engaged in conversation with the voluble Mrs. Fisher but casting "agonized glances in the direction of Miss Bart, whose only response was to sink into an attitude of more graceful abstraction. She had learned the value of contrast in throwing her charms into relief, and was fully aware of the extent to which Mrs. Fisher's volubility was enhancing her own repose" (49)—an evocation of the theatrics of repose under the other's gaze that we've seen before. To convince Gryce of her interest in religion, she agrees to accompany him to church on Sunday, thinking that on the long walk back together she will charm him into proposing, but when Sunday morning comes, Lily oversleeps and Gryce goes to church without her. And then instead of going to meet him along the country path back from the church, Lily decides to take a walk with Lawrence Selden, whom she finds more attractive and amusing than Gryce. Though Lily thinks she has Gryce so firmly under her spell that she can recoup her missed opportunity, she has in fact lost her chance with him forever. As the novel progresses, it becomes clear that Lily's tragic flaw is that, through a combination of vanity and laziness, she lacks the "dramaturgical discipline" to successfully portray (to completely inhabit) the role of a suitable marriage partner for a wealthy man.

Wharton frequently invokes theatrical imagery in the novel to characterize a situation or a person, as when Selden, visiting in Monte Carlo, notes groups of people in the town square "loitering in the foreground against mauve mountains which suggested a sublime stage-setting forgotten in a hurried shifting of scenes" (191). Or later when Selden sees Ned Silverton, the correspondent in a scandalous affair with the married Bertha Dorset, "loitering somewhat ostentatiously about the tables" at the Casino, and Wharton says "the discovery that this actor in the drama was not only hovering in the wings, but actually inviting the exposure of the footlights, though it might have seemed to imply that all peril was over, served rather to deepen Selden's sense of foreboding" (223). Wharton also draws on theatrical imagery when Lily's position in society has begun to slip because Bertha Dorset, in order to protect herself in the matter of Ned Silverton, has begun to spread false rumors of Lily's involvement with Bertha's husband, and Lily finds herself having to associate with people of new wealth, such as the Gormers, who are trying to rise in the New York social world: "The Gormer *milieu* represented a social out-skirt which Lily had always fastidiously avoided; but it struck her, now that she was in it, as only a flamboyant copy of her own world, a caricature approximating the real thing as the 'society play' approaches the manners of the drawing room" (244). The Gormers' set includes not only society types but also theatrical people such as the celebrated actress Miss Anstell, and though Lily, because of Bertha Dorset's rumors, has been "publically branded as the heroine of a 'queer' episode," the Gormers

> instead of shrinking from her as her own friends had done, . . . received her without question into the easy promiscuity of their lives. They swallowed her past as easily as they did Miss Anstell's, and with no apparent sense of any difference in the size of the mouthful: all they asked was that she should—in her own way, for they recognized a diversity of gifts—contribute as much to the general amusement as that graceful actress, whose talents, when off the stage, were of the most varied order. (245)

So Lily in this downscale milieu finds herself having to practice the same arts of social ingratiation as a creature of the demimonde. All of which simply suggests that within the tradition of the American novel of manners Fitzgerald's move, in the wake of *The Vegetable*'s failure, back to writing a type of fiction that had the theatricality of upper-class social interactions as its ongoing subject was not a wholly unpredictable occurrence.

3

Between the publication of *Gatsby* in 1925 and *Tender Is the Night* in 1934, Fitzgerald published two series of short stories, each with an ongoing protagonist. As Jackson Bryer and John Kuehl note in their preface to *The Basil and Josephine Stories*, "Sometime in March of 1928, when he was having great difficulty writing his fourth novel, F. Scott Fitzgerald suddenly and quite surprisingly reached back into his childhood and began a series of stories about his life from 1907 at age eleven in Buffalo, New York, to 1913 at age seventeen, when he entered Princeton University. Transparently concealing himself behind the alias Basil Duke Lee, Fitzgerald wrote eight of these stories between March 1928 and February 1929," all eight appearing in the *Saturday Evening Post* in 1928 and 1929 (Bryer and Kuehl vii). Fitzgerald was unable to sell a ninth Basil Lee story, "That Kind of Party," to the *Post*, and "in an effort" to market "this story apart from the series, Fitzgerald changed the protagonist's name to Terrence R. Tipton; but his attempts . . . were unsuccessful" (Bryer and Kuehl viii), and it was only published posthumously in 1951. The other set of stories has as its protagonist a wealthy young Chicago socialite, Josephine Perry, clearly modeled on Fitzgerald's girlfriend from his prep school days, Ginevra King. Fitzgerald wrote the five Josephine Perry stories between January 1930 and June 1931, all five appearing in the *Saturday Evening Post* in 1930 and 1931 (Bryer and Kuehl viii). As early as the summer of 1928 both Fitzgerald's editor, Maxwell Perkins, and his agent, Harold Ober, had suggested Fitzgerald consider the notion of ultimately collecting the series of stories as a separate book, a notion Fitzgerald agreed with, saying that he had planned the series as "a nice *light* novel, almost, to follow my novel [*Tender Is the Night*] in the season *immediately* after, so as not to seem in the direct line of my so-called 'work'" (Bryer and Kuehl viii). But, as Bryer and Kuehl suggest, once *Tender Is the Night* had appeared and was neither a financial nor critical success, Fitzgerald felt that publishing the Basil and Josephine stories as a book might further detract from his reputation as a serious novelist: he pointed out that the stories too closely resembled the works of Booth Tarkington (e.g., *Seventeen, Penrod, Penrod and Sam*), thus inviting "disadvantageous comparisons," and that "their 'best phrases and ideas' had been used in *Tender Is the Night*" (Bryer and Kuehl x).

Fitzgerald's ultimate opinion of the Basil and Josephine stories notwithstanding, these two series are significant for our purposes because, as the textual bridge between *Gatsby* and *Tender*, they bring into even greater relief the thematic and structural importance of theatricality in Fitzgerald's fiction. As a more or less transparent account of the influences that shaped Fitzgerald's childhood and adolescence, the Basil Lee stories make clear his early and continuing attraction to playwriting, popular songs, musical comedy, and the stage. Not surprisingly, in the nine Basil stories there are, by my count, no less than twenty-one popular songs either cited or quoted from—songs ranging from those in operettas (such as "Every Little Movement Has a Meaning All its Own" from *Madame Sherry* and "Velia" and "I'm Going to Maxim's" from *The Merry Widow*) to Tin-Pan Alley tunes of the day (such as "Basil's tune of tunes," the 1910 "Chinatown, My Chinatown" [*Basil* 169], the 1911 "Oh, You Beautiful Doll," the 1912 "On Moonlight Bay," and the 1913 "Peg o' My Heart").

Even more striking than the number of songs mentioned is the amount of space devoted to Basil's theatrical ambitions and activities. For example, in "The Freshest Boy," set during Basil's freshman year at the East Coast prep school St. Regis, the tale's turning point occurs when Basil attends a Broadway musical. All three acts are described in some detail, along with Basil's emotional response to the play's story of a young man and woman who love each other but are separated by "tragic errors and misconceptions" (71), only to be reconciled in the third act's happy ending. After the performance, Basil follows the young female star of the musical and her beau, the Yale football captain Ted Fay, to a hotel tearoom and overhears their conversation: though the two are deeply in love, she tells him she's going to keep her promise of a year earlier to marry the older man who gave her the leading role in the show and made her a star. When Ted Fay asks her to tell the other man she loves someone else and ask him to release her from her promise, she replies, "This isn't musical comedy, Ted. . . . I'm living up to my responsibility to Beltzman; you've got to make up your mind just like I have—that we can't have each other" (74). Understanding in this incident the distance between romantic stage illusion and the real world, the fifteen-year-old Basil puts the misery of his first year at St. Regis in a more mature perspective and decides to stay in school rather than accompany his mother to Europe.

Clearly, the ongoing subject of the Basil and Josephine stories concerns the sort of lessons one has to learn in adolescence as one's personality and character are forming, those lessons of behavior (appropriate to an upper-middle- or upper-class environment) a young person learns as he or she acquires the verbal and gestural vocabulary of successful social performance. Among the several things Basil learns from his social faux pas, which is to say, the several personal traits he acquires due to humiliations his missteps cause, are "an air of consideration" for others, "which was the mark of his recent re-discovery that others had wills as strong as his, and more power" (92), and a ongoing commitment to the process of "molding . . . his own destiny" (75) no matter the painful cost of lost dreams. At the end of the Basil series, in "Basil and Cleopatra," he realizes that his love, Minnie Bibble, no longer loves him and resigns himself to this in a passage reminiscent of Keats:

> There was a flurry of premature snow in the air and the stars looked cold. Staring up at them he saw that they were his stars as always—symbols of ambition, struggle and glory. The wind blew through them, trumpeting that high white note for which he always listened, and the thin-blown clouds, stripped for battle, passed in review. The scene was of an unparalleled brightness and magnificence, and only the practiced eye of the commander saw that one star was no longer there. (184)

In contrast, Josephine Perry learns quite different lessons, their divergence from Basil's being a function both of her gender and the fact that whereas Basil is upper-middle class ("only comfortable" [46], as Fitzgerald describes Basil's family in "A Night at the Fair"), Josephine's family is "Chicago Society, and almost very rich" (188). (Indeed, in "First Blood," the initial Josephine story, Fitzgerald provides a fuller rendering of the three-generation rule of inherited wealth: Josephine "had no desire for achievement. Her grandfather had had that, her parents had had the consciousness of it, but Josephine accepted the proud world into which she was born. This was easy in Chicago, which, unlike New York, was a city state, where the 'old' families formed a caste" [*Basil* 191].) And in this proud world the lessons Josephine learns are essentially two. The first comes in "A Snobbish Story," in which the teenaged Josephine has become infatuated with an older, married man from a lower social class, the journalist and would-be playwright John Boynton Bailey. Bailey wants to cast Josephine in the starring role of a play he's written, hoping Josephine's wealthy father will back its production by a local Chicago theater group. Josephine invites Bailey to meet her family, but during the visit a policeman arrives with the news that Bailey's wife has attempted suicide, apparently because of her husband's involvement with Josephine. After Bailey departs, Josephine's parents claim they don't understand why Josephine "should have to know people like that. . . . Is it necessary to go into the back streets of Chicago?" And her father concludes, "That young man had no business here . . . and he knew it" (266). At the prospect of appearing in Bailey's serious, professional stage play, Josephine had earlier passed up an opportunity of performing a song-and-dance number with one of her old beaus in an amateur vaudeville night put on and attended by her peers. As she watches another girl perform "the role Josephine would have played" in the song-and-dance number, the first lesson hits home as a realization about herself: "With the warm rain of intimate applause, Josephine decided something: That any value she might have was in the immediate shimmering present—and thus thinking, she threw in her lot with the rich and powerful of this world forever" (268).

The second lesson Josephine learns comes in her final story "Emotional Bankruptcy." Here she finds that inherited wealth, which has given her too much of everything too early, allowing her to run through innumerable affairs of the heart as a teenage girl, has left her emotionally spent when she finally meets the man she wants to marry. She tells him, " 'You're everything I've always wanted. . . . But I've had everything. . . . I've got nothing to give you. I don't feel anything at all.' . . . The love of her life had come by, and looking in her empty basket she had found not a flower left for him" (285–86). Obviously, Josephine forms the link, the bridging figure, between Daisy Buchanan and Nicole Diver, but perhaps less obviously, her character is also the link between Gatsby, who loses his dream before he dies, and Dick Diver, who ends up emotionally spent, remarking that the change in his personality occurred "a long way back—but at first it didn't show. The manner remains intact for some time after the morale cracks" (*Tender* 320).

As I said, what stands out about the Basil and Josephine stories is the degree to which this adolescent learning process, the drama of social performance, is played out against the backdrop of actual stage theatricality. The most extensive use of this theatrical framework occurs in the Basil story "The Captured Shadow." It begins with the fifteen-year-old Basil returning home at midnight from a play and, still under the spell of the performance, immediately starting to work on a play of his own. Basil turns over the pages of his copybook, past the opening pages of two of his previous, unfinished pieces—"MR. WASHINGTON SQUARE A Musical Comedy by Basil Duke Lee Music by Victor Herbert" and "HIC! HIC! HIC! A Hilarious Farce in One Act" (101–2)—before coming to the play he is presently working on: "THE CAPTURED SHADOW A Melodramatic Farce in Three Acts" (103). Fitzgerald makes clear the type of drama Basil is imitating:

> This had been a season of "crook comedies" in New York, and the feel, the swing, the exact and vivid image of the two he had seen were in the foreground of his mind. At the time they had been enormously suggestive, opening out into a world much larger and more brilliant than themselves that existed outside their windows and beyond their doors, and it was this suggested world, rather than any conscious desire to imitate "Officer 666," that had inspired the effort before him. (103).

*Officer 666* was "a melodramatic farce in three acts" written by Augustin McHugh and produced on Broadway in 1912 by the team of George M. Cohan and Sam Harris (both of whom, as we noted earlier, lived in Great Neck during the time the Fitzgeralds were there). The play, directed by Cohan, concerned the comic attempt to capture a gentleman art thief.

This figure of the gentleman thief had first surfaced in the Basil's stories with "The Scandal Detectives." The fourteen-year-old Basil's "favorite character in fiction was Arsène Lupin, the gentleman burglar, a romantic phenomenon lately imported from Europe and much admired in the first bored decades of the century" (18). The French writer Maurice Leblanc (1864–1941) had introduced the character of Arsène Lupin to the world in a 1907 collection of stories *Arsène Lupin, gentleman cambrioleur.* Though a thief, the suave Lupin often steps in to foil criminals more dangerous than himself and always with stylish Gallic wit. So popular was the character of Lupin that it gave rise almost immediately to stage adaptations and to twenty more volumes of his adventures over the next thirty years. Moreover, between 1908 and 1917 there were five silent films alone based on the character, three of them titled *Arsène Lupin* and the other two *The Gentleman Burglar*. In "The Scandal Detectives," Basil, daydreaming about his future, thinks, "next fall he was starting away to school. Then he would go to Yale and be a great athlete, and after that—if his two dreams had fitted onto each other chronologically instead of existing independently side by side—he was due to become a gentleman burglar" (22). But at the story's end Basil "was no longer sure that he wanted to be a gentleman burglar, though he still read of their exploits with breathless admiration" (35). In "The Freshest Boy" this figure recurs in Basil's daydream during the train ride east to his prep school:

> It was a hidden Broadway restaurant in the dead of the night, and a brilliant and mysterious group of *society people*, diplomats, and *members of the underworld* were there. A few minutes ago the sparkling wine had been flowing and a girl had been dancing gaily upon a table, but now the whole crowd were hushed and breathless. All eyes were fixed upon the masked but well-groomed man in the dress suit and opera hat who stood nonchalantly in the door.
>
> "Don't move, please," he said, in a well-bred, cultivated voice that had, nevertheless, a ring of steel in it. "This thing in my hand might—go off." . . .
>
> "Now that my purpose is accomplished, it might interest you to know who I am." There was a gleam of expectation in every eye. . . . "I am none other than that elusive gentleman, Basil Lee, better known as the Shadow."
>
> Taking off his well-fitting opera hat, he bowed ironically from the waist. Then, like a flash, he turned and was gone into the night. (55, italics mine)

One can see that what Blatchford Sarnemington was for Rudolph Miller, and Jay Gatsby was for James Gatz, the Shadow is for Basil Lee—an imaginative alter ego, an idealized other self, that becomes the principal character in Basil's play "The Captured Shadow." Most of the action in Fitzgerald's story of that name focuses first on Basil's maneuvering in casting and then directing the play in rehearsals and then on his intervening during the actual performance to avert a catastrophe. The story ends with Basil basking in the adulation of the crowd, but then "as the crowd melted away and the last few people spoke to him and went out, he felt a great vacancy come into his heart. It was over, it was done and gone—all that work and interest and absorption. It was a hollowness like fear" (119). Basil has found that gaining the object of his desire in this instance—which is to say, capturing that self-projected goal of seeing his play through to a successful performance—has proved to be as insubstantial as a shadow, which is the final meaning of the story's and the play's title.

The importance of "The Captured Shadow" for our purposes is the light it sheds on the origin of the recurring element we've been tracking in Fitzgerald's fiction. Basil's play brings together three registers—show business (because it's a play), high society (because its main character is a "well-bred, cultivated" [55] gentleman), and the underworld (because that gentleman is a burglar)—that we identified in the fictive biography of Curtis Carlyle (who leads a ragtime band, then turns to armed robbery to finance his ultimate goal of achieving "aristocracy") and in the original conception of Jay Gatsby (who is attracted to popular songs and performs one of his own compositions for Nick but ultimately becomes a bootlegger to enable his rise in society). If, as Fitzgerald makes clear, Basil's Shadow derives from Leblanc's Arsène Lupin and if, as Bryer and Kuehl suggest, the Basil stories are based, more or less transparently, on Fitzgerald's own adolescence, then one can see that the figure of "Arsène Lupin, the Gentleman Burglar" (famous from numerous stage and screen adaptations) had captivated the immature Fitzgerald's imagination and became in the imagination of the mature fiction writer the figure of Jay Gatsby, the gentleman bootlegger whose parties are filled with people who work in show business.

4

If, as I have suggested, Gatsby and Fitzgerald are to some degree reciprocals of one another (the former had the money but not the background, education, or manners for the social world he wants to enter, while the latter had all the social qualifications but not the money), then with the character of Dick Diver in *Tender Is the Night* Fitzgerald creates a protagonist much closer to his own situation. Diver is upper-middle class, the son of a clergyman, a graduate of Yale, with an MD degree from Johns Hopkins; he has done postgraduate work in Vienna and published a well-received, first book on psychiatry. He is, in short, a young man with a virtually unlimited professional future. But then, because of a character flaw, he commits the professional sin of marrying a mental patient, the young Nicole Warren, whose family is one of the wealthiest, most socially prominent in Chicago, and the drama of the middle-class professional trying to stay afloat, trying to remain his own man, while moving in the society of the big rich begins. One recalls in this regard Fitzgerald's description in "Pasting It Together" of his own situation as someone who, though always cherishing "an animosity toward the leisure class," lived for sixteen years "distrusting the rich, yet working for money with which to share their mobility and the grace that some of them brought to their lives" (*Lost* 147).

Fitzgerald's use of professional theatricality as an allusive background against which to display the theatrics of social performance gained momentum from its initial appearance in *Gatsby* to its progression in the Basil and Josephine stories, finally coming to pervade *Tender Is the Night*. For the first time in any of his novels, one of the main characters is actually a professional actor, the young movie star Rosemary Hoyt, whose arrival on the French Riviera, her infatuation with Dick Diver, and his attraction to her initiate the book's action. Fitzgerald makes clear just how important a role the interaction of professional theatricality and social/theatrical performance will play in the novel at the very first moment Rosemary catches sight of Dick on the beach at Cap d'Antibes. Her professional eye immediately realizes "that the man in the jockey cap was giving a quiet little performance" for a group of friends gathered under beach umbrellas: "He moved gravely about with a rake, ostensibly removing gravel and meanwhile developing some esoteric burlesque held in suspension by his grave face. Its faintest ramification had become hilarious, until whatever he said released a burst of laughter. Even those who, like herself, were too far away to hear, sent out antennae of attention" (12). Dick is, indeed, giving a show for the members of his set—an in-group composed of Nicole, Abe and Mary North, and Tommy Barban—a performance apparently meant to burlesque the déclassé group of newcomers to the beach—Albert and Violet McKisco, Mrs. Abrams, Luis Campion, and Royal Dunphy. At least that's the way the newcomers interpret it. When Campion, intruding on Rosemary's privacy, introduces himself and the other members of his group, Violet McKisco's first words to Rosemary are "We know who you are" and then "We thought maybe you were in the plot. . . . We don't know who's in the plot and who isn't. One man my husband had been particularly nice to turned out to be a chief character—practically the assistant hero." When Rosemary asks, "Is there a plot?" Mrs. Abrams says, "My dear, we don't *know*. . . . We're not in on it. We're the gallery" (13–14). In this instance Dick's social theatrics serve to enforce a class distinction, and the practical effect of this difference is experienced two days later when Dick invites Rosemary to join his group on the beach. McKisco's group seemed to think that because they knew who Rosemary was, she should naturally reciprocate and want to know them. Dick takes a different tack; when he brings her into his group, he manages "the introduction so that her name wasn't mentioned and then let her know easily that everyone knew who she was but that they were respecting the completeness of her private life—a courtesy that Rosemary had not met with save from professional people since her success" (23). But perhaps McKisco's group felt that since Rosemary was an actress and thus a member of the demimonde, her being permitted to know them would represent a social step up.

Fitzgerald locates the point of view for the book's opening scenes with the teenaged Rosemary in order to give the reader a sense of the external impression made by the Divers at this their most sophisticated and charming moment: Rosemary's

> naïveté responded whole-heartedly to the expensive simplicity of the Divers, unaware of its complexity and its lack of innocence, unaware that it was all a selection of quality rather than quantity from the run of the world's bazaar; and that the simplicity of behavior also, the nursery-like peace and good will, the emphasis on the simpler virtues, was part of a desperate bargain with the gods and had been attained through struggles she could not have guessed at. At that moment the Divers represented externally the exact furthermost evolution of a class, so that most people seemed awkward beside them—in reality a qualitative change had already set in that was not at all apparent to Rosemary. (28)

Rosemary experiences that first day spent as part of Dick's group as a well-planned social drama, its every moment (and their sequence) conceived, directed, and acted in by Dick, bringing to mind Anthony Patch's remark in *The Beautiful and Damned* that a well-planned day should go "marching along surely, even jauntily, toward a climax, as a play should" (51):

> Rosemary felt that this swim would become the typical one of her life, the one that would always pop up in her memory at the mention of swimming. . . . The Divers' day was spaced like the day of the older civilizations to yield the utmost from the materials at hand, and to give all the transitions their full value, and she did not know that there would be another transition presently from the utter absorption of the swim to the garrulity of the Provençal lunch hour. But again she had the sense that Dick was taking care of her, and she delighted in responding to the eventual movement as if it had been an order. (28)

Rosemary's experience here confirms her sense of two days earlier when she'd first come to the beach knowing no one: that the "excitement . . . generating under that umbrella . . . all came from the man in the jockey cap" (17). And her professional actor's awareness that Dick always arranged his social events as if they were mini-dramas grows as she gets to know the Divers. Planning a dinner party at Villa Diana for Dick's set, for Rosemary and her mother, and for the McKisco group, Dick tells Nicole, "I want to give a really *bad* party. I mean it. I want to give a party where there's a brawl and seductions and people going home with their feelings hurt and women passed out in the cabinet de toilette" (35), and Dick almost achieves the entire agenda, with Nicole having an hysterical episode in the bathroom and Tommy Barban and McKisco fighting a duel at dawn. Indeed, when Rosemary had arrived at the party, she sensed that "the Villa Diana was the center of the world" and that "on such a stage some memorable thing was sure to happen" (37). And later in the evening, alone with Dick, she tells him she fell in love with him the first time they met. Dick, attracted but disconcerted, finds himself caught in a "struggle with an unrehearsed scene and unfamiliar words" (46).

The idea of Dick as a social "actor" is reinforced as Rosemary follows the Divers to Paris. In the scene at the Parisian restaurant during which Dick claims to be the only man with repose, the professional actress Rosemary is "quite sure" of it, and Dick realizes "that he never had a better audience." Determined to make Dick interested enough to sexually initiate her, Rosemary says later at their hotel, "Take me," and Dick, frozen rigid with "astonishment," says "Take you where?" Rosemary, "astonished at herself . . . , had never imagined she could talk like that. . . . Suddenly she knew too that it was one of her greatest rôles and she flung herself into it more passionately" (75–76). The encounter between Rosemary and Dick having evolved into a contest between a socially inexperienced, professional actor and a socially experienced, amateur performer, Rosemary decides to play her trump card and turn Dick into a professional like herself. She invites the Divers and Norths to a film studio in Paris for a screening of her movie *Daddy's Girl* and then springs her surprise: she's arranged a screen test for Dick that same day. The Norths can barely suppress their hilarity, while Dick says, "I don't want a test. . . . The pictures make a fine career for a woman—but my God, they can't photograph me. I'm an old scientist all wrapped up in his private life." And "Dick closed the subject with a somewhat tart discussion of actors: 'The strongest guard is placed at the gateway to nothing. . . . Maybe because the condition of emptiness is too shameful to be divulged'" (81). In this regard one recalls Anthony Patch's tirade against professional actors when Gloria first announces her intention to seek a screen test. For both Anthony and Dick, the acting ability, the "dramaturgical discipline," to use Goffman's phrase, that allows one to perform in the highest levels of society is something acceptable, indeed, desirable, but the notion of taking a step down in class into the demimonde of professional acting in order to earn money is something Anthony and Dick, as social performers, reject.

The inherent falsity of much of the social "acting" among the leisure class is brought home to Rosemary when she accompanies Dick to an artistic gathering that Fitzgerald clearly modeled on the salon that the American heiress and lesbian writer Natalie Barney held each week in her Parisian home: "Rosemary had the detached false-and-exalted feeling of being on a set and she guessed that everyone else present had that feeling too. There were about thirty people, mostly women, and all fashioned by Louisa M. Alcott or Madame de Ségur; and they functioned on this set as cautiously, as precisely, as does a human hand picking up jagged broken glass" (83). In this environment "Rosemary suddenly discovered herself to be an insincere little person, living all in the upper registers of her throat and wishing the director would come. There was however such a wild beating of wings in the room that she did not feel her position was more incongruous than anyone else's" (84). Moving among the group, Rosemary overhears a "trio of young women" discussing the theatrical lifestyle of a couple that Rosemary realizes must be Dick and Nicole: "Oh, they give a good show. . . . Practically the best show in Paris. . . . [Y]ou must admit that the party in question can be one of the most charming human beings you have ever met" (84). Later, as Dick and Rosemary become more romantically, though not yet sexually, involved, Rosemary, in a comment that refers both to their romantic role-playing with each other and to their social role-playing meant to hide their involvement from everyone else, says, "Oh, we're such *actors*—you and I" (121).

When Dick rejects Rosemary's offer of a screen test by saying that "the pictures make a fine career for a woman" but not for a man, he implicitly gender codes the roles of observer and observed as masculine and feminine respectively. When Rosemary says that if the screen test had turned out well, she would have taken it to Hollywood, and he could have been her "leading man in a picture," Dick reemphasizes this coding, saying, "It was a darn sweet thought, but I'd rather look at *you*. You were about the nicest sight I ever looked at" (82). This gender coding of professional acting as a feminine role is meant to be read against Rosemary's mother's encouragement of her daughter to make a play for Dick because "you were brought up to work— not especially to marry. Now you've found your first nut to crack and it's a good nut—go ahead and put whatever happens down to experience. Wound yourself or him—whatever happens it can't spoil you because economically you're a boy, not a girl" (49). Though working as a professional actor is a feminine role according to Dick, yet because Rosemary earns her own money and doesn't need to depend on marriage for her support, she is economically male rather than female according to her mother, and no failed love affair could do her working life any damage.

Phrased in that way, we can see that a major part of the significance of Rosemary's character in the novel is the extent to which it is the reciprocal of Dick's. Just as Rosemary, with one hit film to her credit, is at the start of a successful career as a movie actress when she first meets and falls in love with Dick, so Dick, who had one brilliant book to his credit, was at the start of a successful career as a psychiatrist when he met, fell in love with, and married Nicole. And just as Rosemary, in earning her own money, doesn't need to marry to support herself, so Dick, at the start of his career, didn't need to marry to support himself but nonetheless wed a woman with more money than he could ever earn and as a result, in becoming gradually committed to his wife's upper-class lifestyle, has begun to feel like a kept man. Recall in this regard that in Fitzgerald's own case it was his mother's family's money that paid for his prep school and Princeton education and that as a businessman Fitzgerald's father had been an ineffectual failure. Over the course of the novel Nicole's money finally unmans Dick, in effect, feminizes him, his marriage having turned him, economically, from a boy into a girl, or as Tommy Barban phrases it when he tells Nicole that she has "too much money": "That's the crux of the matter. Dick can't beat that" (327). For a time Dick tries, almost pathetically, to remain his own man. He tells himself he will only use Nicole's money for her support and that of their children and that he will, through a series of small economies, manage to pay all his personal expenses out of his own earnings from professional work and publications, but the sheer volume of Nicole's ever-increasing income during the '20s swamps all Dick's good intentions.

The sense of Dick's progressive feminization is one of the subtexts of the novel's numerous allusions to homosexuality, culminating near the book's end in the scene where Lady Caroline Sibley-Biers accuses Dick of being gay. At the party on Golding's yacht, Dick has had too much to drink and begins to make comments about the English, when Nicole notices Lady Caroline:

Nicole thought that she was formidable, and she was confirmed in this point of view as the party rose from table. Dick remained in his seat wearing an odd expression; then he crashed into words with a harsh ineptness.

"I don't like innuendo in these deafening English whispers."

Already half-way out of the room Lady Caroline turned and walked back to him; she spoke in a low clipped voice purposely audible to the whole company.

"You come to me asking for it—disparaging my countrymen, disparaging my friend, Mary Minghetti. I simply said you were observed associating with a questionable crowd in Lausanne. Is that a deafening whisper? Or does it simply deafen *you*?"

"It's still not loud enough," said Dick, a little too late. "So I am actually a notorious—"

Golding crushed out the phrase with his voice saying:

"What! What!" and moved his guests on out. (305)

As Tom Buchanan's self-assurance had bested Gatsby's uncertainty in their confrontation at the Plaza, so Lady Caroline's "sheer strength derived from an attitude" defeats Dick's "ineptness" and his replying here "a little too late." And just as in that former confrontation the ultimate judge of who had won was Daisy, so here it is Nicole: "She was furious at the woman for her preposterous statement, equally furious at Dick for having brought them here, for having become fuddled, for having untipped the capped barbs of his irony, for having come off humiliated" (305).

Dick's sense of the slowly accumulating humiliation of being kept by his wife's money becomes apparent in the novel's most explicit instance of his giving a theatrical performance—a performance not meant to display wealth but to conceal its lack. In Paris Dick goes to a bank to cash a check, drawing on Nicole's account because he doesn't have sufficient funds in his own:

Writing a check, he looked along the row of men at the desks deciding to which one he would present it for an O.K. As he wrote he engrossed himself in the material act, examining meticulously the pen, writing laboriously upon the high glass-topped desk. Once he raised glazed eyes to look toward the mail department, then glazed his spirit again by concentration upon the objects he dealt with.

Still he failed to decide to whom the check would be presented, which man in the line would guess least of the unhappy predicament in which he found himself and, also, which one would be least likely to talk. . . .

As he entered the amount on the stub, and drew two lines under it, he decided to go to Pierce, who was young and for whom he would have to put on only a small show. It was often easier to give a show than to watch one. (103)

But as Dick walks toward Pierce, he sees he's engaged with another customer and that he must present the check to Casasus, a "Spaniard, with whom he usually discussed a mutual friend in spite of the fact that the friend had passed out of his life a dozen years before" (103):

> "How are you, Diver?" Casasus was genial. He stood up, his moustache spreading with his smile. "We were talking about Featherstone the other day and I thought of you—he's out in California."
> Dick widened his eyes and bent forward a little.
> "In California?"
> "That's what I heard."
> Dick held the check poised; to focus the attention of Casasus upon it he looked toward Pierce's desk, holding the latter for a moment in a friendly eye-play conditioned by an old joke of three years before when Pierce had been involved with a Lithuanian countess. Pierce played up with a grin until Casasus had authorized the check and had no further recourse to detain Dick. . . .
> Cutting across the social mood of Casasus with the intensity he had accumulated at the glass desk—which is to say he looked hard at the check, studying it, and then fixed his eyes on grave problems beyond the first marble pillar to the right of the banker's head and made a business of shifting the cane, hat, and letters he carried—he said good-bye and went out. He had long ago purchased the doorman; his taxi sprang to the curb. (104)

If Dick feels feminized enough by using his wife's money that he needs to give a "show" for the men at the bank, then it is no wonder that Dick considers acting in pictures "a fine career for a woman," nor surprising that Fitzgerald has Dick direct the taxi he takes from the bank to drive to "the Films Par Excellence Studio . . . in Passy" (104), hoping to run into Rosemary there. (Recall that Films Par Excellence was the movie company of which Joseph Bloekman was vice-president in *The Beautiful and Damned* and that one of the guests at Gatsby's parties is "Newton Orchid who controlled Films Par Excellence" [50].)

If, as Dick thinks, "It's often easier to give a show than to watch one," then for whose benefit is the show at the bank being given? Dick's rather obvious, social acting—evoked in the detail of his widened eyes and the way he says "California"—is meant to conceal from other men his own sense of humiliation, conceal his self-consciousness by acting out, with practiced charm, a social consciousness of, a personal interest in, the lives of others, as when he discusses Featherstone (a friend whom he hasn't seen in years) with Casasus or engages in byplay with Pierce. And when not involved in this performance, Dick pretends to focus his attention on, to be absorbed by, insignificant details in his surroundings in order to guard himself from having to look at the big picture of what he has become, a gazing that might cause him to reveal his embarrassment. His feigned preoccupation is meant to disguise his own lack of an occupation remunerative enough to insure his financial independence. When Fitzgerald ends the scene by saying Dick "had long ago purchased the doorman" (probably with tips), he makes clear that Dick's performance for the bank men aims to coopt their goodwill, to "purchase" an exemption from any disapproval they might feel, and to buy it with the currency of social bonhomie, his caring treatment of them not as employees in an establishment he deals with but as social equals, fellow gentlemen. In a novel depicting the slow but steady "emotional bankruptcy" of its main character, this bank scene displaying Dick's insufficient funds is both symbolic of his growing depletion of spirit and indicative of its literal cause, Nicole's growing wealth.

Given that Dick's show at the bank is put on largely for his own benefit (his dramaturgical discipline having become a social/psychological defense mechanism), we should look again at that earlier scene at the restaurant during which Dick claims he's the only man with repose. In making this claim Dick is in part showing off for Rosemary, exhibiting for a professional actor his own dramatic skill in standing the gaze of the Other without betraying any unease or awkwardness; yet in explicitly calling attention to his possessing this theatrical quality (recall that in addition to Rosemary, the Norths and two young French musicians are present at the lunch), he also aims to convince himself, by means of the others' ultimate assent, that he does indeed have that absolute self-assurance Fitzgerald considers a marker of social superiority in those of inherited wealth.

A passage in Fitzgerald's essay "My Lost City," bearing the date "July, 1932" (though written in 1933 for *Cosmopolitan* magazine) but unpublished till 1945 (*Crack-Up* 23), is relevant to Dick's implied gender coding of the gaze's wielder and its object as masculine and feminine roles, respectively, and to his sense that is "easier" to give a show (to be the female object of the gaze) than to watch a show (to be its male wielder). As a nostalgic memoir of Fitzgerald's experience of New York City from his teenage years at prep school right through to the first years of the Great Depression, "My Lost City," written during the time Fitzgerald was working on *Tender Is the Night*, makes clear its author's obsessive attachment to all things theatrical. He says, "When I was fifteen I went into the city from school to see Ina Claire in 'The Quaker Girl' and Gertrude Bryan in 'Little Boy Blue.' Confused by my hopeless and melancholy love for them both, I was unable to choose between them—so they blurred into one lovely entity, the girl. She was my second symbol of New York" (*Lost* 106). In those early years in New York, "I had come only to stare at the show, though the designers of the Woolworth Building and the Chariot Race Sign, the producers of musical comedies and problem plays could ask for no more appreciative spectator, for I took the style and glitter of New York even above its own valuation" (107). When he returned to the city after World War I to try to earn enough money to marry Zelda, he says, "I bought cheap theatre seats at Gray's drugstore and tried to lose myself for a few hours in my old passion for Broadway. I was a failure—mediocre at advertising work and unable to get started as a writer" (109). But once his first book was published and he and Zelda were married, they suddenly found that they were celebrities, and with that, New York became an enchanted playground: "The plays were '*Déclassée*' and 'Sacred and Profane Love,' and at the Midnight Frolic you danced elbow to elbow with Marion Davies. . . . We felt like small children in a great bright unexplored barn. Summoned out to Griffith's studio on Long Island, we trembled in the presence of the familiar faces of the 'Birth of a Nation'; later I realized that behind much of the entertainment that the city poured forth into the nation there were only a lot of lost and lonely people. The world of the picture actors was like our own in that it was in New York and not of it" (110). The Fitzgeralds moved to St. Paul for the birth of their daughter, but then came back and settled in Great Neck, Long Island. And here is where the memoir's salient passage occurs: "In a year we were back and we began doing the same things over again and not liking them so much. We had run through a lot *though we had retained an almost theatrical innocence by preferring the role of the observed to the observer*" (111, italics mine).

"Preferring the role of the observed to the observer" represents Fitzgerald's version, in the story of his own life, of Dick Diver's "It was often easier to give a show than to watch one," and the two goals achieved by these preferences— "theatrical innocence" and greater ease—though apparently different are, I would argue, in one sense essentially the same. Let me begin by recalling for a moment the history of the composition of *Tender*. After the publication of *Gatsby* in 1925, Fitzgerald began work on his fourth novel. The original version of the manuscript was the story of Francis Melarkey and his mother,

Charlotte, on a trip to Europe. Francis, who had worked as a film technician and was dominated by his mother, is a weak young man with an uncontrollable temper. Fitzgerald planned that Francis in a fit of anger would ultimately murder Charlotte. The manuscript, which Fitzgerald worked on off and on from 1925 to 1930, had four tentative titles: *Our Type*, *The World's Fair*, *The Melarkey Case*, and *The Boy Who Killed His Mother*. In late 1929 Fitzgerald started on a second version that centered around "a brilliant young motion-picture director and his wife, Lew and Nicole Kelly, who leave for Europe on an extended vacation at the peak of his success because he feels drained" (Bruccoli, *Composition* 60). It was only after Zelda's mental breakdown in 1930 that Fitzgerald began to think about a new story, and in 1932 he would begin work on the third and final version of the manuscript, a version that incorporated many aspects of Fitzgerald's own personal life at this period and that was tentatively called *The Drunkard's Holiday* or *Doctor Diver's Holiday*.

To summarize briefly his construction of this version, Fitzgerald took from the Melarkey manuscript the American couple living on the Riviera whom Francis and Charlotte met there and with whom they traveled to Paris and turned this couple from peripheral characters into the novel's main focus. He then took many of the characteristics of, and incidents involving, Francis Melarkey and distributed them between Rosemary Hoyt and Dick Diver and reconceived the American couple on the Riviera as a combination of Gerald and Sara Murphy and Scott and Zelda. He gave Zelda's mental illness to Nicole, and he gave his own fears about the way his life and career might end up to Dick Diver, the promising physician who had published a brilliant first book but was having trouble getting started on a second—a fear Fitzgerald felt as the brilliant accomplishment of *Gatsby* gave way to his subsequent inability to complete his next novel. The story of the couple's marriage begins with the husband strong and decisive and the wife weak and mentally unstable, and it progresses through a chiasmus in which the woman's psychological neediness as well as her growing wealth gradually deplete the emotional, psychological, and moral resources of her husband until at the end she is the strong one and he is exhausted and discarded. At one stage in the final manuscript Fitzgerald has a character describe Dick as an *homme manqué*, but Fitzgerald came to think of Dick as being more of an *homme epuisé*.

Matthew Bruccoli suggests that Dick's fatal character flaw was "his desire to be all things to all people: husband and physician to Nicole, physician to his patients, and spiritual guide to the American colony," and he goes on to quote as an analogy Fitzgerald's description of Francis Melarkey's desires:

"To achieve and to enjoy, to be strong and yet miss nothing. . . . To harmonize this, to melt it all down into a single man—there was something to be done. The very thought of such perfection crystallized his vitality into an ecstasy of ambition" (*Composition* 51). Elsewhere Bruccoli remarks that Dick's "crack-up is deeply rooted in his character—in his desire to please, in his egotism, and in his romantic view of life" (*Composition* 109). Bruccoli's reading is accurate, though I would add one qualification to his description of Dick as a "spiritual guide to the American colony." Dick's gradual acceptance of the ultimately corrupting, upper-class lifestyle Nicole's money provides reduces him from being a spiritual guide to simply a social guide to the American colony, an arranger and purveyor of expensive, artistically crafted good times for his friends and acquaintances. Fitzgerald sums up the allure of being "included in Dick Diver's world for a while":

> People believed he made special reservations about them, recognizing the proud uniqueness of their destinies. . . . He won everyone quickly with an exquisite consideration and a politeness that moved so fast and intuitively that it could be examined only in its effect. Then, without caution, lest the first bloom of the relation wither, he opened the gate to his amusing world. So long as they subscribed to it completely, their happiness was his preoccupation, but at the first flicker of doubt as to its all-inclusiveness he evaporated before their eyes. (35)

Dick feels an overwhelming need to be of use to others, to be needed, and he responds to others' needs with charm and a fatal pleasingness that, as it draws more and more on his emotional and mental energy, leaves him drained, his heart for caring worn out. And as Fitzgerald makes clear in the three "Crack-Up" essays of 1936, that was the way he had come to view himself during the years he worked on producing his fourth novel: "I began to realize that for two years my life had been drawing on resources that I did not possess, that I had been mortgaging myself physically and spiritually up to the hilt" (*Lost* 141–42), describing his emotional depletion as "a call upon physical resources that I did not command, like a man over-drawing at his bank" (147)—an image underlining the personal resonance of Dick's "show" at his Paris bank.

All of which brings us back to the translation of memoir into fiction, which is to say, the translation of Fitzgerald's preferring the role of the observed to that of the observer (because it allows him to retain an "almost theatrical innocence") into Dick's finding it easier to give a show than to watch one—in effect, brings us back to the question of what sort of *ease* "theatrical innocence" provides. And the answer ultimately lies in what Fitzgerald understood by the "innocence" created through acting. In "My Lost City" Fitzgerald notes that the success of *This Side of Paradise* was such that it gave him almost the celebrity of a theatrical star: "For just a moment, before it was demonstrated that I was unable to play the role, I, who knew less of New York than any reporter of six months' standing and less of its society than any hall-room boy in a Ritz stag line, was pushed into the position not only of spokesman for the time but of the typical product of that same moment" (109–10). As both product and spokesman of the Jazz Age, Fitzgerald was supposed to enact behavior typical of flaming youth and at the same time explain and comment on it. He adds that he and Zelda "did not know exactly what New York expected of us and found it rather confusing. Within a few months after our embarkation on the metropolitan venture we scarcely knew anymore who we were and we hadn't a notion what we were. A dive into a civic fountain, a casual brush with the law, was enough to get us into the gossip columns and we were quoted on a variety of subjects we knew nothing about" until "gradually we fitted our disruptive personalities into the contemporary scene of New York" (110). Suddenly in the limelight, Fitzgerald felt that he and Zelda were expected to play roles representative of their time and place, and so, like children who begin to "act up" or "act out" once they become aware they're being watched by adults, Scott and Zelda began a public exhibition of their "disruptive personalities."

In his biography of Fitzgerald, Scott Donaldson notes that Scott

corresponded in his behavior rather closely to what psychologist Avodah K. Offit has described as the "histrionic personality." Drama is the essence of life to such people. . . . They covet attention and become actors to get it. Their "primary art" is seduction, but since some resist seduction, the histrionic often "turns to less artful but more direct maneuvers for attention," such as bemoaning cruel fate. Often the histrionic personality plays the role Samuel Johnson's dictionary defined as that of a "seeksorrow," one who is certain that no one else has ever suffered so much and determined that others should realize this. No amount of sympathy or attention or love is ever enough to satisfy such a person.

Generally, according to Offit, histrionics tend to be women. Whatever the sex, however, the pattern was much the same: an opening attempt to please others with one's lovableness, and, should that fail, insistence "on the limelight for [one's] black vapors." But how could such people—seductive, demanding,

manipulative, shallow or overemotional, time-consuming and unrewarding—
manage to seem attractive? The answer, Offit believes, lies in their "uncanny
ability to make sensitive and perceptive observations about others," their "intuitive insight into the ways of engaging other people." (188–89)

Fitzgerald's escapades and drunken sprees are, of course, legendary: his attempts to shock or show off, in effect, his attempts to make social gatherings
memorable (or at least more interesting) in the way that Dick Diver describes
wanting to give "a really *bad* party . . . where there's a brawl and seductions
and people going home with their feelings hurt and women passed out in
the cabinet de toilette," became an all-too-frequent part of his social behavior. But such behavior ultimately left only regret at the waste of time, talent,
and energy it resulted in, a remorse the "Crack-Up" essays record: "During
this time I had plenty of the usual horses shot from under me—*Punctured
Pride, Thwarted Expectation, Faithless, Show-off, Hard Hit, Never Again*." By
the time of "My Lost City" in 1932 it seems that Fitzgerald had clearly begun
to think of his more or less public, more or less egregious social doings as
those of a social persona, which is to say, begun to defend himself psychologically against the remorse this waste caused by allowing him to imagine a split
between this persona and the real self. The real self was the serious writer
with high artistic standards whose genre was the modern novel of manners,
while the persona was the social self that gathered the material for this genre
by trying to pass as a member of the leisure class, by trying, even though
"distrusting the rich," to "share their mobility and the grace that some of them
brought into their lives" (147). By inventing an interior narrative that assigned
all his extravagant behavior to this social persona, Fitzgerald sober could feel
less guilty about the conduct of Fitzgerald drunk; for if the real me, the serious writer, was simply enacting a role meant to increase a situation's dramatic
possibilities by creating a scene and thus generating more interesting material, then this explanation of the matter made it psychologically "easier to
give" such a show because it gave him "theatrical innocence." And no matter
how bad his behavior nor how painful its memory, he could always redeem
it by replaying it as fiction. But, of course, theatrical innocence isn't real innocence, it's a psychological trick.

One indication of the accuracy of this reading is the amount of embarrassing material from his own life that Fitzgerald incorporated into his work,
an amount almost unique among major modern fiction writers. Cecelia
Brady, the narrator of *The Last Tycoon*, states the principle: "What people are

ashamed of usually makes a good story" (99). And as Bruccoli has remarked, for Fitzgerald "emotion was not recollected in tranquillity; the emotions he worked with were still raw or at least re-experienced in the act of recollection" (*Composition* 139). Nowhere were his emotions less tranquil than in memories of humiliations, either social or physical—the most obvious example of this in *Tender* being Dick Diver's beating at the hands of the Italian police in Rome, based on a 1924 incident in Fitzgerald's own life. As Arthur Mizener recounts it,

> At one point Fitzgerald, in drunken exasperation, got in a fight with a group of taxi drivers when, at a late hour, they refused to take him to his hotel except for an extravagant fare. After one of his few successful blows struck a plain-clothes policeman who tried to interfere, Fitzgerald was hauled roughly off to jail. . . . The beating had been a severe one and Fitzgerald suffered from it physically for some time. But its effect on his pride and conscience was even more important. . . . [G]radually, as he thought about the experience, he came more and more to blame himself; what had happened to him that he got into drunken brawls with taxi drivers? Thus bit by bit the humiliation of this experience came to seem to him a measure of his own deterioration. (182)

In a letter to the journalist and novelist Howard Coxe some ten years after the event, Fitzgerald says that in writing the episode in *Tender* he aimed at "reproducing what was just about the rottenest thing that ever happened to me in my life" and "that having gone through hell on that occasion, I am often groggy about recalling it, and I do remember, through the dim mist of blood, that it was you as well as Zelda who helped me out of jail." And he adds that when it came time to write this episode he was "perhaps . . . still a little cuckoo on account of the shock of the beating" (*Correspondence* 349). The scene is one of the most painful and powerful in the novel, and Fitzgerald makes clear that it is a turning point in Dick's deterioration: "He would be a different person henceforward" (263).

  Though the episode of Dick's beating is a striking and highly specific instance of Fitzgerald's translating a humiliating incident from his own life into his fiction, it is nonetheless only a small part of the much larger work of translation by which he turned his own sense of personal deterioration (under the simultaneous pressures of alcoholism, mounting debt, Zelda's mental illness, and the inability to finish his fourth novel) into the character of Dick Diver. And in the "Crack-Up" essays of 1936 in which he examines in detail the causes of his own psychological breakdown, Fitzgerald leaves no doubt about his previous translation of biography into fiction. As Bruccoli remarks, "Though Fitzgerald's collapse came in 1936, these symptoms had been developing since at least as early as 1930. In addition to drinking (whether as cause or effect), both his case and Dick's display the same symptoms: a weariness of people, an inability to participate in routine human relationships, irrational antipathies, and a mounting bigotry" (*Composition* 122). What is most striking here is the way Fitzgerald gets double duty out of his own humiliation (his sense of personal decline), first as fiction in *Tender* and then as memoir in the "Crack-Up" essays. And what this method of translating personal humiliation into art recalls is Freud's game of *fort/da* from *Beyond the Pleasure Principle*. Working on a novel whose main character was a psychiatrist while having a wife who would be under psychiatric care from 1930 to the end of her life, Fitzgerald must have read a certain amount of Freud. Indeed, he says that after Dick finished his final year at Hopkins Medical School, he managed in 1916, even though the war was on, "to get to Vienna under the impression that, if he did not make haste, the great Freud would eventually succumb to an aeroplane bomb" (133–34).

Freud theorizes that the game of *fort/da,* which he had observed being played by a small child, was an attempt to imaginatively master the child's feelings of helplessness (caused by his mother's goings and comings) by inventing a game in which the cycle of loss and recovery that had been passively endured previously was now actively initiated by the child as he dispatched and retrieved a symbolic object representing the mother—a spool attached to a string. When the child threw the spool out of sight, he would utter the German word "fort" ("gone"), and when he pulled the string so that the spool reappeared, he would utter the German "da" ("there"): "This, then, was the complete game—disappearance and return" (Freud 15), and its meaning was that "at the outset he was in a *passive* situation—he was overpowered by the experience" of his mother leaving; "but, by repeating it, unpleasurable though it was, as a game, he took on an *active* part" (16). Similarly, Fitzgerald had felt helpless in suffering a beating at the hands of the Italian police, and the memory of "the rottenest thing" that had ever happened in his life would not lie quiet, even causing him when he came to write it to feel "still a little cuckoo" from "the shock"; yet no matter how "unpleasurable" the event, by repeating it in his fiction he changes his position in regard to it from passive sufferer to active initiator. And inasmuch as Freud tends to gender code active and passive roles as masculine and feminine respectively, then this transformation of passive into active through the agency of imaginative repetition easily aligns itself with Fitzgerald's gender coding of the (feminine) object of the gaze (the role of the observed, or in Fitzgerald's case the self as persona) and the (masculine) wielder of the gaze (the role of the observer, or in Fitzgerald's case the real me, the serious writer). And if in Fitzgerald's self-defensive, interior narrative it is his social persona (the one who plays a part, the one who cuts up and to whom unpleasant, humiliating things happen) that ultimately gives him the character of Dick Diver, the brilliant young professional who has been unmanned (feminized), then the real me, the serious writer, reverses that feminization by actively turning his imaginative gaze on the passively endured experiences of his persona.

If choosing the role of the observed, if giving a show, is associated with theatrical innocence, then how should we characterize the role of the observer, the one who is not in the spotlight but who watches the show from the shadows? A comment of Erving Goffman's in *The Presentation of Self in Everyday Life* is helpful here: he notes that "the arts of piercing an individual's effort at calculated unintentionality seem better developed than our capacity to manipulate our own behavior, so that regardless of how many steps have occurred in the information game, the witness is likely to have the advantage over the actor" (9). If the observer has an advantage over the actor's theatrical innocence, then does this suggest a certain lack of innocence, a kind of culpability, on the part of the one who simply watches? Clearly, that is Nick Carraway's sense of his role as the observer, the narrator, of Gatsby's life. In knowing more of the truth of what happened than any of the novel's other characters but acting at crucial moments more for social than moral reasons, Nick ultimately feels he had become contaminated by the "foul dust" that "floated in the wake" (6) of Gatsby's dreams. And this sense of the wielder of the gaze's relative lack of innocence as compared to the theatrical innocence of the gaze's object is given its own filmic resonance near the start of *Tender Is the Night* when the actress Rosemary Hoyt meets the movie director Earl Brady for the first time: "As he took her hand she saw him look her over from head to foot, a gesture she recognized and that made her feel at home, but gave her always a faint feeling of superiority to whoever made it. If her person was property she could exercise whatever advantage was inherent in its ownership" (31). She recognizes the professional gesture: Brady clearly wants to cast her in some future film he means to direct, and he is mentally comparing what he recalls of her filmed image in *Daddy's Girl* with her actual physical person, in effect, he wants to see how the youthful actress of that film has physically matured. (Fitzgerald will return to this difference between an actress's filmed image and the way she looks in real life in *The Last Tycoon* when he has Monroe Stahr note that Kathleen Moore more closely resembled the actual appearance of his dead wife, Minna Davis, than her filmic appearance.) But if Rosemary experiences "a faint feeling of superiority" to anyone who looks her over from head to foot like this, then is it a sense of social superiority, a sense that she has better manners than someone who has allowed a business gesture to intrude on a social situation, a sense that if Brady had been better bred he could have carried out this sizing up of her physical attributes in a more discreet manner?

Near the end of the novel the noninnocent, not to say the malicious, power of wielding the gaze is made explicit when Dick, Nicole, and Rosemary encounter Mary North Minghetti again on the beach at Cap d'Antibes: They saw "a woman sauntering in their direction followed by a small group who behaved as if they were accustomed to being looked at. When they were ten feet away, Mary's glance flickered fractionally over the Divers, one of those unfortunate glances that indicate to the glanced-upon that they have been observed but are to be overlooked, the sort of glance that neither the Divers nor Rosemary Hoyt had ever permitted themselves to throw at anyone in their lives. Dick was amused when Mary perceived Rosemary, changed her plans and came over. She spoke to Nicole with pleasant heartiness, nodded unsmilingly to Dick as if he were somewhat contagious—whereupon he bowed in ironic respect—as she greeted Rosemary" (320). When Mary notices Rosemary and decides to stop, it's clearly because she wants to annex to her small group of social celebrities a real celebrity whom everyone will want to look at, but Rosemary, having seen how Mary had purposely wielded the gaze in order to wound the Divers, snubs her in turn.

If, as I've suggested, Fitzgerald's enacting a social persona conferred on the serious writer the psychological protection of theatrical innocence, then one main cause of the deep uneasiness that required him so often to give a show was that as a writer of the novel of manners (a genre essentially concerned with class), he had to gain his material by moving in social circles to which he felt he was not financially entitled and thus was always pretending to be something he wasn't. Just as Dick Diver was seduced by the lifestyle Nicole's money provided, so Fitzgerald was seduced by the "mobility" and "grace" of the leisure class. Visiting Fitzgerald in February 1928 at Ellerslie, the estate Fitzgerald had rented in Delaware, Fitzgerald's friend Edmund Wilson recorded Fitzgerald's "invincible compulsion to live like a millionaire" that had "led him even more than usual to interrupt his serious work and turn out stories for the commercial magazines" (Bruccoli, *Composition* 55). Indeed, Fitzgerald himself had diagnosed this condition in a comment he made to Tony Buttitta in 1935: "I'm the American success story. I was born a poor boy and made it in the rich man's world. I'm still a peasant deep down, but I have acquired extravagant tastes. I've been corrupted. I'm hopelessly committed to living beyond my means. A kind of compulsion" (Buttitta 29). Certainly, this "invincible compulsion" had been significantly influenced by Zelda's original refusal to marry him until he could support her in the style to which she was accustomed—with the result that after Fitzgerald's first success and his marriage, there was an ongoing psychological pressure to maintain the standard of living that had made that union possible. Given the sense of himself expressed in his remark to John O'Hara that even with "an embryonic history that tied me to the Plantagenets, I would still be a parvenu. I spent my youth in alternately crawling in front of the kitchen maids and insulting the great"—we can judge that Fitzgerald felt his entrée to the leisure class, though it depended to some extent on his writerly celebrity, was perhaps based as well on his tipsy escapades providing a kind of entertainment for his social betters, on the telling of which they could dine out for a week, that he saw himself not only as chronicler but also as purveyor of outlandish behavior for the rich. In this regard Dick Diver's hilarious and largely ineffectual attempt to fire Villa Diana's cook, Augustine, who has been drinking the Divers' good wine, seems to be the fictive rendering of Fitzgerald's own sense of "crawling in front of the kitchen maids."

Given that Dick's pretending to be something he isn't represents to some degree the fictive version of Fitzgerald's own sense of moving among but not really belonging to the leisure class, then Fitzgerald's construction of a social persona would seem to have sprung from an insecurity, from a need, prior to and more basic than that of simply splitting off the embarrassing, alcoholic social self from the serious writing self. With this in mind we can begin to see why Fitzgerald, in order to create the character of Dick Diver, drew on traits taken from himself and Gerald Murphy. Commenting on his January 1950 interview with Murphy, Matthew Bruccoli notes that "so complete" was Fitzgerald's "identification" with Gerald "that when Murphy remarked after reading *Tender is the Night* that he was puzzled by the combination of himself and Fitzgerald in the character of Dick Diver, Fitzgerald assured him that this was not a problem because he and Murphy were, in fact, the same person" (*Composition* 19). Which immediately raises the question of what resemblance Fitzgerald saw between himself and Murphy to prompt this statement.

Obviously, Fitzgerald and Murphy were both Irish American, had both attended Ivy League universities and moved in social circles composed largely of white Anglo-Saxon Protestants. And they were both committed to an artistic life. Though he was a talented painter, Murphy did not actively pursue it as a career and produced very few paintings. His artistic commitment took more the form of the Murphys' turning their home on the Riviera and their life together there into an ongoing aesthetic endeavor, creating a venue and lifestyle that Gerald planned out as meticulously as one of his paintings and that he loved to share with the many friends of his who were artists or writers. In "Pasting It Together," the second of the "Crack-Up" essays, Fitzgerald acknowledges individuals who had served variously as his "intellectual conscience" (Edmund Wilson), his "artistic conscience" (Hemingway), and his social conscience—this last clearly being Gerald Murphy, who, Fitzgerald says,

> had come to dictate my relations with other people when these relations were successful: how to do, what to say. How to make people at least momentarily happy (in apposition to Mrs. Post's theories of how to make everyone thoroughly uncomfortable with a sort of systematized vulgarity). This always confused me and made me want to go out and get drunk, but this man had seen the game, analyzed it and beaten it, and his word was good enough for me. (*Lost* 149)

Fitzgerald's understanding of a person's successful "relations with other people" as a "game" (in effect, a theatrical performance) that Murphy had analyzed and beaten suggests that Fitzgerald suspected Murphy's repose, his social ease and self-assurance, came from his pretending to be something he wasn't. Gerald and Sara Murphy both came from wealthy families (Gerald's father owned Mark Cross, a leather goods company, and Sara's father was part owner of the Ault & Wiborg Company, which manufactured color inks for printing lithographs). Consequently, if Gerald felt he had continually to enact a social role he felt he had no right to, this couldn't have been due, as in Fitzgerald's case, to a sense of financial insecurity. Murphy's lifelong sense of not belonging must have stemmed from another source.

In her biography of the Murphys, Amanda Vaill quotes a 1929 letter from Gerald to Archibald MacLeish explaining why, on a visit back to the States, Gerald had avoided seeing all his old friends:

> I awaken to find that I have apparently never had one real relationship or one full experience. . . . [I]t is never quite possible to believe that *all* that one does

is unreal, or that one is *never* oneself for a moment—and that the residue of this must needs be a sense of unreality, all-pervading. I don't think I hoped to beat *life*. Possibly I thought that mine was one way of living it, among many thousand ways.

My terms with life have been simple. I have refused to meet it on the grounds of my own defects, for the reason that I have bitterly resented those defects since I was fifteen years of age. . . . You of course cannot have known that not for one waking hour of my life since I was fifteen have I been entirely free of the feeling of these defects. . . . Eight years of school and college, after my too willing distortion of myself into the likeness of popularity and success, I was left with little confidence in the shell that I had inhabited as another person.

And so I have never felt that there was a place in life as it is lived for what I have to give of myself. . . .

My subsequent life has been a process of concealment of the personal realities,—at which I have been all too adept. . . .

Thus I have learned to dread (and avoid) the responsibilities of friendship (as being one of the realities of life), believing, as I do, that I was incapable of a full one. I have *become* unworthy of one.

I have never been able to feel *sure* that *anyone* was fond of me, because it would seem too much to claim, knowing what I did about myself. . . .

Have I made myself clear enough to have you see why I could come to America and dread the possibility of seeing you and Ada, and risk disfiguring one of the few phantom realities of my life, my friendship with you both? (222–23)

Vaill notes that "in the first three-quarters" of the twentieth century "the term 'defect' (or 'defect of character') was frequently applied to an attraction for the same sex" and that "although this might not be such an uncommon thing for an adolescent boy in an all-male environment like Hotchkiss, one can imagine how it would have horrified the senior Murphys if they had learned of it, and how it would have frightened their son if he had felt it" (24). But Gerald nevertheless married Sara and fathered three children with her, and there seems to be no doubt that he loved her deeply. Vaill cites a 1936 letter to Sara in which he says that "although his 'defect'" made him "terribly, terribly sorry that I am as I am . . . only one thing would be awful and that is that you might not know that I love only you. We both know it's inadequate (that's where 'life' comes in);—but such as it is it certainly is the best this poor fish can offer,—and it's the realest thing I know" (275). Vaill suggests that because the teenaged Gerald had felt that his interest in the arts was reciprocated by the young Sara Wiborg, he grew to confide some of his most personal feelings to her, Sara's role as Gerald's early confidante being the origin of his attraction to her. It would seem that part of this role of confidante was Sara's nonjudgmental attitude to Gerald's "defect."

Given Gerald's veiled admission to his friend Archibald MacLeish and his further admission in the letter that this was not the first time he had attempted this explanation (he says, "I once tried to tell you that I didn't believe in taking life at its *own* tragical value if it could be avoided. It was this [defect] I apparently meant" [223]), one wonders whether Murphy had made a similarly oblique admission to his friend Scott Fitzgerald or whether Fitzgerald had simply sensed Murphy's awareness of this "difference." In either case we can speculate that the inclusion of Gerald Murphy's character in Fitzgerald's conception of Dick Diver accounts in part for the fact that Dick's sense of being progressively unmanned or feminized ultimately turns into Lady Caroline Sibley-Biers's public accusation that Dick is a homosexual. And if the lifelong anguish about his inclinations had made Gerald feel he didn't really belong to the heterosexual world he moved in, if it had, in effect, turned his "subsequent life" into "a process of concealment," then Fitzgerald, who felt he had never really belonged to the leisure class he moved in, would have had some taste of Murphy's specific anguish, for in 1920s Paris Fitzgerald had been rumored to be a homosexual. As Bruccoli notes, the rumor had been purposely fabricated by Robert McAlmon, "an American writer and proprietor of Contact Editions, a Paris imprint that published expatriate writers." A homosexual himself, McAlmon "envied the success of Fitzgerald and Hemingway, and later spread gossip about them culminating in the fabrication that they were homosexuals" (*Grandeur* 236–37). Bruccoli notes that Hemingway's later misunderstanding with the Canadian writer Morley Callaghan was "complicated by Hemingway's suspicion that Callaghan had repeated Robert McAlmon's gossip about his alleged homosexuality. . . . Fitzgerald believed that McAlmon's gossip about him and Hemingway helped to spoil the friendship. He observed in his *Notebooks*: 'I really loved him, but of course it wore out like a love affair. The fairies have spoiled all that.' Hemingway is not named in this note, but the reference is clear" (*Grandeur* 289). What also disturbed Fitzgerald was his sense that Zelda believed this rumor. In a 1930 "seven-page memo" to Zelda in which Scott attempted "to account for the destruction of their happiness and the collapse of his career—which were intertwined" (*Grandeur* 297) he writes,

You were going crazy and calling it genius—I was going to ruin and calling it anything that came to hand. And I think everyone far enough away to see us outside of our glib presentation of ourselves guessed at your almost megalomaniacal selfishness and my insane indulgence in drink. Toward the end nothing much mattered. The nearest I ever came to leaving you was when you told me you thot [sic] I was a fairy in the Rue Palatine but now whatever you said aroused a sort of detached pity for you. (*Grandeur* 299)

Clearly one needs to read Fitzgerald's characterization of Murphy as his social conscience—the man who "had come to dictate" the "how to do, what to say" of Fitzgerald's social relationships (when they were successful), the man who "had seen the game, analyzed it, and beaten it"—against Murphy's own estimate of himself: "I don't think I hoped to beat *life*[;] . . . after my too willing distortion of myself into the likeness of popularity and success, I was left with little confidence in the shell that I had inhabited as another person," so that "my subsequent life has been a process of concealment of the personal realities,—at which I have been all too adept." This juxtaposition points to the full complexity of Fitzgerald's assertion that "he and Murphy were, in fact, the same person," and it sends us back to Dick's claim of repose, suggesting that Fitzgerald understood this quality as simply being "all too adept" at the "concealment of personal realities." One can well imagine that Fitzgerald, in making the claim that he and Murphy were essentially the same, would have savored the etymological link between them, for the Anglo-Norman prefix "fitz" (from the French "fils" and the Latin "filius") means that Scott's surname is literally "son of Gerald."

Near the end of *Tender*, Fitzgerald specifically focuses on the theatricality of Dick's social persona in at least three scenes depicting his gradual decline. In the first Dick, Nicole, and Rosemary are once again on the beach at Cap d'Antibes, and Rosemary asks the Divers if they've seen her latest pictures. It is a moment meant to remind us of that earlier scene at the movie studio where the professional actress Rosemary screened her film *Daddy's Girl* for the Divers and Norths and then tried to turn the social performer Dick into a professional by having him take a screen test. But in this later moment Rosemary's question about her recent films evokes a lengthy response from Dick about acting technique, the amateur instructing the professional:

Let's suppose that Nicole says to you that Lanier is ill. What do you do in life? What does anyone do? They *act*—face, voice, words—the face shows sorrow, the voice shows shock, the words show sympathy. . . .

But, in the theatre, No. In the theatre all the best comédiennes have built up their reputations by bur*les*quing the correct emotional responses—fear and love and sympathy. . . .

The danger to an actress is in responding. Again, let's suppose that somebody told you, "Your lover is dead." In life you'd probably go to pieces. But on the stage you're trying to entertain—the audience can do the "responding" for themselves. First the actress has lines to follow, then she has to get the audience's attention back on herself. . . . So she must do something unexpected. If the audience thinks the character is hard she goes soft on them—if they think she's soft she goes hard. You go all *out* of character—you understand? . . .

You do the unexpected thing until you've manoeuvred the audience back from the objective fact to yourself. *Then* you slide back into character again. (322)

The very length and detail of this passage suggests the extent to which Dick has thought about the art of acting and thus how much it's influenced his own social performance. But of course Dick is also showing off for Rosemary in this scene, in effect, flirting with her in front of Nicole. Just as she had tried in that earlier scene at the movie studio to get Dick to become a professional actor, Rosemary now turns to the Divers' daughter, Topsy, and says, "Would you like to be an actress when you grow up? I think you'd make a fine actress," but now instead of Dick being the one who rejects professional acting as a career, it's Nicole who thunders, "It's absolutely *out* to put such ideas in the heads of other people's children. Remember, we may have quite different plans for them." Nicole then leaves abruptly, "without a glance at Rosemary whose face was 'responding' violently" (323).

This explicit evocation of Dick's acting ability prepares the reader for two later scenes in which his self-loathing over having to give a show is even more apparent than in the check-cashing scene at the bank. When Dick is awakened in the middle of the night by a phone call from the police informing him that Lady Caroline Sibley-Biers and Mary North Minghetti have been arrested for impersonating French sailors and picking up two girls, Dick immediately goes to their aid. He finds that "the old fatal pleasingness, the old forceful charm, swept back with its cry of 'Use me!' He would have to go fix this thing that he didn't care a damn about, because it had early become a habit to be loved" (338). He acts to save the two from scandal even though Lady Caroline had accused him of being a homosexual and Mary had snubbed Dick a few days earlier. In effect he puts on a show for the French police chief, telling him that Mary, an Italian countess, is the granddaughter "of John D. Rockefeller Mellon" and "the niece of Lord Henry Ford and so connected with the Renault and Citroën companies" and that Lady Caroline is "affianced to the brother of the Prince of Wales—the Duke of Buckingham" (341). But he also puts on a social show for the two women: when Lady Caroline tells Dick that their presumably lesbian escapade was "merely a lark," he

> nodded gravely, looking at the stone floor, like a priest in the confessional—he was torn between a tendency to ironic laughter and another tendency to order fifty stripes of the cat and a fortnight of bread and water. The lack . . . of any sense of evil, except the evil wrought by cowardly Provençal girls and stupid police, confounded him. . . .
>
> Looking at them as though they were the innocents that he knew they were not, he shook his head: "Of all the crazy stunts!"
>
> Lady Caroline smiled complacently.
>
> "You're an insanity doctor, aren't you? You ought to be able to help us."
> (339–40)

Just as Nick Carraway had allowed a social gesture to trump a moral judgment by agreeing to shake hands with Tom even though he knew Tom ultimately bore part of the responsibility for Gatsby's murder, so Dick does the same by giving the impression that he believes the moral corruption of Lady Caroline is just one of her "crazy stunts."

But the full extent of Dick's revulsion at what he has become—that "distortion" of himself, to use Murphy's phrase, "into the likeness of popularity and success" that leaves him "another person" whom he inhabits like a "shell"— becomes clear in the novel's last scene, Dick's farewell to the beach at Cap d'Antibes. He runs into Mary Minghetti on the terrace above the beach, and she says, "'You were like you used to be the night you helped us. . . . Why aren't you nice like that always? You can be.' It seemed fantastic to Dick to be in a position where Mary North could tell him about things" (350). As Mary lectures Dick about his drinking, she begins to enjoy the dramatic possibilities of the situation, and Dick responds by giving one more performance:

> His eyes . . . asked her sympathy and stealing over him he felt the old necessity of convincing her that he was the last man in the world and she was the last woman. . . .

"You once liked me, didn't you?" he asked.

"*Liked* you—I *loved* you. Everybody loved you. You could've had anybody you wanted for the asking—"

"There has always been something between you and me."

She bit eagerly. "Has there, Dick?"

"Always—I knew your troubles and how brave you were about them." But the old interior laughter had begun inside him and he knew he couldn't keep it up much longer.

"I always thought you knew a lot," Mary said enthusiastically. "More about me than anyone has ever known. Perhaps that's why I was so afraid of you when we didn't get along so well."

His glance fell soft and kind upon hers, suggesting an emotion underneath; their glances married suddenly, bedded, strained together. Then, as the laughter inside of him became so loud that it seemed as if Mary must hear it, Dick switched off the light and they were back in the Riviera sun.

"I must go," he said. (350–51)

Having enacted so many emotions he didn't feel in his career as a social performer, Dick finds himself at last unable to feel any emotion, with the result that, as Fitzgerald concludes about himself in the last of the "Crack-Up" essays, "There was to be no more giving of myself—all giving was to be outlawed henceforth under a new name, and that name was Waste" (*Lost* 151–52). The novel's final theatrical flourish occurs in its conclusion—surely one of the most remarkable in American fiction—as Dick is reported to have moved from one small town to another in upstate New York until he seems to vanish into the landscape. The star actor of *Tender Is the Night* doesn't die at the end; he simply steps out of the narrative spotlight (perhaps that's what the remark "Dick switched off the light" in the preceding scene is meant to prefigure). And certainly *Tender*'s conclusion aims to leave us with the same kind of feeling a "Where Are They Now?" segment on *Entertainment Tonight* creates, the sense that for a star performer to be no longer in the public eye, no longer in the spotlight of our gaze, is the theatrical equivalent of death.

## 5

Just as the two series of stories, each with an ongoing character, which Fitzgerald published between 1928 and 1931, formed a bridge between the theatrical/social element in *The Great Gatsby* and that same element in *Tender Is the*

*Night*, so too another series of stories with an ongoing character served much the same purpose between *Tender* and *The Last Tycoon*. The seventeen Pat Hobby stories published in consecutive issues of *Esquire* between January 1940 and May 1941 are each shorter and slighter than the Basil and Josephine stories, but they are clearly part of Fitzgerald's recreating the ambiance of Hollywood movie making, his depicting the studio environment and its various types of employees, from an insider's point of view. And that insider, the down-at-heels screenwriter Pat Hobby—a success in the silent era of the 1920s but a has-been by the '30s with the coming of sound and the Depression (a more extreme version of what Fitzgerald felt had been the trajectory of his own career as a writer)—is, as Fitzgerald told his editor Arnold Gingrich at *Esquire*, "a complete rat" (Gingrich xv) but one trying to survive among the bigger and smaller rats of the film business. Fitzgerald used the Hobby stories as a sort of rough sketch for the class aspect of the studio pecking order that he would develop more fully in *The Last Tycoon*. As the Hobby stories are a view of that world from the bottom of the heap, so *The Last Tycoon* was to be a view from the very top.

In one sense the Pat Hobby stories and *The Last Tycoon* represent a circling back on Fitzgerald's part to the idea of West Egg village in *Gatsby*. That fictive community, populated largely by people who made their living in the theater or films and by a few bootleggers and gamblers, had represented a class of first-generation strivers who used the money they earned and the celebrity they acquired to create among themselves a society that was déclassé compared to the high society of inherited wealth in East Egg. But in Hobby's and Stahr's Hollywood Fitzgerald had a company town, a community in which all class distinctions from high to low were contained within or in some way related to the world of show business. There was no corresponding East Egg village on the West Coast to which it felt inferior, though as Cecelia Brady remarks at the start of *The Last Tycoon*, the East Coast world of Bennington College, where she is a student, clearly looked down on Hollywood: "Some of the English teachers who pretended an indifference to Hollywood or its products really *hated* it." And she notes, "You can take Hollywood for granted like I did, or you can dismiss it with the contempt we reserve for what we don't understand" (3). Cecelia's take on the East/West opposition as it affected talent imported from the East was that "California was filling up with weary desperadoes[,] . . . tense young men and women who lived back East in spirit while they carried on a losing battle against the climate" (80). *The Last Tycoon* also represents a circling back to the theme of *Gatsby* in another way. Gatsby had been a rags-to-riches, self-made man whose commitment to creating an illusionary ideal self had been compared to the work of Broadway producer/ playwright David Belasco, renowned for the realism of his stage sets. And in some sense Stahr, as a rags-to-riches, self-made man who is the chief of production at a major motion picture studio, is a culmination of this figure, for Stahr is committed to creating, with a maximum degree of artistry and realism, a whole series of illusionary ideals that he will purvey to the American public. At one point Fitzgerald describes Stahr watching the daily rushes at the studio, those unedited segments of film shot the previous day, and passing judgment on their suitability as expressions of those ideals: "Dreams hung in fragments at the far end of the room, suffered analysis, passed—to be dreamed in crowds, or else discarded" (56). Explaining filmmaking to the English author George Boxley, who claims that he just doesn't get writing for the movies, Stahr says that each artistic genre has some "condition" attached and that the condition of screenwriting is that "we have to take people's own favorite folklore and dress it up and give it back to them" (106–7). And though Boxley, when he's in the company of other writers, rages against Stahr and the assembly line method of scriptwriting he originated, he nevertheless "recognized that Stahr like Lincoln was a leader carrying on a long war on many fronts; almost single-handed he had moved pictures sharply forward through a decade, to a point where the content of the 'A productions' was wider and richer than that of the stage. Stahr was an artist only as Mr. Lincoln was a general, perforce and as a layman" (107).

In the company town of Hollywood, where virtually everyone works in some aspect of the movie industry, "the fourth biggest industry in America" (*Decade* 204) by the 1930s, as Fitzgerald points out more than once, class distinctions are a function of the type of job one holds, distinctions geographically expressed in neighborhoods. As Cecelia is being driven to the studio one day by the writer Wylie White, they pass through Beverly Hills, and she observes, "Hollywood is a perfectly zoned city so you know exactly what kind of people economically live in each section from executives and directors, through technicians in their bungalows right down to extras. This was the executive section and a very fancy lot of pastry. It wasn't as romantic as the dingiest village of Virginia or New Hampshire but it looked nice this morning" (69–70). A more comprehensive anatomy of Hollywood classes evoked in the novel would start at the top with "the moneymen," the ten men with whom Stahr and the Danish prince Agge, who is visiting the studio, have lunch in a private dining room in the commissary: "They were the rulers. . . . Eight out of ten were Jews—five of the ten were foreign born, including a Greek and an Englishman—and they had all known each other for a long time; there was a rating in the group, from old Marcus down to old Leanbaum who had bought the most fortunate block of stock in the business and never was allowed to spend over a million a year producing" (44–45). As the studio's chief of production, Stahr was foremost among this group, though not all of the ten would have actively produced individual films. For example, old Mr. Marcus, a figure who also appears in the Hobby stories, bears a name probably meant to recall Marcus Loew, who was instrumental in the formation of MGM, the studio of which Irving Thalberg, the model for Stahr, was production chief. Loew had originally come from the exhibition end of the business. In the golden age of Hollywood films each major studio had a theater chain associated with it, the most extensive of these being the Loew's Theaters linked to MGM. Marcus Loew had begun in the first decade of the twentieth century as the owner of nickelodeons where one-reel films were exhibited and by the beginning of the 1920s had the largest chain of theaters in New York. He then began to acquire movie studios as a way of insuring a steady stream of quality pictures for his movie houses, ultimately gaining control of the Goldwyn Company, Metro Pictures, and Louis B. Mayer Productions for whom Irving Thalberg worked. By the mid-1920s all the pieces of MGM were in place, and when Loew died suddenly in 1927 he was generally acknowledged as the most powerful man in the movie industry.

In *The Last Tycoon* just below the moneymen and independent producers are the supervisors who oversee the making of several pictures at a time (and who apparently report directly to Stahr) and the unit managers who oversee a single film at a time. The novel's principal example of the former is Reinmund, "one of the most favored of the supervisors" (37), whom Cecelia describes as "a handsome young opportunist, with a fairly good education":

> Originally a man of some character he was being daily forced by his anomalous position into devious ways of acting and thinking. He was a bad man now, as men go. . . . But he got his pictures out in time and by manifesting an almost homosexual fixation on Stahr, seemed to have dulled Stahr's usual acuteness. Stahr liked him—considered him a good all around man. (38)

The rank below supervisor is director, and the tension between these two classes becomes clear in the conference Stahr holds with Reinmund, the director John Broaca, and the writers Wylie White and Rose Meloney about an upcoming picture Stahr feels has lost track of its original idea. Threatening to shelve the picture before it goes into production, Stahr gradually brings the conferees back to his vision of what it should be. The director Broaca is described as "on the surface . . . an engineer—large and without nerves, quietly resolute, popular," but in fact he is "an ignoramus" whom "Stahr often caught . . . making the same scenes over and over" (37). At one point in the conference as Stahr is explaining to the writers where their script went wrong, the bored Broaca puts "his hand up to his half closed eyes—he could remember 'when a director was something out here,' when writers were gag men or eager and ashamed young reporters full of whiskey—a director was all there was then. No supervisor—no Stahr" (42). When Stahr is satisfied that the conferees thoroughly understand and assent to his vision, he tells them to go ahead with the project:

> Broaca watched as Reinmund fawned upon Stahr. He sensed that Reinmund was on his way up—not yet. He received seven hundred and fifty a week for his partial authority over directors, writers and stars who got much more. He wore a cheap English shoe he bought near the Beverly Wilshire and Broaca hoped they hurt his feet, but soon now he would order his shoes from Peal's and put away his little green alpine hat with a feather. Broaca was years ahead of him. He had a fine record in the war but he had never felt quite the same with himself since he had let Ike Franklin strike him in the face with his open hand. (43)

Fitzgerald evokes distinctions in rank not only geographically but sartorially as well, and he is always alert to the way a physical humiliation renders one "a different person henceforward" (*Tender* 263).

Immediately below the director in the studio's pecking order is the writer, and for Fitzgerald this level, which would of course have been his own, tends to be the perspective from which the ranks above and below it are evaluated, its importance in the novel suggested by the fact that the major business crisis Stahr would have faced in the finished book was the threat of the Screen Writers Guild's trying to usurp some of Stahr's power at the studio. Stahr tells the communist union organizer Brimmer that "this Guild matter . . . looks to me like a try for power and all I am going to give the writers is money" (122). Brimmer had made the case that the writers were "the farmers in this business. . . . They grow the grain but they're not in at the feast. Their feeling toward the producer is like the farmers' resentment of the city fellow" (121). The level below the writers in the studio hierarchy would have been the heads of the various technical divisions, the men who attend along with Stahr the twice-daily screening of the rushes.

Interestingly enough, movie stars seem to occupy an anomalous position in the pecking order evoked in the novel. In terms of visibility or celebrity, they rank higher than the moneymen (indeed, Fitzgerald states, almost as if it were a brag, that Stahr's name has never appeared on the screen in any of his studio's productions), but in terms of salary they come somewhere below the moneymen but a bit above the most successful directors. Yet in terms of power or decision making they seem to have no position at all. And Fitzgerald implies that Stahr, though he likes actors, tends to be skeptical of their maturity or seriousness. At one point in his discussion with Brimmer about the Screen Writers Guild, Stahr says, "Writers are children—even in normal times they can't keep their minds on their work" (121), and one can well imagine Stahr saying much the same about actors, about people who play imaginative roles and look at themselves in the mirror. And indeed, Cecelia does say something like this: "Writers aren't people exactly. Or, if they're any good, they're a whole *lot* of people trying so hard to be one person. It's like actors, who try so pathetically not to look in mirrors. Who lean *backward* trying—only to see their faces in the reflecting chandeliers" (12). While many movie stars are mentioned in passing in the novel—some real and still lustrous in the '30s (e.g., Ronald Colman, Claudette Colbert, Gary Cooper, Carole Lombard), some fictive and faded (e.g. Johnny Swanson and Martha Dodd)—only three have any kind of interaction with Stahr himself: his dead wife, Minna Davis, whose image haunts his waking life and dreams, the unnamed actress borrowed from another studio to star in a picture directed by Red Ridingwood, and the successful male star who comes to Stahr for advice because he has been struck with a temporary bout of impotence, feeling sure that this will undermine his ability to act leading-man roles and thus end his career. Stahr settles the case of the unnamed actress—whose "hair was of the color and viscosity of drying blood" but who had "starlight that actually photographed in her eyes," her name having "become currently synonymous with the expression 'bitch'" (50–51)—in her favor by replacing Red Ridingwood (who could not control her behavior on set or in front of the camera) with another director, though Stahr's ultimate judgment is that the actress "was a necessary evil, borrowed for a single picture" (51).

As for the male star suffering from temporary impotence, Stahr is amused at the craziness of an actor coming to him to solve this problem. At first the actor won't come out and say why he believes he's "washed up," but when Stahr finally catches on, Fitzgerald says Stahr "had an impish temptation to tell him to go to Brady about it. Brady handled all matters of public relations.

Or was this private relations. He turned away a moment, got his face in control, turned back" (35). At this point Fitzgerald cuts away from Stahr's inner office and his meeting with the actor to the outer reception room where the conferees Reinmund, Broaca, Wylie White, and Rose Meloney are waiting, so that we never know what advice Stahr actually gives the actor, but as Stahr and the actor exit his office, the actor's self-confidence seems to have been restored: When Wylie White asks the actor how he's been, he says, " 'Oh, I've had an awful time,' . . . but Stahr interrupted sharply. 'No you haven't. Now you go along and do the role the way I said' " (36–37).

All of which is simply to note that though the novel's Hollywood is a community in which virtually everyone works in some aspect of show business, the same skepticism about the social acceptability of earning one's living as a professional actor expressed in earlier novels by Anthony Patch and Dick Diver, that sense of professional actors as inhabitants of the demimonde, still persists in *The Last Tycoon*. At one point Stahr, trying to track down one of the two women who'd been put off the studio lot after the earthquake, asks his secretary to phone Robinson and see what he remembers about them: "Were they—questionable? Were they theatrical?" (30). The elided equivalence of "questionable" and "theatrical" suggests Stahr's view of actors, for he asks, in effect, were the two women streetwalkers or were they aspiring actresses who had used the disruption caused by the earthquake to crash the studios gates in hopes of being noticed? But of course what the equivalence also assumes is that many of the attractive young women who came to Hollywood to break into pictures ended up becoming call girls to support themselves, as is the case with Kathleen's acquaintance Edna, the other of the two women. Fitzgerald says that at first Stahr "had only wanted to know if they were 'professional' people, if the woman was an actress who had got herself up to look like Minna as he had once had a young actress made up like Claudette Colbert and photographed her from the same angles" (58), for Stahr suspects that the resemblance of one of the women to his dead, movie star wife might be "some elaborate frame-up" (74), a theatrical trick by a young actress to capture his attention and get a role in a film. Indeed, when Stahr finally tracks down Kathleen, he seems clearly relieved to find she isn't an actress and that she looks more like Minna "actually *look*ed than how she was on the screen" (90). Kathleen's nonprofessional status is subtly evoked by her explicit uneasiness under the public gaze: as she tells Stahr, when she entered the Ambassador Hotel for the screenwriters' ball, the crowd out front "looked so strange[,] . . . as if they were furious at me for not being someone famous" (76)—a phenomenon noted by another nonprofessional, Cecelia, who reports that at movie premieres "the fans look at you with scornful reproach because you're not a star" (*Tycoon* 8).

One might conclude that the tendency to be suspicious of, to look down on, movie stars or professional actors in Fitzgerald's Hollywood—even though most of the novel's characters work in a business whose success depends on the effective presentation of performances by highly photogenic actors on thousands of movie screens—springs in part from the fact that in a company town whose various professional callings were subject to insecurity and neediness, painstakingly detailed by Fitzgerald, movie actors represented that most obvious form of such insecurity, which is to say, represented a constant and uncomfortable reminder to their fellow workers of their own less obvious situations. Since a movie star's looks are the essence, the patent expression, of his or her value in the business, a value with a relentless, highly visible time clock attached and an uncertain expiration date, this tendency to disparage professional actors represents a psychological defense mechanism, an affirmation, in effect, that "at least I'm not that."

Fitzgerald had several friends who were professional actors (perhaps most notably Helen Hayes), and yet when Fitzgerald had once attempted to perform before a gathering of professional entertainers in Hollywood, he suffered one of those classic humiliations that, predictably, he would turn into an incident in one of his best short stories, "Crazy Sunday." Attending a Sunday afternoon party at the home of Irving Thalberg and Norma Shearer, Fitzgerald had been moved to exhibit his own talent. As Andrew Turnbull recounts it, "After a few drinks—'his blood throbbing with the scarlet corpuscles of exhibitionism,' like Joel Coles in the story—Fitzgerald had asked to do an act. Thalberg's wife, Norma Shearer, quieted the company and Fitzgerald sang a song about a dog which amused no one. Directly in front of him John Gilbert, the Great Lover of the screen, 'glared at him with an eye as keen as the eye of a potato'" (202). Bruccoli notes that Fitzgerald's "humorous song 'Dog' with a piano accompaniment by Ramon Navarro . . . was booed by John Gilbert and Lupe Velez" and that "Thalberg told Charles MacArthur to take Fitzgerald home. The next day Fitzgerald received a telegram from Norma Shearer," that read: "I THOUGHT YOU WERE ONE OF THE MOST AGREEABLE PERSONS AT OUR TEA" (*Grandeur* 322–23). When Fitzgerald translated this incident into his short story, the young writer Joel Coles, realizing the skit he's performed has flopped, "felt the undercurrent of derision that rolled through the gossip; then—all this was in the space of ten seconds—the Great Lover, his eye hard and empty as the eye of a needle, shouted 'Boo! Boo!' voicing in an overtone what he felt was the mood of the crowd. It was the resentment of the professional toward the amateur, of the community toward the stranger, the thumbs-down of the clan" (*Short Stories* 702). After penning an abject note of apology to his host the next day, Joel receives a telegram from his hostess: "You were one of the most agreeable people at our party. Expect you at my sister June's buffet supper next Sunday" (703).

But as happy and long lasting as Fitzgerald's memories of Norma Shearer and her kindness were, his memory of being booed by John Gilbert was equally long lasting, and it took him another decade to get even with the actor. In the Pat Hobby story "Two Old-Timers," Hobby and the faded film actor Phil Macedon, "once the Star of Stars," get into an auto accident "on Sunset near the Beverly Hills Hotel," and because "there was liquor in the air as they argued" (*Decade* 190), the cop takes them both to the station house. There, Macedon claims not to remember who Pat Hobby is, and Pat decides to remind him by recounting an incident during the filming of Macedon's World War I picture *The Final Push*. In one scene Macedon was playing a soldier trapped in a shell hole during an artillery bombardment: "You got out to the back lot . . . sore as hell because your suit didn't fit," Pat tells him. "Only you didn't have much time to complain about the uniform because that wasn't Corker's plan." The picture's director, Bill Corker, always thought Macedon was "the toughest ham in Hollywood to get anything natural out of—and he had a scheme. He was going to get the heart of the picture shot by noon—before you even knew you were acting. He turned you around and shoved you down into that shell-hole on your fanny, and yelled 'Camera'":

> "I can still hear you: 'Hey, what's the idea! Is this some gag? You get me out of here or I'll walk out on you!'
>
> "—and all the time you were trying to claw your way up the side of that pit, so damn mad you couldn't see. You'd almost get up and then you'd slide back and lie there with your face working—till finally you began to bawl and all this time Bill had four cameras on you. After about twenty minutes you gave up and just lay there, heaving. Bill took a hundred feet of that and then he had a couple of prop men pull you out. . . .
>
> "Corker cut that piece of film and titled it so you were supposed to be a doughboy whose pal had just been killed. You wanted to climb out and get at

the Germans in revenge, but the shells bursting all around and the concussions kept knocking you back in. . . .

"Bill said the best moment in the picture was when Phil was yelling 'I've *already* broken my first fingernail!' Bill titled it 'Ten Huns will go to hell to shine your shoes!'" (*Decade* 192–93)

Like all the Hobby stories, this one was published in *Esquire*, and Fitzgerald wrote to the magazine's editor Arnold Gingrich, "Did you know that last story (Two Old Timers) was the way 'The Big Parade' was really made? King Vidor pushed John Gilbert in a hole—believe it or not" (Gingrich xv). By the time the story was published in March 1941, Gilbert had been dead for five years and Fitzgerald dead for three months, but it suggests that some of the disparaging comments about professional actors in Fitzgerald's fiction expressed the sentiments not only of the characters but of the author as well.

Yet if *professional* acting comes across in *The Last Tycoon* as being considered slightly déclassé, all the book's characters who work in some area of the movie business take for granted a certain level of social theatricality in their personal and professional interactions, indeed, expect a certain dramaturgical discipline from their peers. Almost the first thing we are shown about Stahr in the novel is the theatrical component of his managerial skill: on a flight to Los Angeles he gives the pilot a lesson in the absolute self-assurance a leader has to demonstrate in his decision making in order to inspire confidence in the people he manages. He poses the hypothetical situation of a railroad man who has to send a train track somewhere through the mountains: "You get your surveyors' reports, and you find there's three or four or a half a dozen gaps, and not one is better than the other. You've got to decide—on what basis? You can't test the best way—except by doing it. So you just do it" (20). Though the pilot remains puzzled by Stahr's lesson, later in the novel when Stahr confronts the communist union organizer Brimmer, he finds someone who immediately understands the theatrics of leadership. Claiming that writers "are not equipped for authority," Stahr says,

"There is no substitute for will. Sometimes you have to fake will when you don't feel it at all."

"I've had that experience."

"You have to say 'It's got to be like this—no other way'—even if you're not sure. A dozen times a week that happens to me. Situations where there is no real reason for anything. You pretend there is."

"All leaders have felt that," said Brimmer. "Labor leaders, and certainly military leaders." (122)

And in virtually every professional interaction at the studio Stahr gives a more or less self-conscious theatrical performance of leadership. For example, in the conference Stahr has with Reinmund, Broaca, Wylie White, and Rose Meloney in which he threatens to shelve the film that's just about to start in order to bring them around to his vision of the picture, the veteran writer Rose, who "had been in this game longer than any of them" and had "never taken her eyes off Stahr," knew at a certain point that "it was going to be all right now. If he had really been going to abandon the picture he wouldn't have gone at it like this" (40). Clearly, Rose has seen Stahr give this performance many times before. Similarly, when Stahr decides to remove Red Ridingwood from the picture he's directing he enacts a bit of displeased-executive "business": "Stahr walked past him, heading across the great stage toward a set that would be used tomorrow. Director Ridingwood followed, realizing suddenly that Stahr walked a step or two ahead. He recognized the indication of displeasure—his own métier was largely the 'delivery' of situations through mimetic business" (49). And again, when Stahr is shown viewing the rushes and making almost instantaneous decisions about what is good, what needs to be reshot, or what is to be totally discarded, one of the people present questions whether a scene is too long, and Stahr replies, "Not a bit":

> "Sometimes ten feet can be too long—sometimes a scene two hundred feet long can be too short. I want to speak to the cutter before he touches this scene—this is something that'll be remembered in the picture."
>
> The oracle had spoken. There was nothing to question or argue. Stahr must be right always, not most of the time, but always—or the structure would melt down like gradual butter. (56)

Fitzgerald gives us a glimpse of the cumulative effectiveness of Stahr's theatrics of leadership in the scene where the studio employees mobilize to repair the damage done by the earthquake:

> Men began streaming by him—every second one glancing at him smiling speaking Hello Monroe ... Hello Mr. Stahr ... wet night Mr. Stahr ... Monroe ... Monroe ... Stahr ... Stahr ... Stahr.
>
> He spoke and waved back as the people streamed by in the darkness, looking I suppose a little like the Emperor and the old Guard. There is no world so but it has its heroes and Stahr was the hero. Most of these men had been here a

long time—through the beginnings and the great upset when sound came and the three years of Depression he had seen no harm came to them. The old loyalties were trembling now—there were clay feet everywhere—but still he was their man, the last of the princes. And their greeting was a sort of low cheer as they went by. (27)

As for the dramaturgical discipline of the novel's other characters, Cecelia, for example, playfully rehearses with Wylie White the scene she means to play with Stahr to show him she loves him. Announcing that she's going to throw herself "under the wheels of Stahr's car, this morning" (67) to attract his attention, Cecelia says,

> "He's going to look at me and think 'I've never really seen her before.'"
> "We don't use that line this year," he said.
> "—Then he'll say 'Little Celia' like he did the night of the earthquake. He'll say he never noticed I have become a woman."
> "You won't have to do a thing."
> "I'll stand there and bloom. After he kisses me as you would a child—"
> "That's all in my script," complained Wylie. "And I've got to give it to him tomorrow."
> "—he'll sit down and put his face in his hands and say he never thought of me like that."
> "You mean you get in a little fast work during the kiss." (69)

But when Cecelia goes to Stahr's office and tries to play out the imagined scene, it all turns out wrong. Stahr asks her why she doesn't get married, and Cecelia replies, "What could I do to interest an interesting man?" When Stahr "unexpectedly" says "I'd marry you. . . . I'm lonesome as hell. But I'm too old and tired to undertake anything," Cecelia says, "Undertake me" (70–71). Suddenly realizing she's in earnest, he says that he doesn't have any time for marriage, and Cecelia replies, "You couldn't love me." Then "right out of my dream but with a difference," Stahr says, "I never thought of you that way, Celia. I've known you so long. Somebody told me you were going to marry Wylie White" (71). And indeed this same self-conscious theatrical behavior is apparent even in the novel's minor characters: when Cecelia goes to the writer Rose Meloney trying to get her to invite the faded film star Martha Dodd to lunch so that Cecelia can learn the name of the mystery woman Stahr is involved with, Rose exclaims "with ready theatrical sympathy," "Hasn't that little girl had a tough break though!" (102).

So imbued is Stahr with a sense of the theatrical aspect of social behavior that when he has his first date with Kathleen Moore, even though he is pointedly relieved to find she's not a professional actress, he nevertheless evaluates her physical appearance as if she were: "She had not made a move or a gesture that was out of keeping with her beauty, that pressed it out of its contour one way or another. It was all proper to itself. He judged her as he would a shot in a picture. She was not trash, she was not confused but clear—in his special meaning of the word which implied balance, delicacy and proportion, she was 'nice'" (80). And later after Stahr and Kathleen have made love at Stahr's Malibu beach house, he again appraises her as he would an image on film: "He watched her move, intently yet half afraid that her body would fail somewhere and break the spell. He had watched women in screen tests and seen their beauty vanish second by second as if a lovely statue had begun to walk with the meagre joints of a paper doll. But Kathleen was ruggedly set on the balls of her feet—the fragility was, as it should be, an illusion" (90). That Stahr judges Kathleen's beauty in this way is not only an expression of his highly developed sense of social theatricality and a function of his constantly judging screen tests of aspiring young actresses but also a consequence of the fact that his initial attraction to Kathleen was based on her physical resemblance to his dead wife, movie star Minna Davis, a woman who now exists only as an image on film. In this regard the word "illusion" in the phrase "the fragility was, as it should be, an illusion" takes on an added resonance that suggests a further link between Stahr and Jay Gatsby.

The essence of Gatsby's disillusion is twofold. On the one hand, James Gatz is finally unable to actualize his ideal self as Jay Gatsby in a manner authentic enough to convince Daisy he is what he appears. As Nick says after the confrontation scene at the Plaza, "'Jay Gatsby' had broken up like glass against Tom's hard malice and the long secret extravaganza was played out" (115–16). For Fitzgerald, disillusion comes from facing the discrepancy between an illusory (one might say, dream) image and a real person, between a picture and a physical body. And thus the other half of Gatsby's twofold disillusion comes with his ultimate realization of the gap between his idealized image of Daisy, treasured up and constantly elaborated in his secret heart over the five years of their separation, and the real woman he meets again on Long Island. As Nick observes on the day Daisy visits Gatsby's house the first time, "There must have been moments even that afternoon when Daisy tumbled short of his dreams—not through her own fault but because of the colossal vitality of his illusion. It had gone beyond her, beyond everything. He had thrown himself into it with a creative passion, adding to it all the time, decking it out with every bright feather that drifted his way. No amount of fire or freshness can challenge what a man will store up in his ghostly heart" (75). In effect, James Gatz can only achieve his dream by convincing one illusory, idealized person (Daisy) of the authenticity of another illusory, idealized person (Jay Gatsby), or as Nick phrases it when Gatsby realizes Daisy didn't have a good time at the party she attends, "He talked a lot about the past and I gathered that he wanted to recover something, *some idea of himself* perhaps, that had gone into loving Daisy. His life had been confused and disordered since then, but if he could once return to a certain starting place and go over it all slowly, he could find out what that thing was" (86, italics mine).

If for Fitzgerald disillusion comes from discovering the distance between an imagined image and a real person, then this opposition becomes explicit in *The Last Tycoon* as that between a picture and a physical body. When Cecelia tells Stahr that she loves him, a scene Cecelia had so carefully imagined in advance, and the scene turns out all wrong, Cecelia says, "I'll always think of that moment . . . as the end of childhood, the end of the time when you cut out pictures. What I was looking at wasn't Stahr but a picture of him I cut out over and over: the eyes that flashed a sophisticated understanding at you and then darted up too soon into his wide brow with its ten thousand plots and plans; the face that was ageing from within, so that there were no casual furrows of worry and vexation but a drawn asceticism as if from a silent self-set struggle—or a long illness. It was handsomer to me than all the rosy tan from Coronado to Del Monte. He was my picture, as sure as if he was pasted on the inside of my old locker at school" (71). But perhaps Cecelia's picture imagery had been prompted by Stahr's somewhat flustered response to her offer, "Undertake me": he says he doesn't have any time for marriage because "pictures are my girl" (71).

Stahr's dead wife had been a movie star, a real person part of whose physical presence was a constant awareness of her filmed image, and this distinction between a human body and its picture is emphasized when Stahr notes that Kathleen resembles more the way Minna "actually *look*ed than how she was on screen," even though Stahr appraises Kathleen's beauty "as he would a shot in a picture." When Stahr first sees Kathleen on the night of the earthquake he recognizes "the face of his dead wife . . . across four feet of moonlight[,] . . . warm and glowing" (26–27). And the second time he meets her, Kathleen is framed in a lighted doorway: "There she was—face and form and smile against the light from inside. It was Minna's face—the skin with its peculiar radiance as if phosphorous had touched it" (64). This radiant phosphorescence is clearly influenced by Stahr's memory of Minna's face projected as a lighted image on a silver screen, and of course as a star Minna would naturally be associated with light: as Stahr thinks when he goes to meet the woman he believes is the double of his dead wife, "A childish association of Minna with the material heavens made him, when he reached his office, order out his roadster for the first time this year" (62). This association of a movie star with the material heavens resonates back to the real life models of Stahr, Minna, and their studio—the producer Irving Thalberg, his movie star wife, Norma Shearer, and their studio MGM whose motto, inscribed above its front gates, was "More Stars Than There Are in the Heavens."

Moreover, this association of Minna with light gets transferred to Kathleen when her face is seen first in "moonlight" and then framed in a doorway "against the light from inside" and then implicitly associated with the light from a star when Edna, who's being driven home by Stahr, says, "You see that last highest light—Kathleen lives there. I live just over the top of the hill" (*Tycoon* 64). Fitzgerald underlines this association of Kathleen with starlight when he has Stahr misremember a detail from the night of the earthquake: he thinks that the woman who resembled his dead wife wore "a silver belt . . . with stars cut out of it" (44), but as it turns out, it was Edna who wore the silver belt. As Bruccoli notes, this detail is based on something that actually happened when Fitzgerald first met Sheilah Graham, the model for Kathleen. On July 14, 1937, the writer Robert Benchley gave a party to celebrate the engagement of Graham, a Hollywood gossip columnist, and the Marquess of Donegall: "Fitzgerald dropped in at the party and left early without speaking" to Graham, "but he had noticed her extraordinary resemblance to the young Zelda. . . . Benchley phoned Fitzgerald to rejoin the party after Sheilah and her fiancé had left, and Fitzgerald asked who was still there. When Benchley told him that a blond actress named Tala Birell was there, Fitzgerald returned, thinking she was Sheilah. (He had incorrectly remembered that the girl who interested him had been wearing a silver belt—a detail that went into *The Last Tycoon* for Monroe Stahr's meeting with Kathleen Moore.)" (*Grandeur* 429). But of course in adapting this incident Fitzgerald had added the specific detail of the silver belt having stars cut out of it.

As the green light at the end of Daisy's dock had been for Gatsby a symbol of the distant, idealized woman who is the object of his desire, so the image of a star's light (in the sense both of the radiant phosphorescence of a face and the last highest light in the material heavens) is for Stahr a symbol of the recovery of the image of his dead wife in the living body of a real woman, a picture reincarnated. Recall that in the poetic passage that ends chapter 6 of *The Great Gatsby*, where Gatsby is walking at night with Daisy and sees "that the blocks of the sidewalk really formed a ladder and mounted to a secret place above the trees," he imagines that he could climb up among the stars, "suck on the pap of life, gulp down the incomparable milk of wonder" if "he climbed alone. . . . So he waited, listening for a moment longer to the tuning fork that had been struck upon a star. Then he kissed her. And at his lips' touch she blossomed for him like a flower and the *incarnation* was complete" (86–87, italics mine). In *The Last Tycoon* Fitzgerald obliquely evokes the disillusion inherent in the notion of incarnation/reincarnation in the scene where Stahr fires Red Ridingwood. As Stahr walks on the set, "The eyes and open mouths of a group of visitors moved momentarily off the heroine of the picture, took in Stahr and then moved vacantly back to the heroine again. They were Knights of Columbus. They had seen the Host carried in procession but this was the dream made flesh" (50). The experience of seeing a movie star on screen and then seeing her in person is likened here to the incarnation of the son of God in the communion wafer, but this image of "the dream made flesh" (echoing "the Word made flesh") is immediately undercut when Fitzgerald tells us that the movie-star heroine, though "starlight . . . actually photographed in her eyes," wears "a low gown which displayed the bright eczema of her chest and back. Before each take the blemished surface was plastered over with an emollient, which was removed immediately after the take" (50). Certainly no radiantly phosphorescent skin here.

Just as Fitzgerald's failure as a playwright with *The Vegetable* sent him back to writing fiction that would now more clearly thematize the theatrical element of social behavior in the novel of manners, so his third, largely unsuccessful attempt at making a go of screenwriting, an attempt that began when he moved to Hollywood in the summer of 1937, added a further layer to this social/theatrical theme. The trajectory of Fitzgerald's reputation as a writer had been on a continual rise during the economic boom years of the 1920s with the popular success of *This Side of Paradise* and the critical success of *The Great Gatsby* and then in decline after the stock market crash during the years of the Great Depression of the 1930s. His writings of the '20s had become so closely identified with the Jazz Age and its excesses that when those excesses inevitably led to a bust and people needed someone to blame, critics and the public tended to turn against Fitzgerald's work, as witnessed by the reception of *Tender Is the Night*. As the Depression deepened, many of Fitzgerald's writing contemporaries became more politically engaged on the left, and Fitzgerald's material, which dealt with the leisure class, seemed hopelessly outdated. In trying to annex a degree of political awareness and a concern for social justice to his fiction, Fitzgerald had at one point during the writing of *Tender* considered having Dick Diver at the end of the novel send his son, Lanier, to the Soviet Union to be educated, but he wisely abandoned the idea. One of Fitzgerald's oldest friends, the critic Edmund Wilson, whom Fitzgerald had called his "intellectual conscience" (*Lost* 148) in "Pasting It Together," was, as Bruccoli notes, "deeply involved with communism" (*Grandeur* 348), though not a party member himself. In a January 1933 letter to Maxwell Perkins, Fitzgerald reports that in a recent visit with Wilson he seemed "rather gloomy. A decision to adopt Communism definitely, no matter how good for the soul, must of necessity be a saddening process for anyone who has ever tasted the intellectual pleasures of the world we live in" (*Letters* 230). In an August 1934 letter to his cousin Ceci Taylor, he says that he's "given up politics. For two years I've gone half haywire trying to reconcile my double allegiance to the class I am part of, and the Great Change I believe in. . . . I have become disgusted with the party leadership and have only health enough left for my literary work, so I'm on the sidelines" (*Letters* 417).

While Fitzgerald's reputation as a novelist had been declining in the '30s, the reputation of his sometime friend Ernest Hemingway, the man implicitly identified as his "artistic conscience" in "Pasting It Together," had been on the rise, particularly as Hemingway's fiction had become more engaged in left-wing causes. Although Fitzgerald hoped to work his way out of debt (to his agent Harold Ober, his editor Maxwell Perkins, and his publisher Scribner's) by returning to Hollywood and script work in 1937, he clearly felt this to be a step down in his career. The decline in status became palpable when Hemingway visited Hollywood in July 1937. As Bruccoli notes,

> His embarrassment about his position in Hollywood was intensified by Hemingway's arrival as a conquering hero to raise money for the Spanish loyalists. Fitzgerald was among the guests when Hemingway showed *The Spanish Earth* [the Joris Ivens film for which Hemingway wrote the narration and did the voice-over] at the home of Frederic March on 12 July. After the showing, he offered to drive Lillian Hellman to Dorothy Parker's house, where the party was continuing, but he was intimidated by Hemingway and did not want to join the party. Hellman persuaded him to go in with her and left him in the kitchen talking with Dashiell Hammett and Dorothy Parker. This was the last

time Fitzgerald saw Hemingway, and there is no record that they talked. The next day he sent Hemingway a wire: THE PICTURE WAS BEYOND PRAISE AND SO WAS YOUR ATTITUDE = SCOTT. Fitzgerald understood that their close friendship was over, admitting: "I talk with the authority of failure—Ernest with the authority of success. We could never sit across the table again." (*Grandeur* 425)

In the last year of his life Fitzgerald summed up his feelings about communism and the left in a letter of advice to his daughter Scottie: "The point is that Communism has become an intensely dogmatic and almost mystical religion and whatever you say they have ways of twisting it into shapes which put you in some lower category of mankind ('Fascist,' 'Liberal,' 'Trotskyist') and disparage you both intellectually and personally in the process. They are amazingly well-organized. The pith of my advice is: think what you want, the less said the better" (*Letters* 65). If one explanation for why Fitzgerald wrote the Pat Hobby stories—besides the fact that they produced enough income for him to spend less time doing script work and more time on *The Last Tycoon*—is that they allowed him to try out and develop some of his Hollywood material, another, I would argue, is that that they gave him a way to elaborate on what he terms "the authority of failure," an authority that was linked in his mind to the question of communism and to the incident of the communist union organizer Brimmer trying to infiltrate the Screen Writers Guild in *The Last Tycoon*. Fitzgerald describes Pat's situation in "Pat Hobby's Preview" where the down-at-heels screenwriter suffers an insult that would have been "a crushing blow" to a "rising young screen poet. . . . [B]ut Pat was made of sterner stuff. Sterner not upon himself, but on the harsh fate that had dogged him for nearly a decade. With all his experience, and with the help of every poisonous herb that blossoms between Washington Boulevard and Ventura, between Santa Monica and Vine—he continued to slip. Sometimes he grabbed momentarily at a bush, found a few weeks' surcease upon the island of a 'patch job,' but in general the slide continued at a pace that would have dizzied a lesser man" (*Decade* 158).

Most of the Hobby stories turn around Pat's trying to get temporary work on a script at $250 a week (as compared to his former salary of $1500 a week when he was on top) and then trying either to chisel his way into sharing a screen credit or steal another writer's idea outright. (Recall in this regard that in the three and a half years from the summer of 1937 to December 1940 that Fitzgerald worked on scripts, he had only one shared screen credit for the

Frank-Borzage-directed MGM film of Erich Maria Remarque's *Three Comrades*.) Pat's nefarious schemes usually go awry, often hilariously, but the series of stories ultimately leaves the reader with a sense of Hobby's resilience, his almost indomitable will to survive and his inextinguishable hope of succeeding—that and a sense of the essential dignity, the rehabilitating effect, of work. As Fitzgerald says in "No Harm Trying," "The prospect of a job did something to Pat. It anesthetized the crumbling, struggling remnants of his manhood, and inoculated him instead with a bland, easy-going confidence. The set speeches and attitudes of success returned to him" (*Decade* 165). One can gather from two letters Fitzgerald wrote to his daughter Scottie (one in July 1938 and the other in the spring of 1940) the sort of concerns in his personal life at this period that animated his sense of Hobby's will to survive and his character. In the 1938 letter he complains that Scottie has begun to show signs of being an idler like her mother:

> When I was your age I lived with a great dream. The dream grew and I learned how to speak of it and make people listen. Then the dream divided one day when I decided to marry your mother after all, even though I knew she was spoiled and meant no good to me. I was sorry immediately I had married her but, being patient in those days, made the best of it and got to love her in another way. . . . But I was a man divided—she wanted me to work too much for *her* and not enough for my dream. *She realized too late that work was dignity, and the only dignity*, and tried to atone for it by working herself, but it was too late and she broke and is broken forever. (*Letters* 32, italics mine)

Fitzgerald says that for a long time he had hated Zelda's mother "for giving her nothing in the line of good habit—nothing but 'getting by' and conceit. I never wanted to see again in this world women who were brought up as idlers. And one of my chief desires in life was to keep you from being that kind of person, one who brings ruin to themselves and others." And he continues, "I don't want to be upset by idlers inside my family or out. I want my energies and earnings for people who talk my language. I have begun to fear that you don't. *You don't realize that what I am doing here is the last tired effort of a man who once did something finer and better*. There is not enough energy, or call it money, to carry anyone who is dead weight and I am angry and resentful in my soul when I feel that I am doing this" (*Letters* 32–33, italics mine). The near heroic sense of Fitzgerald's effort—laboring at the sort of writing he knew was neither as fine or good as his fiction but that he had to do to get out of debt, pay for Zelda's medical care, and Scottie's tuition at Vassar—comes up again in his spring 1940 letter to his daughter: "Anyhow I am alive again—getting by that October did something—with all its strains and necessities and humiliations and struggles. I don't drink. I am not a great man but sometimes I think the impersonal and objective quality of my talent and the sacrifices of it, in pieces, to preserve its essential value has some sort of epic grandeur. Anyhow after hours I nurse myself with delusions of that sort" (*Crack-Up* 291). Fitzgerald's sense of persevering through "strains and necessities and humiliations and struggles," of doing whatever it takes to survive, is part of what he pours into the Hobby character, the other part being a wry humor at Hobby's expense meant to cauterize any hint of self-pity. Fitzgerald's portrait of Hobby, evoking in detail the marginalization of the writer in the Hollywood production system, also served perhaps as a defense mechanism, an imaginative exorcism of any fear that he himself could ever sink that low. In "Mightier than the Sword" Hobby explains to an author whose script he's been assigned to rework, "Authors get a tough break out here. . . . They never ought to come." To which the other replies, "Who'd make up the stories—these feebs?" " 'Well anyhow, not authors,' said Pat. 'They don't want authors. They want writers—like me' " (*Decade* 200).

Having fallen several economic rungs in the studio caste system, Pat might seem to be just the sort of writer to whom the communist union organizer Brimmer's notion of writers as "the farmers in this business. . . . They grow the grain but they're not in at the feast" would appeal. But in "Boil Some Water—Lots of It" Pat turns out to be someone who, though he may object to the justice of his present status, doesn't think overthrowing the system is the answer to his problem—probably because he still hopes to be back on top some day. At lunch in the studio commissary Pat is seated near the "Big Table," where by general custom only the important producers and directors are allowed to sit:

> Beside the Big Table stood an extra, a Russian Cossack with a fierce moustache. He stood resting his hand on the back of an empty chair between Director Paterson and Producer Leam.
>
> "Is this taken?" he asked, with a thick Central European accent.
>
> All along the Big Table faces stared suddenly at him. Until after the first look the supposition was that he must be some well-known actor. But he was not.
> . . .
> Someone at the table said: "That's taken." But the man drew out the chair and sat down.

"Got to eat somewhere," he remarked with a grin.

A shiver went over the nearby tables. Pat Hobby stared with mouth ajar. It was as if someone had crayoned Donald Duck into "The Last Supper." . . .

The dozen men at the table, representing a thousand dollars an hour in salaries, sat stunned. (*Decade* 106–7)

The men at the Big Table are slow to act, but "Pat Hobby could stand no more. He had jumped up, seizing a big heavy tray from the serving stand nearby. In two springs he reached the scene of action—lifting the tray he brought it down upon the extra's head with all the strength of his forty-nine years," knocking the man unconscious to the floor as he "stood over him panting—the tray in his hand." " 'The dirty rat!' he cried 'Where does he think he—' " (*Decade* 107). One assumes the interrupted sentence would have continued, "is—Russia?"—since the extra is dressed as a Cossack. But at this point two men from another table rush up shouting, "It was a gag! . . . That's Walter Herrick, the writer. . . . He was kidding Max Leam. It was a gag I tell you!" (*Decade* 108). As people crowd around, Pat lets the tray slip to a chair, and he

caught Max Leam's eye but Max happened to look away at the moment and a sense of injustice came over Pat. He alone in this crisis, real or imaginary, had *acted*. He alone had played the man, while those stuffed shirts let themselves be insulted and abused. And now he would have to take the rap—because Walter Herrick was powerful and popular, a three thousand a week man who wrote hit shows in New York. (*Decade* 108)

Pat, who's been at the studio twenty years, is referred to, or refers to himself, as an "old-timer" (*Decade* 200), and his loyalties, in spite of all the indignities he's suffered, are very much with the establishment and the ancien régime. Fitzgerald had said in his 1934 letter to his cousin Ceci Taylor that for two years he'd gone "half haywire trying to reconcile" his "double allegiance to the class I am part of, and the Great Change I believe in." The class that Fitzgerald was born into and of which he was part was the upper middle class—as Fitzgerald says of Basil Lee's family, they weren't rich, "only comfortable." But the class that Fitzgerald—the novelist of manners, who felt, as his friend Edmund Wilson said, "an invincible compulsion to live like a millionaire"—imaginatively belonged to was the leisure class. If Fitzgerald the man felt a double allegiance both to his class and to the "Great Change" he believed in (the latter apparently involving some massive sociopolitical reorganization that would bring about greater economic equality), then Fitzgerald the writer would certainly have tipped the balance in favor of class, realizing that any communist vision of a proletarian, classless society would destroy the very stuff of the novel of manners. Pat Hobby's violent physical defense of the studio's upper class against what appeared to be a revolutionary interloper with Russian overtones gets translated in *The Last Tycoon* into Stahr's confrontation with the communist union organizer Brimmer and his determination not to give the Screen Writers Guild any bargaining power at the studio.

Stahr prepares for his meeting with Brimmer "by running off the Russian Revolutionary Films that he had in his film library at home. He also ran off 'Doctor Caligari' and Salvador Dali's 'Un Chien Andalou,' possibly suspecting that they had a bearing on the matter. He had been startled by the Russian Films back in the twenties and on Wylie White's suggestion he had had the script department get him up a two-page 'treatment' of the 'Communist Manifesto'" (119). But as Cecelia remarks, "His mind was closed on the subject. He was a rationalist who did his own reasoning without benefit of books—and he had just managed to climb out of a thousand years of Jewry into the late eighteenth century. He could not bear to see it melt away—*he cherished the parvenu's passionate loyalty to an imaginary past"* (119, italics mine). After centuries of the social oppression of his people, Stahr, having risen to the top, wasn't about to let the ladder of class be toppled by a Red, and in *The Last Tycoon* Fitzgerald gives us a variation on the Big Table scene from the Hobby story. Attending the "screen-writers' ball" at the Ambassador Hotel, "Stahr went to the table where he was expected and sat down with the Café Society group—from Wall Street, Grand Street, Loudon County Virginia, and Odessa Russia. They were all talking with enthusiasm about a horse that had run very fast and Mr. Marcus was the most enthusiastic of all. Stahr guessed that Jews had taken over the worship of horses as a supersymbol—for years it had been the Cossacks mounted and the Jews on foot. Now the Jews had horses and it gave them a sense of extraordinary well-being and power" (74). Just as in the Hobby story it had been a writer who, pretending to be a lower-class interloper, had tried to crash the closed circle of the Big Table, so in *The Last Tycoon* it is specifically writers who represent an uprising of the lower orders at the studio, writers banded together in a guild trying to gain bargaining leverage and wrest away some of Stahr's power. In attending the screenwriters' ball, Stahr is clearly in the camp of the enemy, but he sits at the equivalent of the commissary's Big Table. Moreover, where in the Hobby story it had been the writer who was dressed as a Russian Cossack, here at the Café Society table Fitzgerald's invoking the image of the

Cossacks, the Russian czar's cavalry, suggests the way this group of more or less self-made men, after climbing to the top of their business, had taken up the symbolic trappings of the ancien régime, the fallen Russian royalty overturned by the Communist Revolution—in effect, another example of "the parvenu's passionate loyalty to an imaginary past."

This more or less oblique evocation of royalty recalls the numerous instances in which this imagery is attached to Stahr. When Stahr sees Kathleen at the ball, he asks her to dance, and she says that when she returned to her table, the people there "talked as if I been dancing with the Prince of Wales" (74). And much earlier in the novel at the conclusion of the earthquake scene Stahr, receiving the greetings of the studio workers going to repair the damage, is likened to Napoleon, "the Emperor and the Old Guard." And when Stahr meets Kathleen the first time and she finds out he's a producer, she says,

> "I suppose the girls are all after you to put them on the screen."
> "They've given up." he said.
> This was an understatement—they were all there, he knew, just over his threshold, but they had been there so long that their clamoring voices were no more than the sound of the traffic in the street. But his position remained more than royal—a king could make only one queen—Stahr, at least so they supposed, could make many. (65–66)

And this imagery of royalty culminates with Stahr's discovery that Kathleen is the former mistress of a deposed king and her admission to Stahr that "he wasn't much like a king. Not nearly as much as you" (114).

Throughout his fiction Fitzgerald's imagination remained committed to the image—the inherent interest and charm, the larger-than-life quality—of the extraordinary individual—Jay Gatsby, Dick Diver, Monroe Stahr—a commitment that never allowed his imagination to be seduced by an appeal to the notion of collective man. The fact that Stahr, fueled by his innate intelligence and his will, rises to the position of chief of production at his studio by age twenty-two and then becomes the dominant figure in the film industry in the 1930s—or as Cecelia says, "a marker in industry like Edison and Lumière and Griffith and Chaplin" (28)—makes the image of Hollywood royalty for him seem inevitable, but it also recalls, and represents the culmination of, that rags-to-riches career path for the self-made man that Fitzgerald had originally projected twenty years earlier in his story "The Offshore Pirate." Fitzgerald's idea that the two American careers a young man could take up to get rich quick—the half-world of show business and the underworld of crime—met, as we have seen, in the fictive biography of Curtis Carlyle (the orchestra leader turned armed robber), but the goal projected for both paths was an ascension to the very highest level of society (as Carlyle says, "aristocracy"). (Recall that the underworld element would also have entered into Stahr's story: in the final, unfinished portion of the novel Fitzgerald considered having Pat Brady put out a contract to have Stahr killed and for Stahr do the same with Brady.) If Stahr's story represents the final fulfillment of a career trajectory originally imagined for the fictive Curtis Carlyle, then we can see that the twenty-year odyssey through Fitzgerald's fiction of a single thematic structure (the essentially theatrical nature of social interactions, particularly among the upper class) paralleled the working out of this trajectory. One might say that for Fitzgerald the two mottoes inscribed above this trajectory were that if you want to rise and *be* an aristocrat, you must first learn to *act* the role and that, in Thomas Jefferson's words, the true test of a democracy is whether it is able to produce an aristocracy, not of wealth and birth but of virtue and talents.

# CHAPTER FIVE

# Fitzgerald and the Mythical Method

ONE ASPECT OF *The Great Gatsby* that entered my consciousness with
my first reading of the novel and intrigued me ever after—though I
could not have stated it clearly at the time and only became aware of
its importance retrospectively—was the trope of self-invention embodied by
its protagonist. The notion of creating another self, of imagining and objectifying a persona and a life based on one's mental image of an ideal other (*the
real me that ought to be*) was a trope so powerful and appealing that it led to
my ongoing interest in doubling in all its structural and psychological ramifications. And though my first critical book, *Doubling and Incest / Repetition
and Revenge: A Speculative Reading of Faulkner*, was about a different author,
I realize now that my original interest in this structure had been initiated by
Fitzgerald. Doubling in one or another of its several manifestations has been
to some degree the theme of all my five previous books of literary criticism,
particularly in the sense of doubling as the *metasubject* of those writers I
dealt with—metasubject in the sense that the literary artist creates with the
body of his work an imagined and imaginative other self, a *corpus* meant to
embody the author's *real me* (his interior life) and meant, he hopes, to have
sufficient mental and emotional life to survive the moment when his physical body becomes a *corpse*. I was also influenced in this idea of the writing
self producing its written double (in effect, projecting a shadow self created
by black ink on white paper) considered as the metasubject continually at
work in the formation of a writer's corpus, no matter what the ostensible
subject of any individual work, by Faulkner's musings on authorship in his
second novel *Mosquitoes* and by Borges's seminal essay "Borges and I." In
contemplating the involved notion of an author's written self, I'm reminded
of that moment in Salinger's *The Catcher in the Rye* when Holden Caulfield,
after reading Thomas Hardy's *The Return of the Native*, says that he'd like to
phone up Hardy to tell him that he knew just how Eustacia Vye felt. Yet I've
always thought that, strictly speaking, one can never talk to the person who

wrote a book one loves. One might be able to speak to someone bearing the same name as the writer, but the person who wrote the book is a self that only comes out to play when the writer is alone in a room with a blank sheet of paper and a pencil or a typewriter or computer—when the author is by himself with himself. The only way you can meet *that* person is on the printed page. It was in response to this notion that I decided long ago, during the same years I was producing books of literary criticism, to publish my poems under the name John Bricuth, a persona, a written self wholly, and solely, constituted by the words on the page. And it is now this same deep and abiding interest in doubling, originally instilled by Fitzgerald, that leads me back to treat an aspect of that subject in his work.

In the previous chapter I suggested that the quantum leap in quality that Fitzgerald's fiction made with *The Great Gatsby* was due in part to his being able—after the failure of *The Vegetable*—to thematize his interest in drama and the theater by structuring this novel, as well as subsequent novels, around the notion of social theatricality. But there were other things Fitzgerald learned in writing *Gatsby* that were to become recurring elements in his later novels, things that clearly became associated in his own mind with the high artistic level he had achieved in *Gatsby* and that he repeated as a way of replicating that book's critical success.

The first of these elements reflects the influence of T. S. Eliot on Fitzgerald's fiction. It is a critical commonplace that the valley of ashes in *Gatsby* is, as Bruccoli observes, Fitzgerald's imagistic evocation of *The Waste Land* (1922), "which Fitzgerald greatly admired." Bruccoli goes on to note that "Eckleburg can be read as a Long Island version of the blind seer Tiresias, and the ash heaps are actually and symbolically a waste land" (*Grandeur* 209). On the novel's publication, Fitzgerald sent Eliot a copy of *Gatsby* inscribed "For T. S. Eliot Greatest of Living Poets from his entheusiastic [*sic*] worshipper F. Scott Fitzgerald" (*Correspondence* 180) and received in turn a letter from Eliot dated December 31, 1925, saying that the novel "interested and excited me more than any new novel I have seen, either English or American, for a number of years" and that "in fact it seems to me to be the first step that American fiction has taken since Henry James" (*Crack-Up* 310), a comment Fitzgerald treasured, reporting in a February 1926 letter to his editor Maxwell Perkins that T. S. Eliot, "the greatest living poet in any language," had "read *Gatsby* three times and thought it was *the first step forward American fiction had taken since Henry James*" (*Letters* 199). The only time Fitzgerald ever met Eliot was in February 1933 when Eliot gave the Turnbull Poetry

Lectures at Johns Hopkins University. At the time the Fitzgeralds were living in a rented house at La Paix, the Turnbulls' estate, whose grounds adjoined those of Shepherd Pratt Hospital, where Zelda was an outpatient. Knowing that Fitzgerald was an admirer of Eliot's poetry, the Turnbulls invited him to a dinner for the visiting poet, and Fitzgerald reported in a letter to Edmund Wilson "that T. S. Eliot and I had an afternoon and evening together last week. I read him some of his poems and he seemed to think they were pretty good. I liked him fine" (*Letters* 345).

Beyond the valley of ashes and Dr. T. J. Eckleburg as obvious examples of *The Waste Land*'s presence in the novel, an even more important and pervasive Eliotic influence revealed itself in *Gatsby* and became more pronounced in *Tender* and *The Last Tycoon*. One year after the appearance of *The Waste Land* and James Joyce's *Ulysses*, Eliot published an essay in the November 1923 issue of the *Dial* entitled "*Ulysses*, Order, and Myth," in which he details his sense of the major innovation Joyce achieved and the impact the novel would have on all future fiction writing. Noting that one might expect "the significance of the method employed—the parallel to the *Odyssey*, and the use of appropriate styles and symbols to each division . . . to be the first peculiarity to attract attention," Eliot observes that so far this method had been treated by reviewers "as an amusing dodge, or scaffolding erected by the author for the purpose of disposing his realistic tale, of no interest in the completed structure" (*Prose* 175). But Eliot claims "that Mr. Joyce's parallel use of the *Odyssey* has a great importance[,] . . . the importance of a scientific discovery. No one else has built a novel upon such a foundation before: it has never before been necessary" (177). He continues, "The novel ended with Flaubert and with James," but Joyce, being "in advance" of his time, "felt a conscious or probably unconscious dissatisfaction with the form" (177). Eliot then defines what he considers to be the essence of Joyce's "scientific discovery":

> In using the myth, in manipulating a continuous parallel between contemporaneity and antiquity, Mr. Joyce is pursuing a method which others must pursue after him. They will not be imitators, any more than the scientist who uses the discoveries of an Einstein in pursuing his own, independent, further investigations. It is simply a way of controlling, of ordering, of giving a shape and a significance to the immense panorama of futility and anarchy which is contemporary history. It is a method already adumbrated by Mr. Yeats, and of the need for which I believe Mr. Yeats to have been the first contemporary to be conscious. It is a method for which the horoscope is auspicious. Psychology

(such as it is, and whether our reaction to it be comic or serious), ethnology, and *The Golden Bough* have concurred to make possible what was impossible even a few years ago. *Instead of narrative method, we may now use the mythical method*. It is, I seriously believe, a step toward making the modern world possible for art, toward . . . order and form. (177–78, italics mine)

Of course, Eliot's critical essays, particularly those he wrote at the start of his literary career, often had a dual purpose: on the one hand, they single out writers, literary techniques, or artistic innovations he meant to praise (with the specific writers often being invoked as predecessors in a tradition Eliot was constructing for his own work), while on the other hand, they serve as oblique explanations or defenses of his own poetic practice. And "*Ulysses*, Order, and Myth" is no exception; for what Eliot intends by explaining the importance of the new "mythical method" in Joyce's work is an implicit explication of his own technique in *The Waste Land*, published the same year as Joyce's novel. And lest readers think that Eliot had merely copied Joyce's innovation, Eliot notes that this method had been foreshadowed by Yeats, most notably in his drawing on characters from Celtic lore in rendering the political and cultural turmoil of contemporary Ireland.

Eliot clearly had his own practice in *The Waste Land* in mind when discussing Joyce, as evidenced by his claim that the new method was made possible by "psychology . . . , ethnology, and *The Golden Bough*"—the last being a work that Eliot specifically invokes at the start of his notes to *The Waste Land*. Pointing out that "the title[,] . . . the plan and a good deal of the incidental symbolism of the poem were suggested by Miss Jessie L. Weston's book on the Grail legend: *From Ritual to Romance* (Cambridge)," he goes on to note that "to another work of anthropology I am indebted in general, one which has influenced our generation profoundly; I mean *The Golden Bough*. . . . Anyone who is acquainted with these works will immediately recognise in the poem certain references to vegetation ceremonies" (*Poems* 50). But of course Eliot's acknowledgment of Weston's influence was already an implicit acknowledgment of Frazer's, for Weston had said in the preface to her book that "like many others I owe to Sir J. G. Frazer the initial inspiration which set me, as I may truly say, on the road to the Grail castle," specifically citing "the guidance" provided by *The Golden Bough* (Weston vii).

Given that Eliot's *The Waste Land* and Joyce's *Ulysses* both appeared in 1922, that Eliot's essay "*Ulysses*, Order, and Myth" appeared in November 1923, and that Eliot's letter to Fitzgerald thanking him for sending a copy

of *Gatsby* was date 31 December 1925, a striking similarity of phrasing between the essay and the letter suggests that Eliot felt *Gatsby* had in some form
adopted the mythical method: In his essay Eliot contends that "the novel
ended with Flaubert and with James"—by which he means that what he later
calls "the narrative method" in the novel ended with these writers—while the
new mythical method that began with Joyce's *Ulysses* became "a *step* toward
making the modern world possible for art, toward . . . order and form" (italics mine). And in his letter he specifically praises *Gatsby* as "the *first step* that
American fiction has taken since Henry James" (italics mine), the implication
being that what *Ulysses* was for British fiction, *Gatsby* was for American. But
if Eliot identified (and coined the phrase) "the mythical method" in an essay
on Joyce's *Ulysses*, then shouldn't we associate that change in technique we
find in *Gatsby* with Joyce's influence rather than Eliot's? Critics have noted the
influence of Joyce's *Portrait of the Artist as a Young Man* on Fitzgerald's *This
Side of Paradise* and of Joyce's story "Araby" from *Dubliners* on Fitzgerald's
"Absolution," while in *Tender Is the Night* the novel that Albert McKisco is
working on when Rosemary first meets him on the Riviera is, as McKisco's
wife says, "on the idea of Ulysses. . . . Only instead of taking twenty-four
hours my husband takes a hundred years. He takes a decayed old French
aristocrat and puts him in contrast with the mechanical age" (17). But I would
argue that Eliot's influence is both more apparent and more crucial in *Gatsby*
than Joyce's: it is, first, more apparent because of the clear debt the valley of
ashes and Dr. T. J. Eckleburg owe to the imagery of *The Waste Land* and the
blind seer Tiresias and, second, more crucial because it is Eliot's explanation
of the mythical method (i.e., the "manipulating" of "a continuous parallel
between contemporaneity and antiquity" as "a way of . . . giving a shape and
significance to the immense panorama of futility and anarchy which is contemporary history"), as well as his dictum that henceforth it must be the
method of choice for all modern novel writing, that in effect mediates for
Fitzgerald the influence of Joyce's novel.

Yet this is not to suggest that either Joyce's use of Homer's epic or Eliot's of
certain ancient and medieval vegetative fertility stories was the ancient myth
Fitzgerald had begun working his way toward in *Gatsby*. Indeed, for that
mythic structure Fitzgerald looked to the promptings of his own personality,
to what James Mellow in his biography of Scott and Zelda calls Fitzgerald's
"nagging urge to remake and re-educate the women he was involved with—
his wife, his daughter, his mistress" (23). Mellow might have also included
Fitzgerald's younger sister Annabel in this list. When Fitzgerald was a student

at Princeton, he "sent his thirteen-year-old sister . . . an interminable letter that was virtually a charm course on the ways and means of beguiling young men. With total unselfconsciousness, Fitzgerald advised her on such matters as cosmetics and conversation, dress and deportment" (36), even giving her a list of "leading questions" to use in captivating boys and another list ("analyzing the flaws of character and style among the girls he and Annabel knew in St. Paul") of things to be avoided (36–37). Of course, Fitzgerald was particularly fond of making lists, such as the extensive lists of books he made for his daughter, Scottie, and for his mistress, Sheilah Graham (which Graham subsequently published in her book *A College of One*), to read to make them more cultured and thus more interesting for him to be with.

The remaking of Zelda, however, was a more complex affair, involving a kind of symbiotic relationship in which Fitzgerald borrowed traits from Zelda's personality and incidents from her life to create the female protagonists of his fiction, and Zelda in turn tried to mirror and then outdo these fictional representations of herself. As early as *This Side of Paradise* Fitzgerald had, as James Mellow notes, sent Zelda part of the manuscript and told her "the heroine [Rosalind Connage] does resemble you in more ways than four" (74). Mellow goes on to note that in making his final revision of the manuscript Fitzgerald had likely "planned to use Zelda's letters and her borrowed diary for the purpose" (74). Fitzgerald's Princeton friend Alec McKaig noted that Fitzgerald, after marrying Zelda, became as "absorbed in Zelda's personality" as he did precisely because she "supplied him with all his copy for women" (117). And when George Jean Nathan saw Zelda's diaries on a visit to the Fitzgeralds in Westport, Connecticut, during the first year of their marriage, he was so impressed "he suggested publishing portions of them in *The Smart Set*. But Fitzgerald strenuously objected, because he had 'gained a lot of inspiration from them and wanted to use parts of them in his own novels and short stories'" (114). At the extreme point of this appropriative practice, Fitzgerald would use details from Zelda's mental illness and excerpts from her letters and diaries to depict Nicole Diver during her mental breakdown. One can imagine the effect that Zelda's reading this fictional portrait of herself (made by the person who knew her most intimately and whom she loved best) would have had on her own efforts to stabilize her personality.

Given Fitzgerald's ongoing "urge to remake and re-educate the women he was involved with," we can see that the ancient myth that he first uses to structure his fiction in *Gatsby* and returns to in his next two novels is that of Pygmalion and Galatea. The myth would have been well known to Fitzgerald from George Bernard Shaw's 1912 play *Pygmalion* and also perhaps from W. S. Gilbert's 1871 blank verse drama *Pygmalion and Galatea*, both of which were hits in England and America. And of course there was a prose version of it readily available in Bulfinch's *Mythology*. The best-known ancient account of the myth is contained in book 10 of Ovid's *Metamorphoses*. The Cyprian youth Pygmalion, outraged by the sight of prostitutes and "disgusted with the faults which in such full measure nature had given the female mind, . . . lived unmarried and long was without a partner of his couch":

> Meanwhile, with wondrous art he successfully carves a figure out of snowy ivory, giving it a beauty more perfect than that of any woman ever born. And with his own work he falls in love. The face is that of a real maiden, whom you would think living and desirous of being moved, if modesty did not prevent. So does his art conceal his art. Pygmalion looks in admiration and is inflamed with love for this semblance of a form. Often he lifts his hands to the work to try whether it be flesh or ivory. . . . He kisses it and thinks his kisses are returned. (4:81–83)

On the "festal day of Venus" in Cyprus, Pygmalion, bringing a gift to the goddess's altar, says " 'If ye, O gods, can give all things, I pray to have as wife—' he did not dare add 'my ivory maid,' but said 'one like my ivory maid.' " (4:83–85). When Pygmalion returns home, he finds that the ivory of his statue has turned to real flesh:

> The maiden felt the kisses, blushed and, lifting her timid eyes up to the light, she saw the sky and her lover at the same time. The goddess graced with her presence the marriage she had made; and ere the ninth moon had brought her crescent to the full, a daughter was born to them, Paphos, from whom the island takes its name. (4:85)

Though the apparent meaning of the myth centers on man's embodying his ideal image of womanhood in a physical object (the statue) that then becomes a real person, the deeper, less obvious meaning depicts the relationship between an artist and his work of art as a marriage between the male and female aspects of the artist's self. Clearly, in producing his own ideal image of woman, Pygmalion produces an oppositely gendered, reciprocal double of himself and, as Ovid says, "with his own work he falls in love." One can intuit the symmetry that would have attracted Fitzgerald to this myth for structuring *Gatsby*: where the myth depicts Pygmalion's ideal image of womanhood turning into a real woman, the novel evokes Gatsby's turning a real woman

(Daisy) into an idealized image during the five years of their separation in which he dreams of winning her back. As Nick notes, "the colossal vitality" of Gatsby's illusory image of Daisy "had gone beyond her, beyond everything. He had thrown himself into it with a creative passion, adding to it all the time. . . . No amount of fire or freshness can challenge what a man will store up in his ghostly heart" (75). And that growing illusion about Daisy was an illusion about himself as well, an attempt "to recover something, *some idea of himself* perhaps, that had gone into loving Daisy" (86, italics mine), the illusion that he could once again be that earlier, romantic young man untainted by the compromises of the underworld. In effect, Gatsby's work of imaginatively idealizing Daisy becomes an analogue of, becomes Fitzgerald's vehicle for evoking, James Gatz's work of imaginatively idealizing himself, artistically re-creating himself as Jay Gatsby. Gatsby, facing the realization that Daisy may in fact have loved Tom at some point, dismisses it, saying that "in any case . . . it was just personal," and Nick wonders, "What could you make of that, except to suspect some intensity in his *conception* of the affair that couldn't be measured" (119, italics mine). The words "idea" and "conception" both point to the Platonic, ideal nature of Gatsby's illusions and to its inherent flaw—the inevitable disillusion that reality brings. But as Fitzgerald wrote to his friend Ludlow Fowler in August 1924, romantic illusions "give such color to the world," such "magical glory" (*Correspondence* 145), that even if they turn out to be false they are still worth pursuing again and again no matter how many times they fail in an individual life, because without them the world is simply too drab, too despairing a place—"and to this *conception*" Fitzgerald remained "faithful to the end" (*Gatsby* 77, italics mine).

But Fitzgerald would also have been attracted to the Pygmalion-Galatea myth because of its subtext, its parabolic evocation of the male artist's relationship to his work of art considered as a female double. For not only was Fitzgerald, as Alec McKaig observed, "absorbed in Zelda's personality"—she being both wife and muse (the model for so many of his female characters)—but there was also a strong female element in Fitzgerald's own personality, as Scott believed: "I am half feminine—that is, my mind is. . . . My characters are all Scott Fitzgerald. Even the feminine characters are feminine Scott Fitzgeralds" (Mellow 37). And his lover Sheilah Graham remembered him as "gentle" and "sensitive" with "all the intuition usually associated with women" (Graham 72). As Mellow notes, Fitzgerald's "disappointment at the loss of his role" (because of academic ineligibility) in the Princeton Triangle Club's 1915 production of *The Evil Eye* (the role being that "of a seductive show girl") "must have been quite real." (The well-known photograph of a heavily made-up Fitzgerald in drag was the advertising poster for the show.) Mellow adds that "during his winter of exile in St. Paul, Fitzgerald, dolled up in woman's clothes and accompanied by a male friend, attended a fraternity dance at the University of Minnesota. He spent a good part of the evening whirling around the dance floor, presumably giving his partners some of the snappy lines he had suggested to [his sister] Annabel. The entire incident created a stir" (37).

Clearly, Fitzgerald's "nagging urge to remake and re-educate the women he was involved with" represented in part the urge to create an image of what he would have been like had he been born a woman. But this sense of the Pygmalion-Galatea myth as a story of an artist's falling in love with his own work, which is to say, with his own projected self-image considered as the female aspect of his personality, necessarily implicates another myth: that of Narcissus, who falls fatally in love with his reflection in a pool. And I would suggest that the version of Narcissus's story that the Pygmalion-Galatea myth evokes is not only Ovid's in the *Metamorphoses* but also the one contained in Pausanias's *Description of Greece*. In his section on Boeotia, Pausanias describes the summit of Helicon and the river Lamus, noting

> Here is the spring of Narcissus. They say that Narcissus looked into this water, and not understanding that he saw his own reflection, unconsciously fell in love with himself, and died of love at the spring. But it is utter stupidity to imagine that a man old enough to fall in love was incapable of distinguishing a man from a man's reflection. There is another story about Narcissus, less popular indeed than the other, but not without some support. It is said that Narcissus had a twin sister; they were exactly alike in appearance, their hair was the same, they wore similar clothes, and went hunting together. The story goes on that Narcissus fell in love with his sister, and when the girl died, would go to the spring, knowing that it was his reflection that he saw, but in spite of this knowledge finding some relief for his love in imagining that he saw, not his own reflection, but the likeness of his sister. (4:311)

Pausanias's summary of the more common version of Narcissus's story leaves out a key feature of the myth as told by Ovid—that once Narcissus realizes the image he has fallen in love with is his own reflection and not another young man who lives in the world beneath the water as he lives in the world above, Narcissus pines away and dies of love precisely because he sees that his love of a mere image can never be physically consummated. But in Pausanias's version, no such impediment to consummation would have existed while the sister, Narcissus's oppositely-gendered, physical embodiment, still lived. And the suggestion of an incestuous attachment in the brother-sister love of Pausanias's version meshes with the implied incest present in the Pygmalion-Galatea myth, for if Pygmalion creates the ivory statue of the perfect woman from an image in his own imagination, then he has in effect mentally "fathered" the woman he will ultimately marry. And this father-daughter incest motif is made explicit when Ovid immediately follows the story of Pygmalion and Galatea in the *Metamorphoses* with the story of their grandson Cinyras and his daughter Myrrha.

Myrrha is struck with an unnatural passion for her father; as Ovid remarks, "'Tis a crime to hate one's father, but such love as this is a greater crime than hate" (4:87). Trying to resist this passion, Myrrha argues with herself: "If I were not the daughter of great Cinyras, to Cinyras I could be joined. But as it is, because he is mine, he is not mine; and, while my very propinquity is my loss, would I as a stranger be better off? It is well to go far away, to leave the borders of my native land, if only I may flee from crime; but unhappy passion keeps the lover here, that I may see Cinyras face to face, may touch him, speak with him and kiss him, if nothing else is granted" (4:89). Tormented and distraught, Myrrha decides the only way to avoid this crime is death, but as she prepares to hang herself in her chamber, she is interrupted by her faithful nurse. Badgering Myrrha till she admits the cause of her despair, the nurse decides to facilitate the consummation of this passion rather than let Myrrha kill herself. During the annual festival of Ceres when wives "for nine nights . . . count love and the touch of man among things forbidden," the "over-officious nurse," finding "the king's bed . . . deprived of his lawful wife" and "Cinyras drunk with wine, told him of one who loved him truly, giving a false name, and praised her beauty. When he asked the maiden's age, she said: 'The same as Myrrha's'" (4:95). The nurse conveys Myrrha to her father's chamber, and "the father receives his own flesh in his incestuous bed, strives to calm her girlish fears. . . . It chanced, by a name appropriate to her age, he called her 'daughter,' and she called him 'father,' that names might not be lacking to their guilt" (4:97). The two then make love on several nights, and "Cinyras, eager to recognize his mistress after so many meetings, brought in a light and beheld his crime and his daughter. Speechless with woe, he snatched his bright sword from the sheath which hung near by. Myrrha fled and escaped death by grace of the shades of the dark night" (4:97–99). (In the version of the story in Hyginus's *Fabula* Cinyras kills *himself* when he discovers the incest.)

The pregnant Myrrha flees through many countries until she reaches "the Sabaean land" and there she prays to the gods: "I do not refuse the dire punishment I have deserved; but lest, surviving, I offend the living, and, dying, I offend the dead, drive me from both realms; change me and refuse me both life and death" (4:99). The gods grant her prayer and change her into a tree, and "though she has lost her old-time feelings with her body, still she weeps, and the warm drops trickle down from the tree. Even the tears have fame, and the myrrh which distils from the tree-trunk keeps the name of its mistress and will be remembered through all ages" (4:99). At nine months the child in Myrrha's womb is born, bursting forth from the tree trunk, and that child is Adonis, who will become the lover of Venus. And this last conjunction would seem to be the final twist to the generational persistence of incest in these myths, for if Pygmalion, in conceiving the image of a perfect woman, imaginatively *fathered* his wife, Galatea, through his art, then Venus, who transformed Pygmalion's statue into a real woman, could be said to have brought Galatea to birth, in effect, to have been her *mother*. Thus when Venus takes Adonis as her lover, she mates with her own great-great-grandson.

Given the importance of twins in Pausanias's version of the Narcissus myth, it is worth noting that in *The Beautiful and Damned*, when Anthony and Gloria are falling in love, Anthony asks her to tell him "the reasons why you're going to marry me," and she says it's because they're so alike: "You and I are clean like streams and winds. . . . *We're twins*" (115, italics mine). And she continues, "Mother says that two souls are sometimes created together . . . and in love before they're born" (115). This last detail sounds like an allusion to Plato's version in the *Symposium* of the origin of love between the sexes. There Plato imagines that primordial beings with spherical bodies were originally split in two by Zeus and that this splitting and doubling "left each half with a desperate yearning for the other," so that "they ran together and flung their arms around each other's necks, and asked for nothing better than to be rolled into one" (Plato 543). Thus "our innate love for one another . . . is always trying to redintegrate our former nature, to make two into one, . . . and each of us is forever seeking the half that will tally with himself" (544). One should note in this connection that in 1935 Fitzgerald told his friend Tony Buttitta that "I know her [Zelda] better than I know myself. We could be twins" (Buttitta 125). Further, one of Zelda's fantasies during her mental illness was that she and Scott were the same person (as suggested by their single nickname for each other, "Dodo"—much as Dick and Nicole Diver had a single name, "Dicole," with which they signed their joint correspondence). Moreover, in the watercolor sketches that Zelda painted when she was in therapy at the Phipps Clinic in 1934 (sketches that are now housed in Evergreen House at Johns Hopkins University), there is a recurring motif. Many are of human figures that fall into two types: in one type a single human figure viewed from the front is shown dividing into two, or else two halves are merging into one, along a medial line between the right and left sides, and in the other type a single human figure viewed from the front is clearly evoked as an hermaphrodite.

Given the structural connection—through implicit or explicit evocations of incest—between Ovid's stories of Pygmalion and Galatea and of Cinyras and Myrrha on the one hand and Pausanias's version of the Narcissus story on the other, it comes as no surprise that when Fitzgerald once again employs a more elaborated version of the Pygmalion and Galatea myth in *Tender Is the Night* the myth's incest aspect moves front and center—the violation of the sixteen-year-old Nicole Warren by her father, with the guilt she feels from the trauma becoming the cause of her mental illness. And it is Nicole's attraction to Dick (in Freudian terms, her transference to her psychiatrist) that enables Dick to begin her cure, a cure that involves his gradually recreating Nicole as a stable personality, a work of reeducation that must be begun over again each time she has a relapse. Dick tells himself that "he tried honestly to divorce" Nicole "from any obsession that he had stitched her together" (158), yet when Nicole has another mental collapse after the birth of their daughter, Topsy, she thinks in a stream-of-consciousness passage, "When I get well I want to be a fine person like you, Dick" (185). Later when Nicole suffers a hysterical collapse after receiving a letter from a woman who claims that Dick had an affair with her daughter (a patient at Dick's clinic), and Dick tries to calm Nicole by talking her back to that sense of herself he has created for her, she exclaims angrily, "Who do you think you are? . . . Svengali?" (217).

The reference, of course, is to a character in George du Maurier's 1894 novel *Trilby*, one of the most popular late Victorian novels, whose fame had grown even greater through stage and film adaptations. (In the chronology of *Tender* Nicole makes her remark about Svengali in 1927, but for Fitzgerald writing the novel in 1932–33, the most recent incarnation of this figure would have been in the 1931 film *Svengali*, starring John Barrymore in the title role.) Trilby O'Ferrall, the novel's heroine, is an English grisette living in Paris in the 1850s and a sometime model for art students in the Latin quarter. Beloved by three young English painters—William "Little Billee" Bagot, Taffy Wynne, and Sandy McAlister—Trilby is also desired by the master musician and scoundrel Svengali, an adept hypnotist. As the novel progresses, Trilby ultimately falls under the power of Svengali, and though she could never carry a tune, Svengali, hypnotizing her, turns Trilby into the most renowned female singer of her era. When she performs, she is in a mesmeric trance and completely under Svengali's sway. As one character describes it,

> Trilby was just a singing machine—an organ to play upon—an instrument of music—a Stradivarius—a flexible flageolet of flesh and blood—a voice, and nothing more—just the unconscious voice that Svengali sang with—for it takes two to sing like la Svengali . . . —the one who has got the voice, and the one who knows what to do with it. . . . So that when you heard her sing . . . , you heard Svengali singing with her voice, just as you hear Joachim play a chaconne of Bach with his fiddle! (458)

Performing in the capitals of Europe and before royalty, Trilby is universally hailed. But when la Svengali, as she's called, appears for the first time in Paris, the three English painters hear her for the first time and realize that this diva is their old friend, the little grisette who didn't know one note from another. The three are present again at her debut performance in London, but as she is about to begin her first song, Svengali, who is seated in a box directly in front of her, dies of a heart attack, and with his death his mesmeric hold on Trilby vanishes. Suddenly as she begins her song, she is once again the girl who can't carry a tune, and she collapses. When she is revived, she has no memory of her ever having sung in public as la Svengali, and convalescing from the shock, she begins to decline in health. Surrounded by the three loving English painters who try to care for her, she gradually wastes away. She tells the three how she came to be associated with Svengali and how he had cared for her when she first became ill. But though Svengali and Trilby lived together and performed as man and wife—billed as le Svengali and la Svengali—they had never been married, and Trilby says she could never return his passion, that she "used to try and do all I could—be *a daughter* to him, as I couldn't be anything else" (393, italics mine). But that was the unmesmerized Trilby's sense of their relationship. Another character describes how Svengali

> had but to say "Dors!" and she suddenly became an unconscious Trilby of marble, who could produce wonderful sounds—just the sounds he wanted, and

nothing else—and think his thoughts and wish his wishes—and love him at his bidding with a strange unreal factitious love[,] . . . just his own love for himself turned inside out . . . and reflected back on him, as from a mirror[,] . . . *un écho. un simulacre.* (458)

The story of Svengali and Trilby is simply the dark, modern version of the myth of Pygmalion and Galatea, and the image of Trilby as Svengali's mirror, echo, and simulacrum makes clear the modern sense of how deeply the myth of Narcissus inhabits that of Pygmalion and Galatea. (In regard to this imagery, Fitzgerald exhibits in *Gatsby* his own understanding of how much not only the Pausanian but also the Ovidian myth of Narcissus lie at the heart of the myth of Pygmalion and Galatea when he has Nick, after the confrontation scene at the Plaza, observe that " 'Jay Gatsby' had broken up like glass against Tom's hard malice and the long secret extravaganza was played out" [115–16]. This sense of Gatsby's invented self as a mirror image shattered by Tom's revelations evokes Narcissus one last time when Fitzgerald chooses to have Gatsby die in his swimming pool, recalling Ovid's version of the myth where Narcissus dies beside the pool from an unsatisfiable longing to be physically united with his own image. Wasting away, Narcissus's body is transformed into the eponymous flower. Ovid adds, "And even when he had been received into the infernal abodes, he kept on gazing on his image in the Stygian pool" [3:159]). Interestingly enough, Narcissus's words upon realizing that he is in love with his own image recall Myrrha's lament that the object of her love is too close: Narcissus says, "I burn with love of my own self; I both kindle the flames and suffer them. . . . What I desire, I have; the very abundance of my riches beggars me. Oh, that I might be parted from my own body! and, strange prayer for a lover, I would that what I love were absent from me" (3:157).

In the nineteenth century and the early part of the twentieth, many psychiatrists, or alienists as they were called, used hypnosis as a means of treating mental patients. Even Freud tried it for a while during the late 1880s before giving it up. Fitzgerald says that as a psychiatrist "Dick distrusted and seldom used [hypnosis], for he knew that he could not always summon up the mood in himself—he had once tried it on Nicole and she had scornfully laughed at him" (210). Of course physicians are traditional authority figures, individuals from whom one seeks aid because of their expertise and experience. And the psychoanalyst is, in effect, a father figure, the person, as Freud says, to whom one refers one's problems "as to one who knows." The transference (the cathecting of the analyst by the patient, as if the patient were a child and the analyst a parent) is what enables the analyst's words to carry weight with the patient. Thus when Dr. Diver, as a father figure, marries his patient Nicole, he commits what amounts to symbolic father-daughter incest, reinscribing within their relationship the original source of Nicole's trauma. In the myth, the symbolic incest of Pygmalion's marrying the woman he has imaginatively "fathered" is followed by the real incest of their grandson Cinyras with his daughter Myrrha, but in *Tender Is the Night* this order is reversed: the real incest of Devereux Warren with his daughter is followed by the symbolic incest of Dr. Diver and his patient.

The incident that precipitates Dick's retrospective understanding of this pattern is the arrival of Rosemary Hoyt on the Riviera, her falling in love with Dick at first sight, and his growing, reciprocal attraction to her. She makes him aware, in effect, of a repetition-compulsion in his character (driven by his need to be loved) that attracts him to younger women who desire an older, authority figure to educate and mold their personalities. The beginning of this understanding on Dick's part occurs when Rosemary has her film *Daddy's Girl* screened for the Divers and the Norths. As Dick watches the film he is struck by "a lovely shot of Rosemary" and her father "united at the last in a father complex so apparent that Dick winced for all psychologists at the vicious sentimentality" (81). Of course, one of the reasons Rosemary is attracted to Dick once she learns he's "a doctor of medicine" is that, as she says, "my father was a doctor too" (74). As Dick's initial attraction grows and Rosemary throws herself at him, he tries to maintain the composure of an older, more experienced adult, referring to Rosemary as "a lovely child" and saying that everything she does "like pretending to be in love . . . gets across" (74–75). But having just turned eighteen, Rosemary openly avows her love for Dick at the Paris hotel where she and the Divers are staying, saying "now for my birthday present I want you to come into my room a minute while I tell you something." Once inside her room, Rosemary stands close to him, and Dick, sensing the situation has grown dangerous, tries to defuse it:

> "When you smile—" he had recovered *his paternal attitude,* perhaps because of Nicole's silent proximity, "I always think I'll see a gap where you've lost some baby teeth."
> But he was too late—she came up close against him with a forlorn whisper. "Take me."

"Take you where?"
Astonishment froze him rigid. (75, italics mine)

When he had kissed Rosemary in the taxi on the way back to the hotel, Dick had been "chilled by the innocence of her kiss" and had thought that "she did not know yet that splendor is something in the heart; at the moment when she realized that and melted into the passion of the universe he could take her without question or regret" (75). And some three years later in Rome, when Dick reencounters Rosemary, now an established film star and a veteran of several love affairs, he thinks, "She was young and magnetic, but so was Topsy" (his daughter) (236). Yet Dick does ultimately take Rosemary, and the end of this sojourn in Rome makes clear to him the father-daughter aspect both of his marriage to Nicole and his affair with Rosemary. As Dick is being brought into court to face charges for his brawl with Roman taxi drivers and a plainclothes policeman, he is booed by a group of angry bystanders, and when he asks why, someone explains that "a native of Frascati had raped and slain a five-year-old child and was to be brought in that morning—the crowd had assumed it was Dick" (265). Dick says, "I want to make a speech. . . . I want to explain to these people how I raped a five-year-old girl. Maybe I did—" (265). Dick's ultimate judgment about Rosemary is that she "didn't grow up" (334). And some sense of Dick's apprehension about that aspect of his personality that draws him to younger women who are attracted to father figures had been suggested in his earlier remark about his strictness with his own children, particularly his daughter, Topsy: "What do I care whether Topsy 'adores' me or not? I'm not bringing her up to be my wife" (290).

In Ovid's story of Cinyras and Myrrha, the poet evokes the chaos of kinship relations resulting from incest, exhorting Myrrha, "Think how many ties, how many names you are confusing! Will you be the rival of your mother, the mistress of your father? Will you be called the sister of your son, the mother of your brother?" (4:89). Dick Diver experiences a similar confusion from the doubling of his relationship to Nicole:

> The dualism in his views of her—that of the husband, that of the psychiatrist—was increasingly paralyzing his faculties. In these six years she had several times carried him over the line with her, disarming him by exciting emotional pity or by a flow of wit, fantastic and disassociated, so that only after the episode did he realize, with the consciousness of his own relaxation from tension, that she had succeeded in getting a point against his better judgment. (215)

By all accounts Fitzgerald suffered from this same confusing dual relationship with Zelda, who was both his wife and the model for most of the main
female characters in his fiction. When Dick sees that Nicole is getting well
and that the strain of this dual relationship has caused his own deterioration,
he brings about a countertransference, gradually shifting her libido from her
psychiatrist-husband onto Tommy Barban. At one point near the end, Nicole
approaches Dick, trying to comfort him, and Dick says, "I can't do anything
for you any more. I'm trying to save myself." Yet Nicole "began to feel the
old hypnotism of his intelligence, sometimes exercised without power but
always with substrata of truth under truth which she could not break or even
crack" (336–37)—the reference to "the old hypnotism of his intelligence" recalling her earlier remark comparing Dick to Svengali. Dick leaves, returning
to America, and because Dr. Diver's marrying his patient had symbolically
reinscribed within their marriage Nicole's original trauma, her ultimate cure
requires that the marriage be dissolved. The image of Dick heading west,
trying to save himself, must have seemed prophetic to Fitzgerald in 1936, two
years after *Tender* was published, when, with Zelda lodged in a mental hospital in Asheville, North Carolina, Fitzgerald himself went west to California to
work his way out of debt and recover his career as a serious writer, in effect,
to try to save himself—a westward journey that would lead to his third and
final iteration of the story of Pygmalion and Galatea, now annexed to another
myth, as Fitzgerald began collecting material for his last novel.

In the previous chapter we noted that when Fitzgerald first saw Sheilah
Graham at a party in Hollywood he was struck by how much she resembled
the young Zelda and that the Fitzgerald-Graham love affair then became the
model for the relationship of Monroe Stahr and Kathleen Moore in *The Last
Tycoon*. Where Fitzgerald's wife was at this point institutionalized (in effect,
dead to the outside world), Monroe Stahr's wife, the movie star Minna Davis,
was literally dead. And just as Sheilah Graham's resemblance to the young
Zelda made Fitzgerald feel that his wife had in some sense been returned to
him in another incarnation, so Kathleen's uncanny resemblance to Minna was
to make Stahr feel that his wife had come back from the grave. This notion
likely suggested to Fitzgerald that the myth of Orpheus and Eurydice could
now be attached to that of Pygmalion and Galatea, a not-unprecedented association given that the story of Pygmalion and Galatea is preceded by the
story of Orpheus and Eurydice in book 10 of Ovid's *Metamorphoses*. As Ovid
tells the story, Orpheus, the son of the god Apollo and the muse Calliope,
was given the lyre by his father and became so good at singing and playing

the instrument that his song could charm the beasts and enchant trees and stones. Orpheus weds Eurydice, but "while the bride was strolling through the grass with a group of naiads in attendance, she fell dead, smitten in the ankle by a serpent's tooth" (4:65). Using the magical powers of his singing, Orpheus descends to the underworld and petitions Persephone and Pluto to return Eurydice to life again. So moved are the rulers of Hades that they agree to restore Eurydice to her husband but with

> this condition, that he should not turn his eyes backward until he had gone forth from the valley of Avernus, or else the gift would be in vain. . . . And now they were nearing the margin of the upper earth, when he, afraid that she might fail him, eager for sight of her, turned back his longing eyes; and instantly she slipped into the depths. He stretched out his arms, eager to catch her or to feel her clasp; but, unhappy one, he clasped nothing but yielding air. . . . She spake one last "farewell" which scarcely reached her husband's ears, and fell back again to the place whence she had come. (4:67–69)

Appropriately enough, when Stahr first sees Kathleen it is on the night of a Los Angeles earthquake, a splitting open of the earth symbolically evocative of disinterment, the releasing of shades from the underworld. Surveying the damage on the studio back lot, Stahr sees two women on the head of the god Siva floating down an "impromptu river" created by a broken water main: "The idol had come unloosed from a set of Burma" (26). Part of the Hindu trinity, along with the gods Brahma and Vishnu, Siva is a god of destruction and regeneration (a phallic deity), and the fact that the head of Siva the Destroyer is floating down a river evokes this god of death under his inseminating aspect of returning a soul from the underworld. As the two women disembark from the head, Stahr sees

> smiling faintly at him from not four feet away . . . the face of his dead wife, identical even to the expression. Across the four feet of moonlight the eyes he knew looked back at him, a curl blew a little on a familiar forehead, the smile lingered changed a little according to pattern, the lips parted—the same. An awful fear went over him and he wanted to cry aloud. Back from the still sour room, the muffled glide of the limousine hearse, the falling concealing flowers, from out there in the dark—here now warm and glowing. The river passed him in a rush. (26–27)

Just as Pygmalion and Orpheus were artists (the former a sculptor, the latter a musician and singer), so Fitzgerald makes clear that besides being a hard-headed business man, Stahr is also an artist, a film artist who had "led pictures way up past the range and power of the theatre, reaching a sort of golden age before the censorship in 1933" (28). And Fitzgerald shows us Stahr practicing his own form of art when he holds story conferences with writers, watches the daily rushes, and deals with directors, actors, and film editors—the art of pushing all these other artists to make their very best effort and never settling for anything less. And just as Pygmalion had used his art to fashion the image of a perfect woman from his imagination, one can well imagine that Stahr as the production chief of his studio would have exercised equal care in crafting the filmed image of his movie star wife. We know Stahr had this power to create a woman's visual image: Fitzgerald tells us that Stahr "had once had a young actress made up like Claudette Colbert and photographed her from the same angles" (58). And indeed, the fact that his movie star wife is in some sense his self-created, ideal image of the woman perfect for him is one of the things suggested by the homophonic doubling of Stahr and star. And just as the myth of Narcissus inhabits that of Pygmalion and Galatea, so too the relationship of Pygmalion to his sculpted ivory statue figures the artist's relationship to his work (considered as the projection of his own self image, the thing he loves most), an image oppositely gendered so as to permit the fantasy of an ultimate physical consummation. Fitzgerald emphasizes this sense of an artist's true (and perhaps only) love being his art when he has Cecelia throw herself at Stahr and has Stahr reply, "Oh, no. . . . Pictures are my girl" (71). And as Stahr will later admit to Kathleen, "I enjoy working most. . . . My work is very congenial" (7).

Though Stahr's remaking of Kathleen amounts, in effect, to his assimilating her to the image of his dead wife, her reeducation (a detail based on the extensive reading lists Fitzgerald prepared for Sheilah Graham) had already been begun by her previous lover, the painter and deposed king, another artist figure like Pygmalion or Svengali. According to Kathleen, he

> knew everything and he had a passion for educating me. He made out schedules and made me take courses at the Sorbonne and go to museums. . . .
>
> He was a painter of sorts and a hell-cat. And a lot besides. He wanted me to read Spengler—everything was for that. All the history and philosophy and harmony was all so I could read Spengler and then I left him before we got to Spengler. (91)

Reading Spengler together and having her understand his learned allusions had also been the goal of Sheilah Graham's reeducation by Fitzgerald, but

Fitzgerald had departed before they got to Spengler. And just as in *Tender Is the Night*, where a young woman and a slightly older woman (Rosemary and Nicole) both feel Dick's influence reshaping their minds and psyches to his image of what they should be, so too in *The Last Tycoon* Cecelia Brady is the younger counterpart of Kathleen. In discussing her romantic longing to make herself attractive to Stahr, a man who could have any woman he wanted, Cecelia thinks about how she might remake her image into something he could fall in love with, noting that it was "more than possible that some of the pictures which Stahr himself conceived had shaped me into what I was" (18).

Fitzgerald is able to fuse the myths of Pygmalion and Galatea and of Orpheus and Eurydice in *The Last Tycoon* because while the former is a fable of animation, the latter is one of reanimation. In his account, Ovid says that Orpheus lost Eurydice before they had reached the upper earth because he was "afraid that she might fail him" and thus being "eager for sight of her, turned back his longing eyes" (4:69). But the version of the story in Bulfinch's *Mythology*, though based largely on Ovid, adds a detail that may have influenced Fitzgerald's handling of the myth. Bulfinch has Orpheus excuse himself with the thought "how can she blame his impatience to behold her?" (187). Fitzgerald rings a change on this by making Stahr lose Kathleen not by being impatient but by being too patient. At the end of their last meeting, Stahr knows that he wants to marry her,

> but something else said to sleep on it as an adult, no romantic. And tell her tomorrow. . . .
>
> . . . It is your chance, Stahr. Better take it now. This is your girl. She can save you, she can worry you back to life. . . . But take her now—tell her and take her away. . . .
>
> [H]e felt that madness about it akin to the love of an ageing man for a young girl. It was a deep and desperate time-need, a clock ticking with his heart, and it urged him against the whole logic of his life to walk past her into the house now—and say "This is forever."
>
> Kathleen waited, irresolute herself. . . . She was a European, humble in the face of power, but there was a fierce self-respect that would only let her go so far. She had no illusions about the considerations that swayed princes.
>
> "We'll go to the mountains tomorrow," said Stahr. Many thousands of people depended on his balanced judgement—you can suddenly blunt a quality you have lived by for twenty years. (116–17)

And of course, the next day Stahr receives a telegram saying that Kathleen married another man at noon. The additional change Fitzgerald rings on the myth of Orpheus and Eurydice is that Kathleen's resemblance to Stahr's dead wife not only seems to bring Minna back to life; it also has the effect of revivifying Stahr, whom his doctor estimates has anywhere from six months to a year before he will die of overwork.

2

While Fitzgerald employs the myths of Pygmalion and Galatea and of Orpheus and Eurydice (as inflected by the Narcissus myth) in these novels to layer a pair of ancient lovers beneath a modern pair, he simultaneously balances against this mythical substrate a realistic theme drawn from modern American life—the conflict between one's personal relationships and one's work. And this conflict, considered as an ongoing subject matter in his most serious writing, was another theme Fitzgerald took up beginning with *The Great Gatsby*. In my earlier book *Unless the Threat of Death Is Behind Them: Hard-Boiled Fiction and Film Noir* I show how this conflict between an individual's personal and professional life was likewise an aspect of some of the best hard-boiled novels of the 1930s and '40s: Hammett's *The Maltese Falcon*, Chandler's Marlowe novels, Cain's *The Postman Always Rings Twice*, and *Double Indemnity*. Fitzgerald was a reader of detective stories, and with his first mature novel a crime element entered his fiction, for not only is *Gatsby*'s protagonist an underworld figure modeled, as we noted, on Edward Fuller, the real-life stock swindler and Rothstein associate, and Max Gerlach, a real bootlegger, but the novel's climax is a virtual trifecta of manslaughter, murder, and suicide. Further, at one point in the late 1920s when his fourth novel was still titled *The Boy Who Murdered His Mother*, Fitzgerald planned to base the climactic incident in the book on a notorious case of matricide currently in the news. And recall that for the ending of *The Last Tycoon* Fitzgerald had contemplated having Brady and Stahr either blackmail each other or put out a contract on each other's lives in their power struggle for control of the studio.

In *Unless the Threat of Death Is Behind Them* I discuss at some length the various ways Fitzgerald likely influenced Hammett, Chandler, Cain, W. R. Burnett, and Cornell Woolrich, and in turn how hard-boiled fiction's persistent use of the conflict between a man's personal life and his work influenced Fitzgerald in the writing of his last two novels. In Hammett, Cain, and Chandler this conflict presents itself to their novels' protagonists as a choice between *having* and *being*, between their possession of a beautiful, sexually desirable woman (whom one may or may not love but whom one certainly wants) and their allegiance to a professional code of ethics, to the expertise that is their work. The genre evokes the beautiful, often dangerous, woman as something a man may or may not *have*, but it presents his work as what he *is*—the doing that is his being. And the genre imagines two alternative resolutions to this conflict. In *The Maltese Falcon*, for example, the detective chooses his commitment to his work over his attraction to a woman: Sam Spade turns Brigid O'Shaughnessy over to the police for murdering Spade's partner, Miles Archer, rather than accept her sexual bribe to let her escape. Similarly, Chandler's Marlowe rejects the sexual blandishments of any number of beautiful heiresses trying to either "sugar him off the case" or influence his investigation, and he stays true to his code. In Cain's *Double Indemnity*, on the other hand, the insurance agent Walter Huff lets himself be seduced by the sexy, mentally unstable Phyllis Nirdlinger into using his professional expertise to help her murder her husband and collect the insurance, with the result that he is finally destroyed.

The overall moral that attaches to the best hard-boiled fiction of the 1930s is, then, that if a man chooses being over having he remains his own boss and succeeds, and if he chooses having over being he is no longer in control of his own destiny and is ultimately ruined. Clearly, *Tender Is the Night* and *The Last Tycoon* fall into this second category, and it was with the writing of *Gatsby* that Fitzgerald began to explore the importance to his project of producing serious fiction of being able to depict his protagonist's working life. We know from the 1938 letter to his daughter, Scottie, cited in the previous chapter that Fitzgerald had come to believe that "work was dignity, and the only dignity," and we can see that part of his dissatisfaction with his first two novels by the time he came to write his third was that the protagonists of these earlier efforts (Amory Blaine and Anthony Patch) were essentially trivial because they had no real work—a wastrel and a dilettante, respectively. Though Gatsby's work (for and with Wolfshiem) is apparently bootlegging, gambling, and stock and bond swindling, his working life is not depicted in any great detail precisely because part of the sense of Gatsby's remaking himself to win back Daisy is his need to keep hidden the shady dealings that enable his quest. Nevertheless, what this work (questionable though it may be) gives Gatsby is the kind of weight lacking in the characters of Amory Blaine and Anthony Patch. A self-made man, a serious man, Gatsby has been skillful and successful enough in his business to earn in just three years the money to buy his mansion. But with *Tender Is the Night* and *The Last Tycoon* a much more detailed presentation of their protagonists' working lives moves front and center.

In his essay "My Lost City" Fitzgerald says, "I once thought that there were no second acts in American lives" (*Lost* 114). And in his edition of *The Last Tycoon* Edmund Wilson includes the following two notes from among those found after Fitzgerald died that Wilson believes Fitzgerald was making for his novel:

There are no second acts in American lives.

———

Tragedy of these men was that nothing in their lives had really bitten deep at all. Bald Hemingway characters. (163)

As I say in *Unless the Threat of Death Is Behind Them*, I have always assumed that Fitzgerald's statement that "there are no second acts in American lives" means "that Americans, especially American men, have trouble developing emotionally or intellectually, trouble maturing, that they often grow old without ever growing up" (93). Fitzgerald seems to have felt this was true about himself and perhaps even more true about Hemingway, the apostle of American male perpetual adolescence. In the nine years between the publication of *Gatsby* and the appearance of *Tender*, Fitzgerald struggled, with varying degrees of success, to become an adult both in his personal life and his art. He had to face "the difficulty both in his professional life of continuing to grow his talent . . . and in his personal life of becoming . . . a husband and father who had to support and care for an emotionally erratic, and at last, mentally ill, wife, and raise a young daughter, and who had to do all this while making a living and battling alcoholism" (93–94). And I would suggest that his statement to Scottie that "work was dignity, and the only dignity" was crucial to his understanding of what it meant to be an adult, to have a second act in an American life. That's why the professional or working life of Dick Diver and Monroe Stahr figure so significantly in each of their stories.

A brilliant psychiatrist with an excellent first book and an unlimited future, Dick is initially shown practicing his profession assisting Franz Gregorovius with the care of the young Nicole in Dohmler's sanatorium. Later when he and Franz have their own sanatorium, Fitzgerald devotes an entire chapter (chapter 14 of book 2) to following Dick through a typical workday, highlighting his clinical and administrative skills. Dick's downfall comes, in effect, from sacrificing the professional to the personal, from subordinating his career as a psychiatrist to his role as simply his wife's psychiatrist. Nicole's increasing income so dwarfs what Dick makes from his profession that he begins to feel his own work is pointless. About to throw in the towel on his medical career, Dick gives up trying to complete his second book, and Nicole reminds him of what he once said: that "it's a confession of weakness for a scientist not to write" (185) and that "a man knows things and when he stops knowing things he's like anybody else" (186).

Clearly during the writing of *Tender*, Fitzgerald had come to feel that the effect Zelda had on his working life was similar to Nicole's on Dick's. In his July 1938 letter to Scottie, recall that he had explained that as a young man he had "lived with a great dream" but that once he'd married Zelda he "was a man divided—she wanted me to work too much for *her* and not enough for my dream." But when she realized that work was the only dignity, she "tried to atone for it by working herself, but it was too late and she broke and is broken forever" (*Letters* 32). Fitzgerald knew that

> the very stuff of his personal life (his love affair with Zelda, their marriage, and what came after) had always been the basic material of his life as a fiction writer. His professional and personal lives were inextricably entangled precisely because he'd made the latter the subject of the former. . . . Zelda's instability had created constant turmoil in Fitzgerald's life as a writer and as a husband and father, and her increasing jealousy of his work (both because of the time it took away from his being with her and because of her own artistic ambitions) had almost, Fitzgerald felt by the time he finished *Tender*, unmanned him. (Irwin, *Unless* 94)

In struggling to mature, to have a second act to his life, Fitzgerald circularized his efforts by turning process into product, by making the conflict between the personal and the professional that he faced in writing his fourth novel the very subject of the novel. One need only compare Fitzgerald's emphasis on his protagonists' working lives in his last two novels to Hemingway's lack of any serious fictional engagement with this topic to see how much real work, considered as a marker of adult responsibility, had come to influence Fitzgerald's imagination. As I note in *Unless the Threat of Death Is Behind Them*, "If one considers just those Hemingway works that have survived best, works that seem to have engaged his imagination most fully, these are all set at times (vacations, sabbaticals, leaves, convalescences) or in the midst of activities (big-game safaris, fishing trips, fiestas, volunteer service) coded as *nonwork*" (191). In *Green Hills of Africa*, I point out, "the character 'Hemingway' hunts big-game by day and pontificates about literature at the campfire by night" (192). One of his pronouncements is "all modern American literature comes from one book by Mark Twain called *Huckleberry Finn*"; "it's the best book we've had. All American writing comes from that. There was nothing before. There has been nothing as good since" (192). It seems only appropriate that Hemingway, "the singer of that fierce wish to grow old without ever having to grow up, should invoke Huck Finn as the patron saint of his ongoing theme":

> For clearly Hemingway is twentieth-century America's great writer of sty-
> listically sophisticated, highly mannered "boys' stories," narratives whose
> "you-can't-fool-me-'cause-life's-a-bitch-and-then-you-die" tone of rueful yet
> self-congratulatory knowingness has an enormous appeal for adolescents of
> all ages. And all those narratives, with their times, settings, and activities so
> obviously coded as *nonwork*, make clear what the *Huckleberry Finn* compo-
> nent in modern literature amounted to for Hemingway, for if to the childish or
> adolescent mind, work is one great marker of adulthood, then avoiding work,
> playing hooky from its constraints and responsibilities, is one way to keep from
> growing old. (192)

Most of what Fitzgerald knew about the working life of a psychiatrist that he used in *Tender Is the Night* he had picked up from observing Zelda's treatment at various clinics in Switzerland and America, but in representing the world of movies in *The Last Tycoon,* he was drawing on what he knew from working inside the industry on three separate occasions, the last of these for more than three years. Consequently, Fitzgerald spends a great deal more space detailing Stahr's normal work day than he did Dick Diver's: he shows us, for example, Stahr's conference with the English writer Boxley in which he demonstrates how screenwriting differs from novel writing; next he shows Stahr, as studio head, counseling and reassuring a successful male movie star suffering from a temporary bout of sexual impotence (episode 8); then it's Stahr's extended story conference with the producer, director, and writers of a film about to begin shooting who he feels have lost sight of the story line he had originally approved (episode 9); next Stahr's navigating among the studio's other money men during lunch in the commissary and subtly getting his own way (episode 10); and then his firing of a director from the set of a film being shot because the director has lost control of the film's female star (episode 11); and finally Stahr's going over the daily rushes in his projection room (episode 11)—to name a few of the more significant instances.

In *Tender,* Dick Diver's putting his personal life above his professional life had led to his eventual downfall; with *Tycoon*, however, it is not quite clear how Fitzgerald planned to have Kathleen's reawakening of Stahr's dormant personal life ultimately impact his career. What we know from the more or less finished portion of the novel is that his involvement with Kathleen had blunted his intuitive decision making, that "balanced judgement" he had "lived by for twenty years" and on which "many thousands of people depended" (117). The sudden reemergence of his emotional life makes him overly cautious about declaring his love for Kathleen and asking her to marry him, and the immediate impact on Stahr of Kathleen's marrying another man is a subsequent blurring of his professional judgment in dealing with Brimmer, the communist union organizer. During their long confrontation, first at Cecelia's home, then later at a nightclub, Stahr, who never drinks, gets drunk and tries to beat up Brimmer and run him off, telling Cecelia that Brimmer "has an influence . . . over all you young people" (128). Finally Brimmer knocks Stahr out, but it is clear that in Stahr's drunken state, Brimmer had become symbolically identified with the unnamed "American" who had married Kathleen, and when Stahr regains consciousness, he says to Cecelia:

"Where is he?" . . .

"Who?" I asked innocently.

"That American. Why in hell did you have to marry him, you damned fool."

"Monroe—he's gone. I didn't marry anybody." (128)

From Fitzgerald's notes for the unfinished portions of the novel and from his discussions of his plans for the book's completion with various friends, it seems that Stahr was to renew his affair with Kathleen at one point and that her husband (who was called W. Bronson Smith) was to become involved in the power struggle between Pat Brady and Stahr. As Bruccoli suggests, "Brady was probably going to attempt to force Stahr out of the studio by threatening to reveal Stahr's affair with Kathleen, and Stahr would retaliate by using information about Brady's complicity in the murder of his mistress's husband" (Introduction lx). Fitzgerald had clearly planned to have Brady defeat Stahr in their battle over Brady's proposed pay cut for studio employees. Yet however the novel would have ultimately ended, it seems certain that the affair between Stahr and Kathleen was meant to replicate the pattern present in *Tender* of a man's personal life overwhelming his professional one.

Given the significance of this theme shared by Fitzgerald's mature fiction and the best hard-boiled detective novels of the '30s and '40s, we should note yet another important thematic coincidence between the two—hard-boiled fiction's self-conscious insistence on the essentially theatrical quality of personal interactions among members of the criminal class and between members of that class and the detective. Goffman's distinction between "real, sincere, or honest performances" and false ones, the latter being those "that thorough fabricators assemble for us, whether meant to be taken unseriously, as in the work of stage actors, or seriously, as in the work of confidence men" (70), is relevant here. Certainly in hard-boiled detective stories it is not uncommon for characters to assume false roles, pretending to be something they're not to gain information from individuals they're dealing with without in turn giving away information about themselves or their motives. And nowhere is this theatrical quality, this sinister playacting, more in evidence than in the best hard-boiled novel of the period, Dashiell Hammett's *The Maltese Falcon*. Recall that the novel begins when a young woman named Miss Wonderly presents herself at the offices of Spade and Archer, private investigators, and asks them to help locate her seventeen-year-old-sister Corinne who has been seduced by a man named Floyd Thursby and taken from New York to San Francisco. She tells them she's arranged a meeting with Thursby that night at her hotel, and Miles Archer says he'll shadow Thursby after their meeting and find out where he's keeping Corinne. Later that night Sam Spade receives a phone call from the police saying that Archer has been shot to death. When Spade tries to contact Miss Wonderly at her hotel, he learns that she's checked out without leaving a forwarding address. She subsequently phones Spade, saying she's now registered in an apartment under the name Leblanc. When Spade shows up at her apartment, she says she has "a terrible confession to make": "That story I told you yesterday was all—a story." And he replies, "Oh, that. . . . We didn't exactly believe your story. . . . We believed your two hundred dollars. . . . I mean that you paid us more than if you'd been telling the truth . . . and enough more to make it all right" (33). Spade then asks if her real name is Wonderly or Leblanc, and she says, it's neither, it's Brigid O'Shaughnessy. Having admitted to her false role as Miss Wonderly, Brigid immediately launches into a new one under her purported real name, begging Spade to continue to act as her agent even though she won't tell him the reason she's in danger:

> Be generous, Mr. Spade, don't ask me to be fair. You're strong, you're resource-ful, you're brave. You can spare me some of that strength and resourceful-ness and courage, surely. Help me, Mr. Spade. . . . I've no right to ask you to

help me blindly, but I do. Be generous, Mr. Spade. You can help me. Help me. (36)

To which Spade responds by critiquing her acting ability: "You won't need much of anybody's help. You're good. You're very good. It's chiefly your eyes, I think, and that throb you get into your voice when you say things like 'Be generous, Mr. Spade' " (36). Stung by this, Brigid says, "I deserve that. . . . I deserve it, but—oh!—I did want your help so much. I do want it, and need it, so much. And the lie was in the way I said it, and not at all in what I said. . . . It is my own fault that you can't believe me now" (36–37). To which Spade replies, "Now you are dangerous" (37).

At a subsequent meeting with Brigid, Spade notices she seems "more sure of herself than before, though a becoming shyness had not left her eyes" (56), and he asks, "You're aren't . . . exactly the sort of person you pretend to be, are you? . . . Schoolgirl manner, . . . stammering and blushing and all that":

> She blushed and replied hurriedly, not looking at him: "I told you this afternoon that I've been bad—worse than you could know."
>
> "That's what I mean," he said. "You told me that this afternoon in the same words, same tone. It's a speech you've practiced."
>
> . . . "Very well, then, Mr. Spade, I'm not at all the sort of person I pretend to be. . . . But if it's a pose it's one I've grown into, so you won't expect me to drop it entirely, will you?"
>
> "Oh, it's all right. . . . Only it wouldn't be all right if you were actually that innocent. We'd never get anywhere."
>
> "I won't be innocent," she promised with a hand on her heart. (57)

Spade then provides a piece of information he hopes will startle her out of her act, telling her that he's just seen Joel Cairo:

> She got up from the settee and went to the fireplace to poke the fire. She changed slightly the position of an ornament on the mantlepiece, crossed the room to get a box of cigarettes from a table in the corner, straightened a curtain, and returned to her seat. Her face now was smooth and unworried. Spade grinned sidewise at her and said: "You're good. You're very good." (58)

When Brigid asks what he and Cairo talked about, Spade says,

> "He offered me five thousand dollars for the black bird."
>
> She started, her teeth tore the end of her cigarette, and her eyes, after a swift alarmed glance at Spade, turned away from him.

"You're not going to go around poking at the fire and straightening up the room again, are you?" he asked lazily. (58)

Part of the novel's ongoing wittiness revolves around Spade's cynical appreciation of Brigid's role-playing, yet Spade's own acting ability is a match for Brigid's. And it reaches its height near the end of the novel when Gutman, Cairo, and the young gunman Wilmer, with Brigid's help, get the drop on Spade in his apartment, and he must give the performance of his life to convince them that he's as crooked as they are and is in the affair only for the money, willing to turn over the falcon for the fee he and Gutman had agreed on, as long as they provide a fall guy for the police. His performance succeeds so well that he's able to turn them against one another and disarm them. And later when the black statuette proves to be a fake and Gutman and Cairo are clearing out, Spade keeps up his act, accepting a bribe to keep his mouth shut. After telephoning the police and turning in Gutman, Cairo, and Wilmer, Spade waits in his apartment with Brigid for the cops to arrive and tells her he's turning her in for killing Miles Archer. Thinking that their sexual liaison had bribed Spade into covering up for her, Brigid suddenly realizes that he has also been giving a performance: "You've been playing with me? Only pretending you cared—to trap me? You didn't care at all? You didn't—don't—don't—l-love me?" (223–24). And though Spade admits that he may have fallen in love, he says he won't play the sap for her, adding that if she was taken in by his performance as a crooked private detective, she may be laboring under a misapprehension: "Don't be so sure that I'm as crooked as I'm supposed to be. That kind of reputation might be good business—bringing in high-priced jobs and making it easier to deal with the enemy"—an explanation for the detective's role-playing that resonates through virtually all hard-boiled detective fiction.

## 3

In a 1940 letter to Scottie, Fitzgerald wrote, "What little I've accomplished has been by the most laborious and uphill work, and I wish now I'd *never* relaxed or looked back—but said at the end of *The Great Gatsby*: 'I've found my line—from now on this comes first. This is my immediate duty—without this I am nothing'" (*Letters* 79). Just as Fitzgerald repeated in his last two novels structures he had originally adopted in *Gatsby*, so he was also to repeat in these later works two distinctive, stylistic devices that originated there. The first of these involves Fitzgerald's delaying the narrator's initial meeting with, or recognition of, the novel's protagonist, so that the protagonist's introduction to the reader is achieved by a sort of indirection. Of course, Gatsby's name occurs in the title, and by the novel's fourth paragraph we know he's the protagonist of Nick's narrative. At the novel's start, when Nick begins writing, the events of the narrative are already over, yet later, in the course of the narrative, Nick tells us that when he first met Gatsby, he didn't know who he was. After moving into his Long Island bungalow, Nick sees one night a man he takes to be the owner of the mansion next door, but he doesn't speak or introduce himself, with the result that at the first Gatsby party Nick attends, there's an awkward moment. Nick finds himself sitting at a table with Jordan Baker as well as "a man of about my age and a rowdy little girl who gave way upon the slightest provocation to uncontrollable laughter." At a "lull in the entertainment" the man strikes up a conversation with Nick and invites him to go up in his hydroplane (*Gatsby* 39). Nick says,

> "This is an unusual party for me. I haven't even met the host. I live over there—" I waved my hand at the invisible hedge in the distance, "and this man Gatsby sent over his chauffeur with an invitation."
> For a moment he looked at me as if he failed to understand.
> "I'm Gatsby," he said suddenly.
> "What!" I exclaimed. "Oh, I beg your pardon."
> "I thought you knew, old sport. I'm afraid I'm not a very good host." (39–40)

Similarly, in *Tender Is the Night* Rosemary, on her first day at the beach in Cap d'Antibes, notices "a fine man in a jockey cap and red-striped tights," realizes that he's "giving a quiet little performance" for a group of friends gathered under a beach umbrella and that the "excitement generating under that umbrella . . . all came from the man in the jockey cap." And it is only when Rosemary has fallen asleep in the sun, and the man in the jockey cap wakes her, saying "It's not good to get too burned right away" (18), that Dick Diver's name first appears, some three thousand words into the narrative, though Dick doesn't introduce himself to Rosemary until some fifteen hundred words later.

The opening of *The Last Tycoon* repeats this pattern: on board a transcontinental flight to the West Coast, Cecelia Brady strikes up a conversation with the screenwriter Wylie White who is standing in the aisle when "another man brushed by him . . . and went forward in the direction of the cockpit," saying "Watch your step, Wylie!" (6). Cecelia doesn't see the other man's face and asks the stewardess if he's the assistant pilot. The stewardess says, "No. That's Mr. Smith. He has the private compartment, the 'bridal suite'—only he has it all alone" (6). The plane is grounded in Nashville by a storm, and Cecelia, Wylie White, and Mannie Schwartze visit the home of Andrew Jackson before they return to the airport to reboard the plane, and only then, some four thousand words into the novel, does the novel's protagonist appear by name. Cecelia says, "In the corridor of the plane I ran into Monroe Stahr and fell all over him, or wanted to" (15). This oblique way of introducing a principal character is given a further twist in the case of Kathleen Moore when Stahr confuses the woman resembling his dead wife with the woman wearing a silver belt with stars cut out of it—a mistake that leads him to Kathleen's friend Edna. Only when Edna realizes that Stahr is looking for the woman who resembles Minna Davis does she ask him to take her to Kathleen's house.

Fitzgerald uses this device in *Gatsby* and *Tycoon* as a way of subtly emphasizing at the very start of the book's action the narrator's first-person limitedness, as a means of underlining the fact that the narrator starts out with no "privileged" insight into the protagonist's mind or heart, that indeed at this point the narrator either doesn't recognize the protagonist on sight or isn't aware of his near presence. As a narrative device, the protagonist's oblique or delayed presentation is also meant to capture the reader's interest, surprising us with a slight shock of recognition. In the case of Nick and Gatsby, the surprise is heightened for the narrator (and thus for the reader) by the fact that Nick has heard so many wild rumors about his neighbor that he'd "expected that Mr. Gatsby would be a florid and corpulent person in his middle years"— heightened as well, of course, by Nick's embarrassment at not recognizing his host. When Gatsby leaves their table, Nick says he "turned immediately to Jordan—constrained to assure her of my surprise" (40). Since Nick had never seen Gatsby before in daylight, it's no wonder he doesn't recognize him at the party. But given the virtually nonexistent physical description of Gatsby in the novel, it's doubtful that any reader could recognize its protagonist without his proper name being given. All we're told by Nick about the way Gatsby looks is that he is "an elegant young rough-neck, a year or two over thirty, whose elaborate formality of speech just missed being absurd" (40) and that in a photograph of him as a youth he combed his hair in a pompadour. Daisy says he resembles "the advertisement of the man," presumably, as we noted, the young men with chiseled features in J. C. Leyendecker's drawings for Arrow collar ads—but there the description is already shading off into the only detailed descriptions of Gatsby Fitzgerald gives, which is to say, descriptions of his shirts, suits, his yellow roadster, and his mansion.

One wonders if this lack of physical description, this near invisibility of Gatsby's physical person, which was probably meant at the novel's start to create an air of mystery about him, was also in some sense an unconscious reaction on Fitzgerald's part to his own failure as a playwright: a technique meant to emphasize the difference between seeing a play and reading a novel. As written forms, novels and plays both have a visual presence for the reader, but when a play is performed, its protagonist (in the person of the actor) is physically present to the audience, which recognizes him in every scene he appears, whether he's given a proper name or not. By contrast, in a prose narrative, particularly one in which the protagonist's physical description is sparse enough to render his visual presence for the reader largely indeterminate, the protagonist has to be named to permit the reader's ongoing sense of recognition. As Fitzgerald turned away from writing plays, there was perhaps an element of defiance in his making Gatsby a visually indeterminate figure, which is to say that Fitzgerald may have set out to show that if he couldn't write successful plays, at least he could do something in prose fiction that plays couldn't: he could employ a device for concealing and thus delaying the reader's recognition of the protagonist's identity in a way that could never be achieved in a theatrical or filmic performance where the audience goes in already knowing who the protagonist is because they recognize the star actor. But more of this later when we examine the intriguing visual aspect of *The Last Tycoon*'s hero.

At the start of *Tender Is the Night* Rosemary Hoyt, in whom the narrative viewpoint is initially located, has to notice the Divers' group on the beach, become attracted to the "excitement . . . generating" under their umbrella, and judge their group as superior to the McKiscos' in order to pique the reader's interest in being part of the Divers' world, as much as it does the budding celebrity Rosemary's. The reader sees the Divers' sophistication and charm (patterned, in Fitzgerald's words, on a leisure "class . . . at their truly most brilliant & glamorous" [*Composition* 76] as represented by Gerald and Sara Murphy) through the eyes of a seventeen-year-old girl who is "unaware of its complexity and its lack of innocence." Though Fitzgerald identifies the man in the jockey cap as Dick Diver near the end of chapter 2 of book 1, Dick does not, as we noted, tell Rosemary his name on that occasion. That occurs only after he invites her to join his group at the start of chapter 4 in book 1. In between these two incidents Rosemary tells her mother, "I fell in love on the beach," and when her mother asks with whom, she says, "First with a whole lot of people who looked nice. Then with one man" (19). As a young actress whose first film was a hit, Rosemary is immediately recognized by everyone on the beach: they all know her name, but she doesn't know theirs. Yet as someone whose professional celebrity is a function of her visual attractiveness, she is herself at once visually attracted to "a whole lot of people who *looked* nice" (italics mine) and then to "one man," the charm of whose physical appearance will later be emphasized when Rosemary wants Dick to take a screen test. Certainly, it cannot be mere coincidence that in *Tender* Fitzgerald, in employing this same device of delaying our recognition of the protagonist (of delaying the narrator's learning his name), does so specifically from the narrative viewpoint of an *actor*, a representative of the world of stage and screen where a character has the kind of immediate physical recognizability that no character in prose fiction ever has. Which brings us to Monroe Stahr.

As Jay Gatsby's real name was James Gatz, so in *The Last Tycoon* Mr. Smith, the man who brushes past Wylie White in the airplane aisle, is really Monroe Stahr, traveling incognito. Though White and Mannie Schwartze see his face, and Wylie speaks to him, they don't mention his name, and Cecelia, who notices Smith only after he's passed by, doesn't realize who he is. Even after she reboards the plane in Nashville and runs into Stahr, she still doesn't make the connection. But when Wylie White gives Stahr the note that Mannie Schwartze had written him, Cecelia says, "I must be slow, for only then did I realize that Stahr was Mr. Smith" (16). All of which draws our attention to Stahr's real name. Though he's in the movies (indeed, Fitzgerald evokes him as the uncrowned king of Hollywood), Stahr has never appeared in a film. Moreover, when the stewardess says, "That Mr. Smith—or Mr. Stahr—I never remember seeing his name," Cecelia replies, "It's never on any pictures" (19). So it's not just his image that's never on screen, it's his name as well. "Stahr" and "star" are homophones and so are indistinguishable when spoken. The only way to differentiate between the two—to know that Stahr (though a major figure in films who had even been married to a movie star) is not himself a star—is to see his name in print. But since Stahr never allows his name to appear on any of his pictures, there's only one medium in which his named acquires this distinction—printed prose.

The second stylistic device Fitzgerald adopted in *Gatsby* and repeated in his two subsequent novels is to some extent related to the first. Whereas the first device involves Jay Gatsby's physical description being negligible enough that, as a character, he would be unrecognizable by the reader apart from his proper name, this other device involves the insertion, on two occasions, into each narrative of a nameless character who is identified only by a distinctive physical trait or behavior. I refer, of course, to the man that Nick and Jordan encounter in Gatsby's library at the first party Nick attends: "a stout, middle-aged man, with enormous owl-eyed spectacles, . . . sitting somewhat drunk on the edge of a great table, staring with unsteady concentration at the shelves of books" (37–38). Later that evening when Nick is leaving the party, he notices that the passenger in a car whose front wheel has come off exiting Gatsby's driveway is this same man, whom he now refers to as "Owl Eyes" (44). The second and final occasion on which Nick sees him is at Gatsby's interment: "I heard a car stop and then the sound of some one splashing after us over the soggy ground. I looked around. It was the man with owl-eyed glasses whom I found marvelling over Gatsby's books in the library one night three months before" (136). And it is that last phrase, "one night three months before," that suggests the main purpose of this nameless but physically recognizable character: he is a temporal gnomon, a measuring stick who appears near the beginning and again near the end of the narrative to make the story's arc more perspicuous, causing the reader to register how much has occurred between his two appearances. As the device of delaying the protagonist's introduction to the narrator is meant to emphasize the first-person limitedness of the narrative's starting point, so the temporal gnomon's second appearance is meant to evoke the godlike omniscience of its end point, meant to direct the reader's attention to how much we have come to know of the protagonist's mind and heart between the gnomon's two appearances.

   In *Tender Is the Night* the temporal gnomon first appears in book 1, chapter 21, as Dick Diver is pacing up and down outside a movie studio in Paris hoping to run into Rosemary. Dick is accosted by "a thin-faced American, perhaps thirty, with an air of being scarred and a slight but sinister smile" (106). Dick placed him as a type he'd known "since early youth—a type that loafed about tobacco stores" and that was "intimate to garages, where he had vague business conducted in undertones, to barber shops, to the lobbies of theatres" (106). When Dick asks what he's doing in Paris, he says he's in business here, "selling papers" to American tourists: "The contrast between the formidable manner and the mild profession was absurd." But the man assures Dick he'd made plenty of money last year and hands him "a newspaper clipping" of a "cartoon" showing "a stream of Americans pouring from the gangplank of a liner freighted with gold" (107). The nameless newspaper seller makes his second appearance near the novel's end when Dick, Nicole, and Tommy Barban are sitting at a sidewalk café on the Riviera discussing Dick and Nicole's separation and Tommy's becoming Nicole's protector. They are "suddenly interrupted by an insistent American, of sinister aspect, vending copies of The Herald and of The Times fresh from New York. . . . He brought a grey clipping from his purse—and Dick recognized it as he saw it. It cartooned millions of Americans pouring from liners with bags of gold" (345). In this case it is both the reader and the protagonist who experience the shock of recognition at the gnomon's second appearance.

As contrasted with *Gatsby* and *Tender,* in which the temporal gnomon is nameless, *The Last Tycoon*'s equivalent character has a name, Johnny Swanson. As Cecelia arrives at the studio on the night of the earthquake, she notices that "there were still some extras in the drug store across" the street: "'Old' Johnny Swanson stood on the corner in his semi-cowboy clothes staring gloomily past the moon. Once he had been as big in pictures as Tom Mix or Bill Hart—now it was too sad to speak to him and I hurried across the street and through the front gate" (21). Though Fitzgerald didn't live to write the episode involving Swanson's second appearance in the novel, we know what he had planned. In her March 6, 1941, letter to Edmund Wilson, who was editing the unfinished novel for publication, Sheilah Graham wrote,

> I think the final scene of all was to have been Stahr's funeral. And Scott was going to use an actual incident that happened at Thalberg's funeral. Harry Carey, a well-known actor in the old silents and popular in the early talkies, had been unable to get a job in pictures for several years before Thalberg died. He did not know Thalberg and was surprised to receive an invitation to act as pallbearer at his funeral. It was considered a great honor and only the most important and most intimate of Thalberg's friends (all of them important) were asked to be pallbearers. Harry Carey—slightly dazed, accepted and big shots at the funeral were amazed when they saw Carey, presuming he had an inside track of some sort with Thalberg, and as a direct result he was deluged with picture offers and has been working ever since. The invitation was a mistake. It was meant for someone else. (liv)

As Owl Eyes had suddenly shown up as one of the three mourners at Gatsby's burial, so Johnny Swanson was to have been, by mistake, one of the pallbearers at Stahr's funeral, the revival of Swanson's career demonstrating, as Bruccoli notes, that Monroe Stahr was "a star-maker even in his coffin" (Introduction lxvi).

Given the three large structures (social theatricality, the mythical method, the personal/professional conflict) and the two stylistic devices that Fitzgerald adopted in writing *The Great Gatsby* and then continued to develop in his next two novels, we can perhaps gain a further insight into his wish voiced in his 1940 letter to his daughter, Scottie, that he "had *never* relaxed or looked back—but said at the end of *The Great Gatsby*: 'I've found my line—from now on this comes first.'" With *Gatsby* he had created for his own special talent the essential elements of what his high-art fiction would be, elements he would repeat whenever he tried to write at that level, and at that length, again.

# CHAPTER SIX

# On the Son's Own Terms

THIS CONCLUDES THE THIRD BOOK of a trilogy devoted to the works of four writers—Poe and Borges in the first volume, Hart Crane in the second, and Fitzgerald here. The rationale for this grouping is my contention that these writers' works share, to a greater or lesser degree, an ongoing structure governing each author's relationship to his art, a relationship thematized in their work. As I explained in the preface to *The Mystery to a Solution*, this structure grew

> out of each writer's engagement with Platonic idealism, specifically, their more or less conscious understanding of the allegory of the cave as a womb fantasy that translated the notion of origin (and thus of the self) from a physical to a mental plane and their further understanding that this fantasized return to origin could be assimilated to another structure governing their relationship to their art: that sense of the male artist's ability (personified in the muse) to conceive and give birth to the work, the artist's identification with the muse as mother. What animates the art of these four writers in varying ways is a structure whose underpinning is the desire for a total return to the matrix (the space of origin and of original power), but a return *wholly on the son's own terms*. (xv–xvi)

The most explicit reference to Platonic idealism in Fitzgerald's work appears, of course, in chapter 6 of *The Great Gatsby*, where Nick, noting that Gatsby's "parents were shiftless and unsuccessful farm people," claims that James Gatz's "imagination had never really accepted them as his parents at all," and that Jay Gatsby "sprang from his Platonic conception of himself. He was a son of God—a phrase which, if it means anything, means just that" (76–77). As I note in chapter 3, Fitzgerald had given this same belief—that he was not the son of his parents—to Rudolph Miller (the figure of Gatsby as a child) in "Absolution," a belief that Rudolph describes as a sin of pride in confession and that Father Schwartz paraphrases as "you mean you thought you were too good to be the son of your parents" (*Short Stories* 262). And Fitzgerald was to come back to this childhood belief in a memoir he published in *Esquire* in July 1936 called "Author's House." Cast as a celebrity house tour, the essay invokes the gothic notion of the old dark house as a symbol of a person's psyche and family history, with Fitzgerald leading us through a series of personal revelations like those in "The Crack-Up" essays (also published in *Esquire* that same year). He begins with the cellar, a subterranean space containing "everything I've forgotten—all the complicated dark mixture of my youth and infancy that made me a fiction writer instead of a fireman or a soldier" (*Lost* 168). At one point the person taking the tour notices a "too-recent mound of dirt in the corner that . . . made you think of certain things in police reports" and asks about it. The author says,

> "That is where it is buried." . . .
> "What's buried?"
> "That's where I buried my love after—" he hesitates.
> "After you *killed* her?"
> "After I killed *it*."
> "I don't understand what you mean."
> The author does not look at the pile of earth.
> "That is where I buried my first childish love of myself, my belief that I would never die like other people, and that I wasn't the son of my parents but a son of a king, a king who ruled the whole world." (169)

Significantly, this description of the death of his childish self-love and his belief that he would never die is immediately preceded by the author's pointing out another "dark corner" in the cellar and explaining that "three months before I was born my mother lost her other two children and I think that came first of all though I don't know how it worked exactly. I think I started then to be a writer" (169). In his memoir "The Death of My Father," written "shortly after the death of Edward Fitzgerald" (Bruccoli, *Composition* 123) in January 1931 but unpublished until 1951, Fitzgerald recalled,

> I loved my father—always deep in my subconscious I have referred judgments back to him, [to] what he would have thought or done. He loved me—and felt a deep responsibility for me—I was born several months after the sudden death of my two elder sisters and he felt what the effect of this would be on

my mother, that he would be my only moral guide. He became that to the best of his ability. He came from tired old stock with very little left of vitality and energy but he managed to raise a little for me. (*Composition* 124)

When Fitzgerald translated this incident from his own life to Dick Diver's, he reproduced much of this passage's language, but he also made explicit "what the effect of this would be" on both mother and son: "Dick was born several months after the death of two young sisters and his father, guessing what would be the effect on Dick's mother, had saved him from a spoiling by becoming his moral guide" (232).

If the effect of losing her two daughters (ages one and three) just before the birth of her first son meant that Mollie McQuillan Fitzgerald would lavish love enough for three children on the one surviving child, then Edward Fitzgerald realized that Scott had to be protected from this avalanche of maternal affection, that he must be the one to teach Scott right from wrong, to deny him those things his mother never could. But in this, his father was not particularly successful. As Bruccoli notes, "Mollie spoiled Scott. Sent to nursery school in Buffalo in 1900, he cried so vociferously that he was withdrawn after the first morning. Edward tried to compensate for Mollie's indulgence by teaching his son standards of conduct from his Southern background" (*Grandeur* 17). But since Edward was a financial failure and more or less dominated by his wife, he was never particularly successful in moderating Mollie's desire to use her family's money to indulge her only son. Certainly, Fitzgerald, looking back in later life, blamed his own self-indulgence and bad behavior in part on his mother's spoiling him as a child, but by the time of the 1936 "Author's House" he had come to believe that the death of his two elder sisters shortly before his birth and the consequent flood of unqualified maternal affection he inherited at birth was what had led him to become a writer, though he claimed not to "know how it worked exactly." Yet that last is perhaps disingenuous, for as a child Fitzgerald would have been exposed to two opposing models and would have had little doubt about which he was drawn to: his father, Edward, who after losing his job at Proctor & Gamble in 1908 when Fitzgerald was eleven, would forever after be considered a failure by his son, and his mother, Mollie, whose family money kept them afloat and whose overwhelming love gave her son the sense that he was someone special, someone who could become anything he imagined. Sheilah Graham recalled from her conversations with Fitzgerald that his mother "was so much in love with her beautiful, blond, blue-eyed boy that she could deny him nothing. As far as she was concerned he could do no wrong. 'No matter what awful thing I did, I was just a bad brownie,' Scott explained. It is my belief that in all the drunken escapades throughout his life, he maintained the image of himself as the little bad brownie, whose charm could always win a woman's tolerance and forgiveness" (Graham 39). Yet as Fitzgerald grew older, that level of maternal love, coupled with his mother's eccentricities, began to make him uncomfortable. As Bruccoli notes, "As a child he had discouraged his mother from visiting him at camp and had entertained the fantasy that he was a royal foundling," and then later "as a young literary star he was embarrassed by his mother because she did not fit the glamorous image that was evolving about him. He loved his father, but Fitzgerald was always sensitive to—and perhaps resentful of—Edward's failure" (*Grandeur* 153). And Sheilah Graham remembers, "The indulgence of Scott's mother did not . . . endear her to him. In my time with him he considered her a fool—not because she loved him but because she did it with so little style. He was ashamed of her terrible clothes and ghastly manners" (Graham 39).

Yet if as a child, Fitzgerald fantasized that he was not the son of his parents, then who did he imagine he *was* the son of? By the time of *Gatsby*, he would have claimed that as an artist, a writer, he had fathered himself through an act of imaginative autogenesis, that the written body of his work, his corpus, was his shadow self (created by black ink on white paper), and that this was his real self because it bore the impress of his imagination and thus would preserve his essential spirit and name beyond the death of his body. Recall that Nick says it was specifically Gatsby's "imagination" that "had never really accepted" these "unsuccessful farm people" as "his parents." And while Gatsby, springing "from his Platonic conception of himself," was "a son of God," Fitzgerald in the 1936 "Author's House" believed as a child he was "the son of a king who ruled the whole world." Yet if by the time of his third novel he felt that as a writer he had imaginatively fathered himself, at the time of his first novel Fitzgerald had begun reimagining his own parents to make them more suited to his exalted sense of his own personality, reimagining them in the parents of Amory Blaine. The first chapter of *This Side of Paradise* bears the title "Amory, son of Beatrice," and the chapter's first sentence runs, "Amory Blaine inherited from his mother every trait, except the stray inexpressible few, that made him worth while" (11). On the novel's opening page Amory's father is written off with a lick and a promise: his given name is never mentioned, and he is described as "an ineffectual, inarticulate man with a taste for Byron" (11). We know that Edward Fitzgerald, whom Scott thought of as

198 F. Scott Fitzgerald's Fiction

ineffectual, read the poems of Byron and Shelley to his son as a child, but the main alteration Fitzgerald makes in turning his own father into Amory's is that Amory's has money—though, predictably enough, not money acquired through his own initiative. Rather, he "grew wealthy at thirty through the deaths of two elder brothers, successful Chicago brokers" (11). One wonders whether this detail of the two elder brothers whose deaths endowed Amory's father with material wealth represented a conscious or unconscious transformation of Fitzgerald's two elder sisters whose deaths endowed him with a wealth of maternal love. At any rate, Amory's father is virtually gone from the novel by the end of its first paragraph, and the second paragraph begins, "But Beatrice Blaine! There was a woman!" (11).

Whereas Fitzgerald's reimagining of his father had simply involved making the financial failure Edward rich, his reimagining of Mollie Fitzgerald as Beatrice amounts to a complete makeover. As James Mellow notes,

> Mollie McQuillan, educated at the Visitation Convent [in St. Paul] and then at Manhattanville College in New York, had traveled extensively; had toured Europe four times. Family photographs of her reveal . . . a woman with a wan smile and a distracted, faraway look. She was an indiscriminate reader of innocuous novels and sentimental poetry. She had a liking for the maudlin verses of Alice and Phoebe Cary. Friends considered Mollie McQuillan eccentric and rather careless about dress. She was apt to arrive for a visit wearing one black shoe and one brown, because she preferred to break in a new pair one shoe at a time. An acquaintance described her as "dressed like the devil, always coming apart." (13)

Apparently Mollie's convent, finishing-school education had left her largely unfinished. She was known for making remarks in social situations that in their frankness bordered on the tactless, if not the zany, while her conversation otherwise could range from the eccentric to the bizarre, as could her taste in clothes, particularly in hats. In Fitzgerald's memoir/story "An Author's Mother," published in *Esquire* in September 1936, this last detail begins his description of her: "She was a halting old lady in a black dress and a rather preposterously high-crowned hat that some milliner had foisted upon her declining sight" (*Price* 736). In reimagining his mother as Beatrice O'Hara Blaine, Fitzgerald took the facts of his mother's life and polished them to a brilliance befitting the parent of a rising literary star. "Early pictures" of Beatrice taken . . . in Rome at the Sacred Heart Convent—an educational extravagance that in her youth was only for the daughters of the exceptionally wealthy—showed the exquisite delicacy of her features, the consummate art and simplicity of her clothes. A brilliant education she had—her youth passed in renaissance glory; she was versed in the latest gossip of the Older Roman Families; known by name as a fabulously wealthy American girl to Cardinal Vitori and Queen Margherita and more subtle celebrities that one must have had some culture even to have heard of. (11)

Fitzgerald tells us that "when Amory was five he was already a delightful companion" for his mother, indeed, one whose companionship she clearly preferred to that of her husband, and the first interaction between mother and son shown in the novel depicts Beatrice spoiling him:

> "Amory."
> "Yes, Beatrice." (Such a quaint name for his mother; she encouraged it.)
> "Dear, don't *think* of getting out of bed yet. I've always suspected that early rising in early life makes one nervous. Clothilde is having your breakfast brought up."
> "All right." (12)

Amory always addresses his mother by her first name, and their conversations, which make the two seem as if they were equals, often border on the flirtatious. During these early years Amory was in the process of "deriving a highly specialized education from his mother" (12), and a large part of this education was in the arts: "She fed him sections of the 'Fêtes Galantes' before he was ten; at eleven he could talk glibly, if rather reminiscently, of Brahms and Mozart and Beethoven" (13). Then, when Amory goes away to prep school in the East, Beatrice, set on encouraging his intellectual and artistic development, arranges for him to have a surrogate father in the person of one of her former suitors, who "had gone through a spiritual crisis, joined the Catholic Church, and was now—Monsignor Darcy" (14). Darcy, based on Fitzgerald's own surrogate intellectual and artistic father Monsignor Sigourney Fay to whom *This Side of Paradise* was dedicated, is described entering a room "clad in his full purple regalia from thatch to toe" looking like a "Turner sunset" and attracting "both admiration and attention" (29–30). He had written two novels, one before and one after his conversion: "He was intensely ritualistic, startlingly dramatic. . . . Children adored him because he was like a child; youth revelled in his company because he was still a youth and couldn't be shocked. In the proper land and century he might have been a Richelieu" (30). At Darcy and Amory's first meeting, "the jovial, impressive prelate who could dazzle an embassy ball and the green-eyed, intent youth, in his first long trousers, accepted in their own minds a relation of father and son within a half-hour's conversation" (30). So within the first thirty pages of his first novel, the boy who didn't believe he was the son of his parents has created out of his own imagination a new set of parents—brilliant, socially adept, better educated, and better dressed.

## 2

One can well imagine that Mollie Fitzgerald, with her taste for sentimental novels and the maudlin poetry of Alice and Phoebe Cary, would have early on instilled in her son an interest in imaginative literature and that his initial efforts in this area would have been encouraged by her unqualified love. Which raises the question of what form a male writer imagines his muse as taking. Of course, the classical Muses were the nine sister goddesses in Greek mythology who presided over poetry, music, the arts, and sciences, their mother being the goddess Mnemosyne (Memory). Yet for all practical purposes, the notion of the muse, considered as an inspiring or evocative other, usually assumes for a male writer the form of an imagined ideal reader for whose understanding and approval he labors. And if the writer is very good, then this ideal reader is imagined as being a person of refined and educated taste, subtle perception, and wide experience, someone who possesses the highest artistic standards and can appreciate when the writer meets or exceeds these. Though Mollie Fitzgerald would surely have been the person whose admiring approval Fitzgerald sought for his first efforts at storytelling or poetry, it seems clear that by the age of twelve or thirteen he had begun to doubt her taste and judgment in literature. Which is to say, he had begun to see that the kind of writing he liked and wanted to do, his mother neither understood nor cared for, had begun to sense that Mollie's early encouragement of his efforts had been less a matter of aesthetic judgment than unqualified mother love—all of which would have left him with an early sense of his muse as a mother figure, but an uncomprehending one. (Indeed, even Amory "had no illusions about" his mother [12]: "Amory became thirteen, rather tall and slender, and more than ever *on* to his Celtic mother"

[15].) Moreover, as Fitzgerald reached his teenage years, his mother, no doubt reacting to her husband's lack of success in business, ceased to encourage, and perhaps even actively to discourage, her son's "literary ambitions, hoping that he would become a successful businessman" (Bruccoli, *Grandeur* 23). In an August 1939 letter to Morton Kroll, Fitzgerald recalled, "My mother did me the disservice of throwing away all but two of my very young efforts—way back at twelve and thirteen, and later I found that the surviving fragments had more quality than some of the stuff written in the tightened-up days of seven or eight years later" (*Letters* 593).

One need look no further than Fitzgerald's autobiographical story "An Author's Mother," written a month or so before Mollie's death in September 1936 and published that same month in *Esquire*, to see how this melancholy sense of his mother as uncomprehending muse (as that earliest reader whose understanding and informed approval he could never gain for his later, authentic work) stayed with him to the end of her life. In the story the "halting old lady in a black silk dress and a rather preposterously high-crowned hat" goes down to a department store to buy her son a birthday present. Though she intends to get him a bathrobe, she passes through the store's book department and wonders if he wouldn't like a book instead:

> Her son was a successful author. She had by no means abetted him in the choice of that profession but had wanted him to be an army officer or else go into business. . . . An author was something distinctly peculiar. . . . Of course if her son could have been an author like Longfellow, or Alice and Phoebe Cary, that would have been different. . . . [A]s she lingered in the bookstore this morning her mind kept reverting persistently to the poems of Alice and Phoebe Cary. How lovely the poems had been! Especially the one about the girl instructing the artist how to paint a picture of her mother. Her own mother used to read her that poem.
>
> But the books by her son were not vivid to her, and while she was proud of him in a way, and was always glad when a librarian mentioned him or when someone asked her if she was his mother, her secret opinion was that such a profession was risky and eccentric. (*Price* 736–37)

The old lady asks the salesman if he has the poems of Alice and Phoebe Cary, but he says he's never heard of them. As she's leaving the store, the old lady becomes dizzy, faints, and falls, cutting her forehead, and an ambulance is called to take her to the hospital. She doesn't recall what happened, and when the doctor tells her she had a fall, her reply is, "My son will write about it." The doctor then says, "Don't talk for just a moment. . . . I want to keep this little cut together till we can make a suture":

> Nonetheless she moved her head and said in a determined voice:
> "I didn't say my son was a suture—I said he was an author."
> "You misunderstood me . . . I meant about your forehead. A 'suture' is where someone cuts themselves a little—"
> Her pulse fluttered and he gave her spirits of ammonia to hold her till she got to the hospital floor.
> "No, my son is not a suture," she said. "Why did you say that? He's an *author.*" She spoke very slowly as if she was unfamiliar with the words coming from her tired mouth. "An author is someone who writes books."
> . . . She raised herself to a supreme effort and remembering the only book she knew really in her heart announced astonishingly, "—my son . . . who wrote 'The Poems of Alice and Phoebe Cary—.'" (*Price* 738–39)

As she loses consciousness for the last time, the intern accompanying her "could not know what she was thinking . . . and would never have guessed it was that Alice and Phoebe Cary had come to call upon her, and taken her hands, and led her back gently into the country she understood" (739). At once comic and melancholy, the situation involves both the humorous byplay of "suture" and "author" and the ironic counterpoint by which the mother's particularly liking a Cary poem about "the girl instructing the artist how to paint a picture of her mother" becomes a self-referential detail in Fitzgerald's verbal painting of his own mother's picture. Indeed, one wonders whether he compared this late, realistic portrait to that early, idealized one of Mollie as Beatrice Blaine.

One can begin to see that Fitzgerald's realization as a teenager that this figure of the muse-as-mother was not an ideal reader but an uncomprehending one and his attempt, through his art, to create in the character of Beatrice Blaine an idealized image of a mother more suited to an artist are both linked to the myth of Pygmalion and Galatea that structures his mature novels. Recall James Mellow's comment about Fitzgerald's "nagging urge to remake and reeducate the women he was involved with—his wife, his daughter, his mistress" (23)—a group that also included his younger sister Annabel, the eighteen-year-old starlet Lois Moran with whom he was romantically involved in Hollywood in the mid-1920s, Beatrice Dance with whom he had an affair in Asheville in 1935, and Sheilah Graham with whom he had a three-year liaison in Hollywood. The form this reeducation invariably took was Fitzgerald's prescribing books for the women to read and then discussing with them the things he admired in these works. Judging by Fitzgerald's letters to Scottie when she was at Vassar and by the course of study described in Sheilah Graham's *A College of One*, we can say that though the books he recommended were not exclusively works of literature, the lion's share of titles *were* fiction and poetry, and the goal of this reeducation was to broaden the women's literary knowledge and shape their literary taste so it replicated his own. The narcissism that lies at the heart of the Pygmalion myth can, as indicated in the previous chapter, account for Fitzgerald's impulse to remake the women he was involved with. But I would suggest that what also lay behind this impulse was his sense that he had never really been able to accomplish this reshaping of literary judgment and taste with the very first woman he had ever loved, that though he had in his first novel imagined such a reshaping, imagined a mother who "fed" her son sections of Verlaine's and Debussy's *Fêtes galantes* "before he was ten," he had to face the fact that his real mother, up to the very time of her death, never understood or appreciated what her author son wrote, that he could well imagine her last words being "my son . . . who wrote 'The Poems of Alice and Phoebe Cary.'"

Yet if Fitzgerald's earliest image of his muse was that of an at-first encouraging and then uncomprehending and discouraging mother figure, his second image of this inspiring other, once he'd fallen in love with Zelda and they'd married, exhibited a similar alteration—but from a different cause. (Recall in this regard that Gatsby specifically cites Daisy's incomprehension, her lack of understanding of his dreams, as the reason she fails to correspond to his idealized image of her: he tells Nick, "And she doesn't understand. . . . She used to be able to understand. We'd sit for hours—" [86].) Something of Zelda's character and personality traits went into most of Fitzgerald's memorable female protagonists, and her imaginative excitement and vitality, which mirrored Fitzgerald's own, generated virtually all of the social situations that were his material. Zelda was the muse not as mother but as lover. And while she was an inspiring figure for Fitzgerald early in their marriage, by 1924 during the writing of *Gatsby* on the Riviera, when Zelda became attracted to the French naval aviator Edouard Jozan and Fitzgerald felt betrayed, this began to change. In the nine agonizing years between the publications of *Gatsby* and *Tender*, Fitzgerald felt that Zelda had progressed from being a distracting presence to being a disruptive influence on his work; instead of helping him by arranging a lifestyle that would give him the time and domestic tranquility to write, she hindered him because she had become jealous of his work—jealous, at first, of the time it took away from his entertaining her and then even more jealous of the fact that he *had work* while she had none. What Fitzgerald discovered was that his efforts to remake and reeducate Zelda in his own image had succeeded only too well, that his shaping of her literary taste had made her want to (and believe she could) be a professional writer too. And not only this: he also discovered that while he was struggling to finish his novel of psychiatry and insanity, she had secretly begun writing a novel on the same subject.

The showdown came on May 28, 1933, when Fitzgerald, Zelda, and Zelda's psychiatrist, Dr. Rennie, met for a joint session with a stenographer present. In the extract from the typescript that Bruccoli reproduces in his biography, Fitzgerald begins, "I say I am a different sort of person than Zelda, that my equipment for being a writer, for being an artist, is a different equipment from hers. Her theory is that anything is possible and that a girl has just got to get along and so she has the right therefore to destroy me completely in order to satisfy herself" (*Grandeur* 349). Fitzgerald argued that their life together was not their joint imaginative property and that Zelda must stop writing her novel because its publication would kill the impact of his own. He tells her that "everything that we have done is mine—if we make a trip—if I make a trip to Panama and you and I go around—I am the professional novelist and I am supporting you. That is all of my material. None of it is your material" (*Grandeur* 350). Referring to the economic impact on their family if *Tender* should be a financial failure because Zelda's book had preempted his subject, he goes on to invoke the tough times of the Depression: "I have got all the worries that everybody also has of making a living and I find an enemy in the family, treachery behind my back, or what I consider that" (*Grandeur* 350). The ultimate solution was that Zelda turned her novel's manuscript over to Scott, and after he edited and recast certain aspects, he recommended it to Maxwell Perkins at Scribner's. Speaking of Zelda's *Save Me the Waltz*, Fitzgerald told Tony Buttitta in 1935 that "writing *Waltz* seemed to have calmed some of her egomania and freed her from competitive drives," but "it's a bad novel, not a bad book. A psychiatric document of the schizophrenic mind in action. A mind gone berserk, evidently not with a natural drive or ambition, but consumed by a passion to dazzle and show off. I know her better than I know myself. *We could be twins.* She pushed herself beyond the limit, hoping to blaze a trail as I did. I made it, she broke down" (Buttitta 125, italics mine).

Fitzgerald's statement that he and Zelda "could be twins" evokes the narcissistic component of the Pygmalion and Galatea myth according to which the artist in sculpting his image of the perfect woman creates an oppositely-gender mirror image of himself. In the myth, as we have noted, this union of the fathering artist with his own self-generated image (once it has come to life) is implicitly understood as a kind of father/daughter incest, a content made explicit in the story of Cinyras and his daughter Myrrha. And we saw how in *Tender Is the Night* this component surfaced in the incest of Nicole and her father, which was symbolically reinscribed in the marriage of a doctor as a father figure and his patient. If Fitzgerald's earliest image of his muse was a mother figure whose unconditional love was at first encouraging of his artistic bent but whose later incomprehension was discouraging, and if Fitzgerald's later image of the muse, based on Zelda, was that of a lover and spouse who ultimately showed this same alteration of response, then this similarity in their effect suggests that, by the time of his writing *Tender*, a further assimilation of the figures of mother and lover was taking place in Fitzgerald's image of the muse. All of which sheds light on what would seem an otherwise puzzling manipulation of Freudian symbolism in *Tender*.

Having just returned from the war, Dick begins to help Franz Gregorovius with his treatment of Nicole at Dohmler's sanatorium, and after a few weeks Franz asks him where matters stand, since "apparently the girl is in love with you." Dick says, "I like her. She's attractive. What do you want me to do . . . devote my life to her? . . . I'll do whatever Doctor Dohmler says" (159–60). But Dick, who has already begun to suspect he is falling in love with Nicole, has

> little faith that Dohmler would throw much light on the matter; he himself was the incalculable element involved. By no conscious volition of his own, the thing had drifted into his hands. *It reminded him of a scene in his childhood when everyone in the house was looking for the lost key to the silver closet, Dick knowing he had hid it under the handkerchiefs in his mother's top drawer.* (160, italics mine)

A key is, of course, a standard Freudian phallic symbol, and in this memory the son places it inside an enclosure belonging to his mother. The key's phallic significance is reemphasized when Nicole, on the night of the dinner party at Tarmes, suddenly excuses herself from the table and Mrs. McKisco finds her later "in her bedroom dissolved in crazy laughter," telling her "she could not go in the bathroom because the key was thrown down the well" (192).

As critics have noted, Fitzgerald begins using phallic symbolism in relation to Dick at the very start of book 2, when Dick makes his way to Vienna in 1916 while Freud is still alive and takes a room on "the Damenstiffgasse" (West's emendation of the 1934 first edition's "Damenstiff Strasse"). Whether it is "Strasse" ("street") or "Gasse" ("lane") is of less importance than the proper name "Damenstiff." According to Frommer's online guide to a walking tour of Vienna, there is a Damenstiftstrasse in the city; the name "Damenstift"—a "ladies' foundation" or a "ladies' institution"—designates an upper-class ladies' finishing school, such as the Savoysches Damenstift (Savoy Foundation for Noble Ladies) founded in 1688 by the Duchess of Savoy-Carignan, where, according to Frommer, "countless generations of well-born Austrian damsels struggled to learn 'the gentle arts of womanhood.' " Though the German word "Stift" can mean "foundation, institution, convent," there is also a word "Stift" that means a "nail, spike, or peg," and Fitzgerald clearly intends a phallic pun here, with the name's evocation of penile rigidity being linked to the word for "women"—a rigidity underlined in Fitzgerald's choice of "Damen-*stiff*" rather than "Damen*stift*." And this phallic pun is made explicit a few sentences later when Fitzgerald shows Dick (a slang word for penis) walking around his room on the street named "Damenstiff," repeating to himself, "Lucky Dick, you big stiff" (134) as he congratulates himself on having made the psychological discoveries that will constitute his first book—the same implied sexualization of superior "knowledge" connoted by Dick's childhood memory of the key, as we shall see. This imagery that symbolizes the potency of Dick's intellect and spirit at the start of his career, reappears later but only to imply his growing psychological impotence: "Between the time he found Nicole flowering under a stone on the Zurichsee and the moment of his meeting with Rosemary" in Rome "the spear had been blunted" (229).

Returning to the detail of the phallic key hidden "in his mother's top drawer," we can see that Fitzgerald means to evoke several things with this sudden irruption of a seemingly extraneous memory. First of all, the reminiscence crops up just as Dick is beginning to realize the depth of his attraction to Nicole and as he is about to confront a psychiatric authority figure (the sanatorium's owner, Doctor Dohmler, in whose care Nicole's father has placed his daughter), a figure who wants to know about Dick's growing romantic attachment to Nicole. Second, it is, in good Freudian fashion, specifically a memory of childhood that seems to rise unbidden from the unconscious: in the sentence that leads into the memory he says that his involvement with Nicole had come about "by no conscious volition of his own." And finally this unbidden memory, symbolically evoking a son's incestuous attraction to his mother, serves at the same time to sexualize, in relation to his mother, the notion of superior knowledge: "Everyone in the house was looking for the lost key to the silver closet," but only Dick *knew* where it was. When this childhood memory recurs, Dick is about to speak to Doctor Dohmler because Dohmler and Franz, realizing that the improvement in Nicole's case has been the result of her transference to Dick, want him to bring the transference to an end, but they want to know how emotionally involved Dick has become. When Dick says, "It's certainly a situation," Dohmler thunders, "But it is a professional situation." When Dick admits, "I'm half in love with her—the question of marrying her has passed through my mind" (161), Dohmler realizes that Dick's superior professional knowledge of Nicole as a patient is on the point of turning into the carnal knowledge of a spouse, a literal sexualization of superior knowledge that resonates both with Dick's childhood memory and the Damenstiff pun and with Fitzgerald's relationship to his own mother. For by the time Fitzgerald was a teenager their relationship involved a love based on differing degrees of knowledge: on the one hand, the love of an uncomprehending mother for a son, a love characterized by the mother's not knowing who her son really was, and on the other hand, the son's superior knowledge of who his mother really was and what her love for him actually amounted to—for like Amory Blaine, Fitzgerald "was *on* to his Celtic mother."

The full meaning of Dick's seemingly extraneous childhood memory, symbolically evoking a son's incestuous desire, is elaborated later by another seemingly extraneous detail that pops into Dick's mind at the time of his father's death: that his father, "guessing what would be the effect on Dick's mother" of the death of Dick's two young sisters just before his birth, "had saved him from a spoiling by becoming his moral guide." One sense of this passage is that the father feels he has to stand as a buffer between the mother's overwhelming love and the surviving child to prevent the damage that that level of maternal affection could cause. But another, implicit sense (reinforced by Dick's earlier description of his childhood memory) is that the father, the authority figure who forbids, also stands between son and mother to prevent the son's libido from becoming too attached to the mother, to prevent the son's desire to reciprocate that overwhelming maternal affection from becoming so sexualized that it damages the son's future development, affecting his ability to find a spouse.

This possibility was clearly on Fitzgerald's mind during the time he was working on *Tender*: in his short story "Babylon Revisited," published in 1931, Fitzgerald has the protagonist Charlie Wales, who is trying to regain custody of his daughter, Honoria, in the wake of his wife's death and his own break-down, imagine what his life with his daughter would be like if he succeeds: "The present was the thing—work to do and someone to love. But not to love too much, for he knew the injury that a father can do to a daughter or a mother to a son by attaching them too closely: afterward, out in the world, the child would seek in the marriage partner the same blind tenderness and, failing probably to find it, turn against love and life" (*Short Stories* 628). This passage reflects Fitzgerald's own realization that with Zelda's breakdown, he was going to have increasingly to stand between Zelda and their daughter, Scottie, between the erratic behavior of the mother and the possible effect of this on their daughter, that he would have to take on a buffering role very like that which his father had assumed in relation to Mollie and himself. And Fitzgerald's concern, like Charlie's, is that his expanded, more intensive role in Scottie's life might attach his daughter too closely to him, that he might be tempted to spoil his daughter to make up for the absence or absent-mindedness of her mother, and that he must therefore guard against this by being more exacting about her upbringing. Or, to recall what Dick Diver says when de-fending his strictness in raising his children, particularly his daughter, Topsy, "Either one learns politeness at home . . . or the world teaches it to you with a whip and you may get hurt in the process. What do I care whether Topsy 'adores' me or not? I'm not bringing her up to be my wife" (290).

One can see, then, that, when Dick suddenly recovers a childhood mem-ory symbolically portraying a son's incestuous desire for his mother at pre-cisely the moment that he acknowledges to a professional authority figure his sexual desire for a patient (a symbolic daughter), Fitzgerald, in effect, evokes his sense of a generational reciprocity of incestuous desire: the idea that a child's desire for an oppositely-gendered parent repeats itself once that child has become a parent as an incestuous attraction to an oppositely-gendered child. All of which suggests that Fitzgerald's rendering of Nicole as a victim of actual and symbolic father-daughter incest seemed to him necessarily to entail an evocation of Dick's incestuous attraction to his mother, and since Dick and Nicole were modeled in large part on Scott and Zelda, one has the sense that in writing *Tender* Fitzgerald was dealing with the way his mother's spoiling him as a child had likely caused him, as he says in "Babylon Re-visited," "to seek in the marriage partner the same blind tenderness." (Just as the adult Fitzgerald repeatedly blamed his willful, selfish behavior on his mother's spoiling him, after Zelda's breakdown, he consistently blamed Zel-da's similar behavior on her mother's spoiling her. No doubt that is one of the senses of his remark that he and Zelda "could be twins.") All of which in turn suggests that during the writing of *Tender* Fitzgerald was also dealing with the way that his image of the muse had become an amalgam, an overlay, of two figures, both mother and lover.

3

Earlier we suggested that for a male writer the figure of a muse is, practically speaking, a self-generated image of his ideal reader, one who completely comprehends what the writer is doing, who, in effect, knows the writer's *real self* as embodied in his work. Such an ideal reader is an imaginary other, the male writer's self-projected double or shadow self, there being in actuality no person other than the writer himself who understands his book as fully or in exactly the same way as he does. And the idealized or fantasized figure of a male writer's muse is characteristically imagined as female because what the writer desires from the ideal reader is not only that this imaginary other comprehend the real self contained in his book but also that the other admire and *love* that self. In this regard there are two moments in *Gatsby* that evoke the kind of idealized knowledge and love that a male writer imagines an ideal reader providing. When the narrator Nick Carraway (the story's fictive writer) first meets Gatsby, his description of Gatsby's smile embodies that ideal of perfect understanding of oneself that one seeks in an idealized other: "It understood you just so far as you wanted to be understood, believed in you as you would like to believe in yourself and assured you that it had precisely the impression of you that, at your best, you hoped to convey" (40). But of course Nick's interpretation of that smile is an imaginary self-projection of reciprocated desire.

The second moment in *Gatsby*—one that depicts a real reciprocated desire but that also figuratively represents the way a male writer's ideal of a female muse can be periodically embodied in an actual woman who attracts his libido—occurs at the end of chapter 6 when Gatsby kisses Daisy. Since at the start of this chapter Gatsby is said, as "a son of God," to have sprung from "his Platonic conception of himself," it is only predictable that this imagery would recur at the chapter's end when Gatsby embodies in Daisy his idealized image of the perfect female response to his desire, his female double: when Gatsby projects his ideal "unutterable visions" onto Daisy, weds them to her real "perishable breath," Nick says Gatsby knew "his mind would never romp again like the mind of God." And that detail of the embodied ideal's "perishable breath" naturally brings us to the further evolution of the image of Fitzgerald's muse in *The Last Tycoon*.

At the time Fitzgerald began writing *The Last Tycoon*, his mother was dead and his wife—institutionalized and unable to function on her own—was, in effect, dead to any shared married life. At this point he had already projected the image of his muse onto a new woman, Sheilah Graham, who resembled the young Zelda and whose literary reeducation he had taken on—a younger woman who by all accounts revived Fitzgerald's creative libido in much the same way that Kathleen Moore brought back Stahr's sexual desire. The myth of Pygmalion and Galatea translated into that of Orpheus and Eurydice shows how the power of an artist to bring a mental image to life becomes the power of an artist to bring a shade back to life, and the fact that Fitzgerald had the Orpheus and Eurydice myth in mind is apparent from his choice of time and setting for the scene in which Stahr finds the woman who resembles the dead Minna. The setting is the back lot of Stahr's movie studio, which Cecelia describes as "thirty acres of fairyland," a place that "looked like the torn picture books of childhood, like fragments of stories dancing in a open fire. I never lived in a house with an attic but a back lot must be something like that and at night of course in an enchanted distorted way, it all comes true" (25). The mention of fairyland and the torn picture books of childhood evoke this as a place of dream images and unconscious affect, and it is there in the immediate aftermath of an earthquake that Kathleen first appears. Fitzgerald makes the earthquake serve two symbolic purposes: it breaks a water main and floods the back lot, evoking Eliot's "freeing-of-the-waters" motif from *The Waste Land*—a figuration of restored sexual potency foreshadowing Stahr's renewal of sexual desire with the appearance of Kathleen—and it breaks open the earth and disinters things, conjuring up the return of shades from the underworld. We should note that Fitzgerald has Cecelia compare the picture maker's back lot—this place where the picture book images of childhood are stored—to the attic of a house, a comparison that recalls Fitzgerald's earlier use of the gothic "old dark house" trope in his July 1936 memoir "Author's House"—except that there the region of the house where childhood memories were stored was not the attic but the cellar, the subterranean place where Fitzgerald buried "my first childish love of myself, my belief that I would never die like other people, and that I wasn't the son of my parents" and where in a "dark corner" lurk his two sisters who died before he was born, leading to his own birth as a writer. This subterranean space of death and birth, in effect, assimilates two classical subterranean realms, the underworld of shades and

Plato's cave, and it is in relation to this second image that we must look again at Fitzgerald's engagement with Platonic idealism.

The best-known text in which Plato presents his theory of "forms" or "ideas" is, of course, the "allegory of the cave" from book 7 of *The Republic*. As I noted in *Hart Crane's Poetry*:

> In the allegory of the cave, Plato figures the relationship between a three-dimensional object and its ideal form as being like that between an object and its shadow outline projected on a flat surface, a comparison that transfers to the ideal form the attributes of a shadow, of a schematic two-dimensionality associated with Euclidean plane geometry. Since a Platonic ideal form is basically an apotheosized mental image that has been translated from an individual mind into an imaginary, independent realm of absolute intelligibility, and since Plato's visual model for the relationship of a material object to its mental image is that of shadow projection, the ideal form's *bodilessness* (by which I mean its lack not of a bodily outline but of an opaque third dimension) is simply a means of imaging the *difference* between the *visible* world of objects and the *invisible* world of ideas as the *visible difference* between three dimensions and two.
>
> In a similar manner, an ideal form's *transparency* figures its pure intelligibility, its complete openness to sight as opposed to the opacity of a material object. What Plato does in translating the model of shadow projection from the dark cave of material objects to the bright realm of intelligible ones is to reverse the priority (the causal relation) between a body and its shadow, so that an ideal form becomes more "substantial" than its material object by becoming the original from which the object derives, as if the *object* were simply the form's *material shadow*. Moreover, in its translation from the lower world to the higher, the projected shadow, considered as the visual representation of a mental image, undergoes a symbolic color change: We traditionally imagine an ideal form as not a shadowy but a luminous outline (in keeping with the imagery of intelligibility as light), literally as a glorified shadow ("glory" in the sense of an aureole or nimbus, the light about a sacred body). (88)

In this same passage I further suggested that

> It requires little imagination to see that Plato's "subterranean cavern" . . . , with its fettered inhabitants, is a figurative telluric womb, particularly since this same trope lies behind the famous passage from the *Theaetetus* in which the Socratic method of leading people from the cave of shadow images to the sunlit realm

of intelligible objects is compared at length to the art of midwifery (practiced by Socrates's mother), with Socrates remarking that his art is to assist "the soul that is in travail of birth." . . . It requires, however, somewhat more imagination to see that the realm of intelligible objects (i.e., of Platonic forms considered as reified ideas) represents an intellectual transfiguration or sublimation of the womblike cavern of shadow images, sublimation in the sense both of a raising of something up to and beyond a threshold and of a purifying that transforms a solid body into a diaphanous substance (as in the chemical sense of subliming a solid directly to a gas without passing through the liquid state). (87–88)

Of course, Plato's otherworld of ideal forms became the paradigm for Christianity's imaging of the afterlife of disembodied spirits, and just as Plato's image of ideas (considered as two-dimensional shadow outlines) made the transition from dark to light when the ideas moved from the subterranean cave to the bright realm of ideal forms, so the classical notion of dead souls as "shades" in the underworld was transformed in Christianity into the image of souls as glorified, two-dimensional bodily outlines in heaven.

Now consider all this in relation to Jacques Lacan's notion of the mirror stage, that "phase in the constitution of the individual located between the ages of six and eighteen months" (Laplanche and Pontalis 250). As Jean Laplanche and Jean-Bertrand Pontalis explain,

Though still in a state of powerlessness and motor incoordination, the infant anticipates on an imaginary plane the apprehension and mastery of its bodily unity. This imaginary unification comes about by means of *identification with the image of the counterpart* as total *Gestalt*; it is exemplified concretely by the experience in which the child perceives its own reflection in a mirror.

The mirror phase is said to constitute the matrix and first outline of what is to become the ego. (250–51, italics mine)

In *Doubling and Incest/Repetition and Revenge* I suggested that, as far as I knew,

infants between the ages of six and eighteen months don't spend all that much time looking at themselves in mirrors. Rather, they spend most of their waking hours with their mothers. Consequently, Lacan says that the image with which the infant identifies is that of "its counterpart" or of its own reflection in a mirror. In filling the role of the infant's counterpart at that age, the mother acts as the child's living mirror image. And it is from its interaction with this image of its self that the child learns the basic constituents of all human interaction—duplication (both visual and vocal) and reciprocity—indeed, learns the principle on which learning itself is based, mimicry. The infant discovers in the mirror of the mother's face that a smile begets a smile, a laugh a laugh, a frown a frown. It learns that the proper response to a hug is a hug, a kiss a kiss, and so on. In short the child learns . . . through this process of mimicry . . . the basic expressive elements in the vocabulary of human emotion. (212).

But a difficulty arises: "The principles of duplication and reciprocity would be reinforced by the child's reflected image in a mirror" only up to that point, emphasized in Ovid's version of the myth of Narcissus, "when the child tries to make physical contact" (212) with its reflected image. Recall that in Ovid when young Narcissus falls in love with his image in the pool, he at first mistakes what he sees for another youth who inhabits the world below the surface of the water, as he does the world above. Gazing into the pool, Narcissus says, "I am charmed, and I see; but what I see and what charms me I cannot find . . . and, to make me grieve the more, no mighty ocean separates us," but "by a thin barrier of water we are kept apart." Addressing what he takes to be this other youth, he says,

> Some ground for hope you offer with your friendly looks, and when I have stretched out my arms to you, you stretch yours too. When I have smiled, you smile back; and I have often seen tears, when I weep, on your cheeks. My becks you answer with your nod. (3:157)

This passage of gestural reciprocity leads to a moment of terrible realization that occurs at the border between the visual and the vocal registers: "And, as I suspect from the movement of your sweet lips, you answer my words as well, but words which do not reach my ears.—Oh, I am he! I have felt it, I know now my own image. I burn with love of my own self; I both kindle the flames and suffer them" (3:157). Understanding that he can never consummate this love, can never be physically joined with his image, Narcissus wastes away with hopeless longing beside his pool, and his body is transformed into the eponymous flower.

As Laplanche and Pontalis note, "Concerning the infant's behaviour when confronted with its reflection in a mirror . . . Lacan draws attention to [the child's] 'triumphant assumption of the image, with the accompanying jubilant mimicry and the playful complacency with which the specular identification is controlled'" (251), and Lacan considers the mirror stage as "the setting up of the first roughcast of the ego." In identifying with its image (a finite unified form), the infant "anticipates a bodily unity which it still objectively lacks," and "this primordial experience is basic to the imaginary nature of the ego, which is constituted right from the start as an 'ideal ego'" (251). Not only does the infant's identification with its image present the ideal of that bodily motor control it will eventually achieve; it also presents an external unified form by means of which, that is, in relation to which, the ceaseless flux of ideas, sensations, emotions, memories that constitutes a being's interior life can be associated and unified. The infant's identification with its image is the first step in a movement of inner to outer and back to inner that will ultimately stabilize a being's interior life as individual self-consciousness.

For Lacan the mirror stage corresponds to "the onset of" what Freud terms "primary narcissism" (Laplanche and Pontalis 251), that "early state in which the child cathects its own self with the whole of its libido" (Laplanche and Pontalis 337). But just as in Ovid's myth of Narcissus the recognition of and identification with his image brings a sense of self-alienation, a sense that he cannot be conjoined with his image, so Lacan, as Laplanche and Pontalis explain, sees the "ideal ego" (which begins to take shape in the mirror stage) as "an imaginary agency in which the subject tends to become alienated. . . . For Lacan, in so far as the intersubjective relationship bears the mark of the mirror phase, it is an imaginary, dual relationship inevitably characterised by an aggressive tension in which the ego is constituted as an another and the other as an *alter ego*" (251). In this regard Lacan notes in "The Mirror Stage as Formative of the Function of the *I* as Revealed in Psychoanalytic Experience" that the "first analysts" who had developed the conception of "primary narcissism" had tried to define "the dynamic opposition between this libido and the sexual libido" by invoking "destructive and, indeed, death instincts, in order to explain the evident connection between the narcissistic libido and the alienating function of the *I*, the aggressivity it releases in any relation to the other, even in a relation involving the most Samaritan of aid" (6). And Lacan goes on to remark that the first analysts "were encountering the existential negativity whose reality is so vigorously proclaimed by the contemporary philosophy of being and nothingness" (6). The allusion is, of course, to Sartre's *Being and Nothingness* and to the self-alienating effect of the Other's gaze, to the sense, as I suggested in chapter 3, that the subject knows that the external aspect of its being exists as an image in the Other's subjectivity and that the Other's subjectivity is unknowable, so that implicit in the act of identifying oneself with one's physical image is the awareness that "being-seen constitutes me as a defenseless being for a freedom that is not my freedom" (Sartre 358).

Turning back to Plato's allegory of the cave as a means of understanding Fitzgerald's engagement with Platonic idealism, we can see that as the figurative space of origin the cave merges two images of human inception. On the one hand, there is the birth of the physical body evoked by the image of people huddled in a telluric womb who are brought from the interior darkness to the exterior light through Socrates's practicing his mother's art of midwifery, the maieutic method. And on the other hand, there is the origin of the individual self (i.e., of self-consciousness) implied by the fact that the people huddled in the cave are looking at *projected images*, at shadow images of objects cast by the fire behind them on the wall in front of them; and just as the people in the cave are to be brought from darkness into the realm of intelligible light by the Socratic method, so the projected image itself makes a similar journey from a dark shadow outline in the cave to a bright, transparent outline in Plato's otherworld of ideal forms. Moreover, this transition from darkness to light, from misunderstanding to full comprehension, initiated by the activity of gazing at a projected image implicates that further understanding achieved by Narcissus when he gazes at his own projected image, an image created not by the interruption of light (like a shadow) but by its *reflection*. And this ultimate goal—inherent in the activity of gazing at a projected image (i.e., the goal of self-reflection)—is confirmed by the further evolution of Plato's realm of ideal forms: Christianity's use of it as a model for depicting the otherworld of an afterlife, an otherworld in which the survival of an individual's immortal, bodiless *self* is imagined as a bright, transparent, bodily outline.

The way that the myth of Narcissus inhabits Plato's cave allegory provides a background to understanding the influence of Platonic idealism on the trajectory of Fitzgerald's work: a trajectory that runs from his first novel, in which the author (who believed as a boy that he wasn't the son of his parents) imagines the parents that someone as special as himself should have had, to his third novel, where the protagonist (who also doesn't believe he's the son of his parents) creates a new persona out of his own ideal mental image of himself and then, in the wake of this godlike autogenesis, proceeds to repeat this process by projecting his image of an ideal woman onto a real one, a process Nick describes as an "incarnation." (Recall that Ovid himself imagistically links this activity—the projection of an ideal image of oneself onto a woman—to the myth of Narcissus: when he narrates the story in book 10 of the *Metamorphoses* of Pygmalion's sculpting "a figure out of snowy ivory" [4:81] to represent his ideal female, Ovid expects the reader to remember that in book 3 when Narcissus first sees his own image, "He looks in speechless wonder at himself and hangs there motionless in the same expression, like a statue carved from Parian marble" [3:153–55].) One can see that in contrast to the first novel, which imagines alternative parents, the third novel imagines that the self-invented Gatsby is, in effect, his own ideal father and mother.

In annexing the myth of Pygmalion and Galatea to *Gatsby* Fitzgerald codes the process of projecting the image of an ideal woman onto a real one as specifically that of a visual artist creating his embodiment of this ideal in a work of art (a statue). And this coding further annexes the literary artist's projection of his ideal reader as his muse (that imaginary other who represents the twin ideals of a complete intellectual and sexual knowledge) to Fitzgerald's subsequent novels, to work psychologically fueled by the writer's "nagging urge to remake and re-educate the women he was involved with."

Of course Gatsby's projection of his image of an ideal woman onto the real Daisy had predictably disastrous results, and Fitzgerald's projection of the image of his muse onto an initially encouraging but subsequently uncomprehending mother and then onto an exciting, highly imaginative spouse who later turned into, Fitzgerald felt, a destructive competitor produced difficulties that provided the emotional impetus for his fourth novel. This similarity in the muse's reversal from initial encouragement to subsequent discouragement no doubt helped, as we noted earlier, to blend the images of mother and spouse in Fitzgerald's imagining the figure of an ideal reader and may have given him the sense that such a reversal of response was something he was psychologically fated to see repeated in his choice of muses.

In setting Stahr's first glimpse of Kathleen against the background of the earthquake with its evocation of the underworld splitting open and a shade returning, Fitzgerald makes the epicycle of desire that began when Gatsby sprang from his own platonic idea/ideal of himself come full circle. Imagistically, it is a short associative step from Plato's subterranean cavern (filled with people watching shadow images cast on a wall) to a subterranean world of shades pent up in Hades. And it is another short step from the image of Socrates practicing his mother's art of midwifery as he helps bring people up from the telluric womb into the lighted realm of pure intelligibility to the image of an imaginative artist bringing a shade up from the underworld to the light of day. Further, we can see that the godlike status of the imagination implied by Fitzgerald's deific appellation for Gatsby reaches a sort of culmination in *Tycoon*'s scenario of an artist figure symbolically restoring the image of a dead spouse to life—a raising of the dead characteristically attributed to God's Son.

If Plato's cave of shadow images is evoked as a figurative telluric womb and if that cave and the underworld of shades were for the classical world cognate formations, based, no doubt, on the notion of a body's personal survival after death being thought of as analogous to the persistence of a person's mental image in the minds of those who knew and loved her, then we can see that *The Last Tycoon*'s scenario of image projection (an artistic activity particularly appropriate to a movie maker) and of a consequent resurrection served as Fitzgerald's fictive expression of a narcissistic desire to correct two previous incarnations of his muse by symbolically bringing back the images of two women, one dead, one among the living dead in an asylum, so as to have another chance at creating an ideal form that would combine the figures of mother and spouse. An ideal form that in combining the two would serve to amend his sense of a personal origin (his mother) who had never understood who he really was and thus whose unqualified love for him was always in some sense misplaced, amend it by projecting an origin that had been reeducated so as to possess superior knowledge and thus the absolute appreciation and love such knowledge brings. The form, then, that the artist's fantasized return to the womb (the space of origin and the site of original power) took for Fitzgerald was a sublimation of the real maternal space of origin into Plato's telluric womb (the mental space of origin, of ideal images), a space out of which are born, as these mental images move from darkness into light, the luminous ideal forms, a space within which the artist's narcissistic, godlike power to father (and also bring to birth) his own self-image and to project such images on others makes him, in effect, "a son of God." Indeed, this is what it means to imagine a return to origin on the son's own terms.

Bruccoli, Matthew J. *The Composition of "Tender Is the Night": A Study of the Manuscripts*. Pittsburgh, PA: University of Pittsburgh Press, 1963.

———. Introduction to *The Love of the Last Tycoon*, by F. Scott Fitzgerald, xiii–xcvi. Edited by Matthew J. Bruccoli. Cambridge: Cambridge University Press, 1993.

———. *Some Sort of Epic Grandeur: The Life of F. Scott Fitzgerald*. New York: Harcourt Brace Jovanovich, 1981.

Bryer, Jackson R., and John Kuehl. Introduction to *The Basil and Josephine Stories*, by F. Scott Fitzgerald, vii–xxv. New York: Scribner, 1973.

Bulfinch, Thomas. *Bulfinch's Mythology*. New York: Avenel, 1979.

Buttitta, Tony. *After the Good Gay Times: Asheville—Summer of '35, a Season with F. Scott Fitzgerald*. New York: Viking, 1974.

Conrad, Joseph. *Youth: A Narrative, and Two Other Stories*. Edited by Morton Dauwen Zabel. Garden City, NY: Doubleday, 1959.

Dickens, Charles. *A Tale of Two Cities*. London: Oxford University Press, 1967.

Donaldson, Scott. *Fool for Love: F. Scott Fitzgerald*. Minneapolis: University of Minnesota Press, 2012.

Du Maurier, George. *Trilby: A Novel*. New York: Harper and Brothers, 1894.

Edel, Leon. Introduction to *The Tragic Muse*, by Henry James, vii–xvii. New York: Harper and Brothers, 1960.

Eliot, T. S. *The Complete Poems and Plays, 1909–1950*. New York: Harcourt, Brace and World, 1958.

———. *Selected Prose of T. S. Eliot*. Edited by Frank Kermode. New York: Harcourt Brace Jovanovich, 1975.

Fitzgerald, F. Scott. *The Basil and Josephine Stories*. Edited by Jackson R. Bryer and John Kuehl. New York: Scribner, 1973.

———. *The Basil, Josephine, and Gwen Stories*. Edited by James L. West III. Cambridge: Cambridge University Press, 2009.

———. *The Beautiful and Damned*. Edited by James L. West III. Cambridge: Cambridge University Press, 2008.

———. *The Correspondence of F. Scott Fitzgerald*. Edited by Matthew J. Bruccoli. New York: Random House, 1980.

———. *The Crack-Up*. Edited by Edmund Wilson. New York: New Directions, 1962.

———. *The Great Gatsby*. Edited by Matthew J. Bruccoli. Cambridge: Cambridge University Press, 1991.

———. *The Great Gatsby: A Facsimile of the Manuscript*. Edited by Matthew J. Bruccoli. Washington, DC: Microcard Editions Books, 1973.

———. *The Last Tycoon*. Edited by Edmund Wilson. New York: Scribner, 1941.

———. *The Letters of F. Scott Fitzgerald*. Edited by Andrew Turnbull. New York: Scribner, 1963.

———. *The Love of the Last Tycoon*. Edited by Matthew J. Bruccoli. Cambridge: Cambridge University Press, 1993.

———. *The Lost Decade: Short Stories from Esquire, 1936–1941*. Edited by James L. West III. Cambridge: Cambridge University Press, 2008.

———. *My Lost City: Personal Essays, 1920–1940*. Edited by James L. West III. Cambridge: Cambridge University Press, 2005.

———. *The Price Was High: The Last Uncollected Stories of F. Scott Fitzgerald*. Edited by Matthew J. Bruccoli. New York: Harcourt Brace Jovanovich, 1979.

———. *The Short Stories of F. Scott Fitzgerald*. Edited by Matthew J. Bruccoli. New York: Scribner, 1989.

———. *Tender Is the Night: A Romance*. Edited by James L. West III. Cambridge: Cambridge University Press, 2012.

———. *This Side of Paradise*. Edited by James L. West III. Cambridge: Cambridge University Press, 1995.

———. *Trimalchio: An Early Version of "The Great Gatsby."* Edited by James L. West III. Cambridge: Cambridge University Press, 2000.

Freud, Sigmund. *The Standard Edition of the Complete Psychological Works of Sigmund Freud*. Vol. 18. Translated by James Strachey et al. London: Hogarth Press, 1978.

Gingrich, Arnold. Introduction to *The Pat Hobby Stories*, by F. Scott Fitzgerald, ix–xxiii. New York: Scribner, 1962.

Goffman, Erving. *The Presentation of Self in Everyday Life*. Garden City, NY: Doubleday, 1959.

Graham, Sheilah. *The Real F. Scott Fitzgerald: Twenty-Five Years Later*. New York: Warner, 1976.

Hamilton, Sharon. "The New York Gossip Magazine in *The Great Gatsby*." *F. Scott Fitzgerald Review* 8.1 (2010): 34–56.

Hammett, Dashiell. *The Maltese Falcon*. New York: Vintage, 1972.

Irwin, John T. *Doubling and Incest / Repetition and Revenge: A Speculative Reading of Faulkner*. Exp. ed. Baltimore, MD: Johns Hopkins University Press, 1996.

———. *Hart Crane's Poetry: "Appollinaire lived in Paris, I live in Cleveland, Ohio."* Baltimore, MD: Johns Hopkins University Press, 2011.

———. *The Mystery to a Solution: Poe, Borges, and the Analytic Detective Story*. Baltimore, MD: Johns Hopkins University Press, 1994.

———. *Unless the Threat of Death Is Behind Them: Hard-Boiled Fiction and Film Noir*. Baltimore, MD: Johns Hopkins University Press, 2006.

James, Henry. *The Complete Plays of Henry James*. Edited by Leon Edel. New York: Lippincott, 1949.

———. *The Tragic Muse*. New York: Harper and Brothers, 1960.

Kees, Weldon. *Weldon Kees and the Midcentury Generation: Letters, 1935–1955*. Edited by Robert E. Knoll. Lincoln: University of Nebraska Press, 1986.

Lacan, Jacques. "The Mirror Stage as Formative of the Function of the *I* as Revealed in Psychoanalytic Experience." In *Écrits: A Selection*, 1–8. Translated by Ann Sheridan. New York: Norton, 1977.

Laplanche, Jean, and Pontalis, Jean-Bertrand. *The Language of Psychoanalysis*. Translated by Donald Nicholson-Smith. New York: Norton, 1973.

Le Vot, André. *F. Scott Fitzgerald: A Biography*. Garden City, NY: Doubleday, 1983.

Mellow, James R. *Invented Lives: F. Scott and Zelda Fitzgerald*. Boston: Houghton Mifflin, 1984.

Meyers, Jeffrey. *Scott Fitzgerald: A Biography*. New York: Harper Collins, 1994.

Mizener, Arthur. *The Far Side of Paradise: A Biography of F. Scott Fitzgerald*. New York: Vintage, 1961.

Ovid. *Ovid in Six Volumes*. Translated by Frank Justus Miller. Cambridge, MA: Harvard University Press, 1976.

Pausanias. *Pausanias: Description of Greece*. 4 vols. Edited by W. H. S. Jones. Cambridge, MA: Harvard University Press, 1979.

Plato. *The Collected Dialogues of Plato*. Edited by Edith Hamilton and Huntington Cairns. Princeton, NJ: Princeton University Press, 1973.

Porter, Cole. *The Complete Lyrics of Cole Porter*. Edited by Robert Kimball. New York: Da Capo, 1992.

Sartre, Jean-Paul. *Being and Nothingness: An Essay on Phenomenological Ontology*. Translated by Hazel E. Barnes. New York: Washington Square Press, 1971.

Turnbull, Andrew. *Scott Fitzgerald*. New York: Scribner, 1962.

Vaill, Amanda. *Everybody Was So Young: Gerald and Sara Murphy, a Lost Generation Love Story*. New York: Broadway Books, 1998.

Veblen, Thorstein. *The Theory of the Leisure Class*. New York: Dover, 1994.

Weston, Jessie L. *From Ritual to Romance*. Garden City, NY: Doubleday, 1957.

Wharton, Edith. *The House of Mirth, The Reef, The Custom of the Country, The Age of Innocence*. Edited by R. W. B. Lewis. New York: Library of America, 1985.

Wilson, Edmund. Introduction to *The Last Tycoon*, by F. Scott Fitzgerald, 134–63. Edited by Edmund Wilson. New York: Scribner, 1941.

Names followed by "(ch)" indicate fictional characters. In subentries, real persons are alphabetized by last name and fictional characters by first name.